Natalie Savvides is a full-time mum, living in south-west London with her husband and two young children. Having spent a lot of time searching for love, adventure and excitement, as well as for herself she eventually found happiness in the least expected place. Natalie believes destiny played a big part in bringing her to where she is now and feels that her years of diary keeping simply prove it.

Full Circle

NATALIE SAVVIDES

Full Circle

Vanguard Press

VANGUARD PAPERBACK

© Copyright 2016
Natalie Savvides

A CIP catalogue record for this title is
available from the British Library.

ISBN 978 178465 084 1

Vanguard Press is an imprint of
Pegasus Elliot Mackenzie Publishers Ltd.
www.pegasuspublishers.com

First Published in 2016

Vanguard Press
Sheraton House Castle Park
Cambridge England

Printed & Bound in Great Britain

For my wonderful Mum xx

ACKNOWLEDGEMENTS

Thank you to my husband for inspiring me and enabling me with the time, confidence and conclusion to write this book. Thanks to Mum for her patience in my constant bombardment for advice, and to Dad for his constant support and endless printing. Thanks to Lena for helping me cut down over twenty years of diaries to a manageable size. Thank you to Florina, Connie, Noemi and all those helping at home, allowing me time to write and to all my friends for their encouragement. And thank you to all those of you who have walked through my life in one way or another providing the content for this work and leading me to where I am today.

Contents

PROLOGUE

I just can't keep control of my feelings; that's why I keep a diary.

It was a glorious, hot summer's morning in Italy. I was there on one of my many visits and had just woken up after yet another weekend of constant partying and general self-destruction, when I decided that's it. Enough.

Oh I loved it, the days of endless aperitifs, dinners, the beach, cocktails and dancing on podiums until the early hours. It was great, but it was gnawing away at me inside. I wasn't happy with who I was. As I lay in the lower of my friends' daughters' bunk, barely remembering how I got there, head pounding, riddled with guilt, I questioned why I kept doing this to myself. The vulgarity of it simply accentuated by the innocence and purity of my surroundings, a pretty six-year-old's bedroom, church bells and birdsong framing a beautiful home in a beautiful place, and what was I? No less than a grim stain on it all.

If I'd enjoyed it – genuinely enjoyed it – it would have been different. But deep down I knew it was getting me nowhere. The frustration of entrapment was increasing, yet I knew no other way to release my insecurities. I was searching... like we all do. The pursuit of fulfilment, for that last piece to complete the puzzle was killing me and it had been for some time. Every time I thought I'd found it, it either slipped through my fingers or wasn't for me. No matter how hard I tried, that 'longing' persisted.

Outwardly I seemed together: I was slim, tanned, pretty, popular and even achieved that near impossible task of getting my highlights exactly right. What more could a girl want? But something was missing.

If you look you don't find... is that it?

I had to do something about it. Find something satisfying, gratifying, with a purpose. Something to stop me retreating into such destructive behaviour, willingly, making the same mistakes over and over, chasing every opportunity to escape the void I was so unsuccessfully trying to fill. I was lost and somehow I had to figure out the way. I needed to steady myself but I realised that first I'd have to look back, to see where it all went wrong.

You can't know where you're going until you know where you've been.

I've kept diaries for as long as I can remember. Consoling myself, trying to make sense of the chaos in my head. Simple words they may be but they contained truth and looking back through them was enlightening. In a moment of panic where I felt the need to grab onto something tangible and potentially beneficial, I decided to put it all together in a book, this was the answer. A book would be constructive. It may even bring balance and some form of satisfaction.

And so I began... reflecting my words on paper yet again though this time with a different purpose, a real purpose.

I started by creating a clear picture of where I was, before ploughing through years of journals to piece the travelled road together, hoping to shed some light on where that first domino fell, clear the blur from my vision as to where I might actually be headed and with any luck, make sense of the continuous quest for whatever it was I was furiously searching for.

I've compiled my findings on the pages that follow. Parts are best told through diary excerpts themselves and part from memory. Tied together with the wisdom of hindsight, they paint the picture and reveal what only time could tell.

CHAPTER ONE
The Early Days

Tuesday 16 May 1989.

I can't stand people being over attention seeking and trying to take over every situation. I've been in such a mess lately getting really wound up with Tanya. She's been annoying me so much, when we're out etc. She's false, really loud — over bubbly and completely overpowering to try and get all the attention. She doesn't give me any space to be myself — just pushes me right out of the way. So frustrating. For ages now she's really cramped my style. I hate that sort of thing, can't breathe! She does it on purpose to outshine me and steal the limelight. And then it's like I'm always there to be her best friend after she's upset me. Well it's just not me.

I'm not going to let people make me retreat into myself and suffocate me! No way!

**Don't fear the enemy that attacks you
but the fake friend that hugs you.
(Unknown)**

Looking back perhaps that evil bitch Tanya was destiny, sent to me in my formative years to make me strive that little bit harder. All I know is that she spent a lot of time making me feel bad; her back-stabbing and manipulative ways reaching new heights with the dawn of every school year. Somehow she'd transformed from never-say-boo to a goose wallflower to scheming demon, and the bane of my teenage years. Later, as I found myself in professional environments I realised there were lots of Tanyas, women who would scheme and bitch and do their best to make you feel inadequate. Even if they were not so active in undermining me as she was in our youth, they would never be my friend or ally. They would just be there, reminding me that while I had female friends I could trust my life to, there were women who were smiling at me, and not because they liked me. If adolescence is, as they say, finding out who you are, then it is just as much about finding out who other people really are and what they are capable of.

School is supposed to prepare you for life. I'm not so sure it does in the way it's supposed to but it certainly does prepare you for the inequalities and unfairness of life. What better place could there be to discover that someone else would always be more beautiful, richer, smarter and seriously bitchy than a North London private establishment, seething with spoiled princesses? That's where I was, in the airless environment of a Catholic school with such high fees that the only people who could afford it were mainly the Jewish families who lived nearby. Their daughters exhibited an enviable, though not always attractive, confidence, the kind that comes with a combination of money and strong extended family network. They felt they were seriously better than us and they wanted us to know it. You sort of had the feeling you were not meant to be there, on their territory. Suddenly, as Catholics, we were the minority in what was supposed to be a Catholic school. We could only marvel at the stuff they had. Make-up, jewellery, clothes were lavished upon them. They had those huge watches, Armani sunglasses and jeans and proper handbags, though this was even before the great handbag era of the last ten years. Their parents drove Rollers, Bentleys and Porsches, their holidays were spent in villas in Spain or France and they would never want for anything. They almost seemed older because of it all. Whatever they were, they were different, or we were, or I was anyway.

I used to wonder how my parents felt about being amongst all this. We were very comfortable and we lived in a lovely house but these girls lived in the palaces of Hampstead Heath and Highgate. Comparisons are the stuff of growing up and visiting a house where there were numerous rooms that nobody used, gleaming gold taps in the bathrooms and four-car garages brought home the fact that we were just kind of ordinary. Mum never seemed to be fazed by any of it when she picked me up from parties or met the mothers at the front gate. Perhaps she knew that it would take a lot more to join that particular club than a mansion: we would not, ever, be part of their circle and I would never be a princess.

We had a decidedly unhealthy quota of popular girls who set the agenda. Whilst at times they could be annoying, I wasn't afraid of them. The same could not be said about the twins, non-identical but horribly similar in demeanour and personality – one with long, lank, dark hair and the other with short, mousy hair. They were a fearsome duo, precisely because they were not part of the glamorous set, and so you always felt they came from a place you didn't understand. They looked like they had secrets, dark secrets. They knew they didn't fit in with the tanned, bouncy-haired, diamond-clad, Jewish set; even in religious terms they were on the outside as their mum had converted so they were almost, kind of. They reminded me of scheming, cartoon characters, who today you might encounter in a computer game, guarding the gates to the enchanted kingdom.

They had this precise way of doing things, which made them even scarier. They were very controlled in everything, the way they used their pencils and returned them to their designer pencil cases with cold deliberation. I always imagined that when not at school they must've communicated in some strange language that nobody knew. I did my best to avoid them, but it wasn't enough and somehow, despite my best efforts to stay out of their way, I came onto their radar and they soon decided that they owned me. They set about giving me rules and I was simply too scared to argue. I was not allowed to talk to the other crowd (the glamorous ones) I'd befriended, which really upset me, as I was proud of being in with the cool girls. It got worse when the twins ordered me to check in with them on a daily basis and seek permission before I spoke to anyone else. Somehow I got caught up in it like a trap, I did it because I felt I had no choice. I was afraid of them because they were an unknown quantity. I had no idea what they were capable of, so couldn't know if they were messing around or whether they really would punish me. The cool set were mystified and told me not to listen to them. But I had no choice. I didn't want enemies; the one thing you did want, was these people on your side. Entangled in a tug of war between the two groups, I was clearly not going to win. I retreated into myself and looked forward to a day when I could be free of the twins, free of all the girls who it seemed were judging and manipulating me while I had no interest in doing that to anyone.

Then fate intervened on my behalf. Despite the large fees it attracted, the school seemed to have trouble paying its way and so it closed down and we were all split up. I was thirteen, in third year. My parents despatched me to another convent school in Hertfordshire – this time a properly Catholic one with bona fide Catholics in it, and not so much obvious wealth, a breath of fresh air. None of the hard-core princesses from the previous school were there, except for the terrible twins who, fortunately by now, had new targets to conquer and were no longer interested in me. In fact, finding themselves in the minority in a new environment, they became overly friendly, which was annoying in itself. There was already a resident nasty crew and we were warned about them, but compared to what I'd experienced at the previous school they were fluffy, soft bullies, so I was able to ignore them and simply laugh it off. And instead of a single sex coach trip there and back, there was a train with real, live boys on it. There were multiple advantages to this, not least being that we had train money to spend, since we cunningly evaded the fare most of the time with me as cheerleader. This was going to be good – a new school, fresh start. While inside I might have felt reticent and fragile, early on, all that disappeared when the fun started and if there was any chance of that happening I was probably the person igniting it. I enjoyed being the instigator of high jinks. It made me feel good to see everyone was having a good time and I'd started it. I didn't do it to be the centre of attention as that's a characteristic I find unappealing in others. I didn't want to control the fun anyway: I wanted to create it.

As we hit the sixth form, school was pretty much a sideshow to the fun. We had a good gang. There were the three musketeers: Karl, Ravi and Charlie, who went to the conveniently located, boys' school down the road, the same school as my brother. Karl lived up the road from me, Irish, small, skinny with spiky blond hair and transparent skin. Ravi, Indian, was short, stocky and had the kind of black eyes that could charm the socks off anyone. Charlie was English but with his olive skin and brown hair had a continental air about him. He was easy-going and wore great clothes and had just returned from the States, which added to his casually confident air. Additions to the group often included Simon, notable because he always brought his sidekicks Tobias and Bunny, two super cool types with long, curly hair they wore tied back. Both had that air of trouble and hence, they obviously sparked my imagination, especially Bunny.

Saturday 24 June 1989
Life's as good as you make it!
So, other than exams, which no doubt I could have done a lot better in, this year has been a total doss. We've had no proper lessons as courses were finished so we've been sunbathing at the lake every day eating McDonalds and messing about with the boys. Before each exam we'd all get kicked out of St Albans library for being rowdy, all of us girls and the boys too – Ravi, Karl, Charlie – Tobias, Bunny and the rest!

There was no getting past the fact that I liked boys but not just in the hormonal sense. Boys represented freedom, a different way of doing things and most of all, pure fun. They seemed to have none of the constraints that girls placed on themselves and it was always easier to have a good time when they were around. One of the earliest objects of my affections was Brandon; I must have been about seven when I first set eyes upon him in the school playground. I soon found out that he was in my brother's year and they were friends. He was my dream. An angelic, long-limbed, glossy-haired, delicate, dark-skinned hotty. He lived just around the corner, which meant every time I left the house there was the suspense of a potential sighting. From the outset I felt he was out of my league but I daydreamed about him and he was the one I had my first pretend cuddles with at night.

Dominic was completely Brandon's opposite in every respect. He wasn't a full blown Goth but he had that air about him: short, skinny with yellowish-tinged skin and a hangdog look effected by his big, lost eyes. He had bits of chains and string hanging off him, wore ripped jeans, obligatory Doc Martens and a permanent cigarette hanging from the corner of his mouth which, no matter when you saw him, always seemed to be at exactly the same stage. If he'd been a straightforward guy I probably wouldn't have been interested in him, a theme that was to recur often in my life. Anyway, we got together and perhaps it was our differences that made it hard but things quickly became problematic. It all came to a head on one of those joint boys/girls school trips to Wales, one of those touchy-feely excursions where you are supposed to 'open up' and tell everyone else what you are feeling. This always struck me as odd since half the time I wasn't even sure what I was feeling or it was all mixed up with other feelings that I could not sort out from the rest, but anyway everyone told their story as they saw it and Dominic's was pretty heart-breaking. He had no relationship with his family, his father had died, he hated his stepfather and basically the guy was bereft of any love whatsoever. I'm ashamed to admit that at first it was totally incomprehensible to me but why should I have understood? My own family was a functioning, happy unit, strong on love, support and values and so to hear this... well, of course it brought out the middle class do-gooder in me and maybe it just made him that little bit more interesting, who knows?

Letter from Dominic:
Natalie,

I'm really sorry about having a go last night. I didn't really say everything I wanted to, and what I did say didn't really come out right.

All I know is that I like you very much, not only in a romantic way. I don't know how to describe it really. In a funny kind of way I feel really close to you, and I so much want to develop an understanding and openness with you — that frustrates me because I can't on my own.

If you feel you could use the friendship too, help me out please.
Love, Dominic.

"Sorry, Nat, need to talk to Dominic for a minute... in private." Tanya edged her filled-out little frame between us. Sweeping the coy, blonde wave from her face, she peered up over her shoulder and opened her eyes up big. It was her 'sincere' look, but so fake.

Dominic seemed powerless to refuse her. I could feel the tears come to my eyes.

How does it get to this? How did everyone start playing games, cruel games? People whispering, people eyeing up other people's boyfriends, plotting around tables in the pub; how quickly it had gone from innocence to complication, competition and deceit.

I was at a loss to understand why Tanya did this: we'd had such laughs, shared secrets and been or at least I thought, always wholly open with each other. And then she'd turned. She hadn't become my enemy but something far worse. A friend who really doesn't care if she hurts.

It was Dominic who first warned me about Tanya. Even when we were having our problems together, he always found time to put a protective arm around my shoulder and give me some wise words. She'd been with me at the previous school but honestly you wouldn't have even known she was there, you never heard a word out of her. She was short, tubby, blonde, had blue eyes and an air of 'butter wouldn't melt'. We hadn't been friends back then at all but the new school seemed to pull us together. At first it was OK, she seemed to just be part of our group, one of an ever-growing gang who all got on well, made mischief, went to each other's houses and parties. But then things changed. She became very intense and while I didn't notice it, Dominic had picked up on it and he wasn't the only one. Charlie, who I'd got very close to and who seemed to take interest in me beyond the usual obvious, hormonal guy stuff had pointed it out too.

Sunday 10 September 1989.

I've never had a completely intense friend like that – it's not me. I got dragged into it before I even noticed what was happening. I need to break away. I can be so much more myself, relax, let myself go, when she's not around! Charlie noticed it too. Said it was really obvious I'm not the sort for a serious intense friendship like that, but Tanya needs it. He also says you can tell I'm much more myself, my good old bubbly fun self when she's not around me all the time! Well, basically, I need my space.

What had begun as friendship dotted with the usual sleepovers, movies and general mucking around became something far more complicated. She was coming into her own and not in a good way. It's inevitable where boys are involved that girls will change their behaviour but boy did Tanya transform from her previous angelic persona. She was out to win whatever she could and instead of being important to her as a friend – if I ever really was – now what mattered was what I did. She followed my interactions with pathological interest and it became weird. She seemed to hate it when I made the boys laugh which I often did. I was a bit of a tomboy and I guess lots of them felt comfortable with me. Tanya clearly saw this popularity as a threat and it had the effect of transforming her into a sly, calculating creature, a girl who wanted to be the centre of attention but who didn't do it with charm, joy and a sense of fun: she just monopolised situations and gradually wore everyone down, especially me.

If she saw me speaking to one of the boys, she would find a way of intervening. It was all so contrived, the way she'd drag them away from me saying she had to speak to them in private. I couldn't go anywhere without the threat of Tanya turning up, like some sort of bizarre policeman. She didn't just turn up when boys were present; she did it with girls as well. She just didn't want me to have anything of my own. She made me miserable; even just the thought she might turn up upset me. I now know that you should not let one person manipulate you whether it's personal or professional. Nobody should be that significant that they throw you off your path. But I was young and for whatever reason had never been that confident so it affected me and seriously undermined what little confidence I had.

I had taken up with Dominic for the umpteenth time and it was going kind of OK, as well as it might with two totally different people, one of whom was a strange freak from a dysfunctional family. When it got shaky again, guess who popped up? I discovered Tanya had been talking to Dominic behind my back, gradually doing her best to take him from me. Despite him being one of the first people to warn me about her, she muscled her way in and eased me out. I was devastated not so much by losing Dominic, but more by the disloyalty, the sheer nastiness and manipulation from Tanya. This was more than an adolescent spat; it was a watershed moment in my life. My family began to notice changes in me and they were right. I retreated into myself a bit and began being picky and very strict with my food. People close to me began to ask me if I was OK. The deceit and hurt Tanya had caused led me to seriously doubt myself and my self-esteem took a beating. Though I still enjoyed the life I had with other friends at school it cast a shadow over me that was to endure.

Feeling like I was losing control of so many aspects of my life, I tried to grab on to the few areas where it seemed possible to gain control. I needed to feel like I was steering this vehicle at least where I could amidst these periods of unease. I decided I would make myself untouchable. I would find things that were mine and that nobody else could take away from me. I'd regain control by transforming myself, making myself totally and utterly perfect, perfect in every sense. Absolutely irresistible! The object of everyone's desire, starting point: *Vogue*, it wouldn't just be Nat Saunders saying 'You look like you've just stepped off a page of *Vogue*'. Everyone would!

I bought all the glossies and began to devour the articles on fashion and beauty voraciously. I decided I would mould myself on the inspiring array of what were simply the most beautiful women in the world. I devised a strict eating plan and lavished in the marvellous discovery of alcohol to numb the mind, the hunger and create a pleasant, hazy film over what was actually quite a struggle, physically and mentally.

CHAPTER 2
Italy

My father's Greek and my mother's Italian, well half-Italian but that was enough for me to take ownership of the nationality. I'd been to Italy many times as a child and adored it. There I was made to feel special, fussed over and generally treated like a princess from foreign parts. From my early teens there began a ritual whereby I would be shipped off to Vicenza for a couple of weeks, the birthplace of my Italian grandmother so that I could improve my Italian, a choice that was as much mine as my parents'. I would spend one week with family and one sitting in the local school next to Emilia. Emilia was a little older than me, she was warm, funny, open and positive, quite a contrast to many of the girls I'd left back home in North London. We were kind of semi-relatives actually; our grandparents had been neighbours, and so the association had continued between our mothers and now us. Emilia gave me Italy and I gave her a taste of my convent school in London in return. For the life of me I had no idea what pleasure she could take from being in London and this particular school, relatively dreary by comparison. Fortunately though, her curious and quaint devotion to Laura Ashley, afternoon tea, the Monarchy and all things British, stuff that frankly I barely noticed, made her experience a very enjoyable one.

For me though, Italy wasn't just another country, or experience; it was another universe altogether. I'd come from the colourless world of a single sex school where life was regimented; everyone wore dark uniforms and rarely smiled. All of a sudden I was Alice, well I guess this was Italy so I was Alicia, in Wonderland. I found myself in a classroom that bore no resemblance to the grey, official buildings I spent my time in back in the UK. The air was filled with gorgeous singsong Italian voices, easy laughter and cries of *"Dai Prof.."* and *"Secchione".* There was a lightness to the atmosphere there; it didn't feel like I was dragging myself around as I did in London. The desks, which of course didn't look like desks at all but were cool looking tables populated with brightly dressed, attractive, tanned kids. Lessons were punctuated by interruptions and jokes and the snack breaks – *merende* – they called them were unbelievable. A couple of times a day we'd be treated to the most delicious snack, the 'Kinder brioche'. Layers of soft cake, with a jammy filling and a thin dark chocolate covering, the variety of which was endless. It all seemed so carefree. The days were short and filled with the luminous sunlight that seeped through the windows, then led us out each afternoon, as the bell sounded at one, into the streets of this most enchanting of Palladian cities. I drank it all in: the aroma of fresh coffee, bread and pastries oozed from the chic bars, the bustle of people going about the *passeggiata* as mopeds weaved between them along the cobbled roads. Beauty, sophistication and style surrounded me from morning until night. Everyone there was incredibly lovely to me, probably initially because I was different but also because I wasn't a typical, precious Italian girl, obsessing over shoes and handbags or giggling at every tiny thing, so everyone wanted to take me out, invite me to places, I felt more welcome there than I had anywhere.

There was none of the strictness or austere attitude I felt in the UK, I felt happy there. More than that I realised I liked who I became in Italy. I felt good and perhaps because of that I was perceived differently, more positively than I was in the UK. Of course we take ourselves with us wherever we go and we can't change who we are but while I didn't dislike the UK and London, I felt I'd been born in the wrong place for me. Italy awakened me at every touch-point: visual, verbal and visceral. It worked its way into my heart and penetrated my soul, inviting me to belong. I simply devoured every experience put before me and eagerly sought more. I just couldn't get enough of it. Year on year, I'd return to the birthplace of my maternal grandmother, to be my Italian self and that part of me grew with each visit. When not staying with Emilia I'd be travelling and staying with other relatives, most commonly my Aunt Rosalie, who was almost a bit like a second mother. I'd stay at her magnificent villa with their name boldly engraved at the entrance on a gold plaque that sat to the left of the towering, black, shiny gates. Every time they picked me up and we drove in, I relished the moment those gates would open ever so slowly, unveiling a world of luxury and glamour. Inside there was a five-car garage and a lush courtyard with the healthiest lemon trees I'd ever seen; terracotta vases were heaving with fragrant flowers and bougainvillea spilled from the windows above onto perfectly trimmed hedges and fig trees. A sweeping stone stairway led to the enormous front door. The house itself built on hilly land meant that you couldn't see all of it from any one perspective. By any standards it was massive, a house made for entertaining with a large reception filled with softly coloured sofas and an impressive semicircular, luscious bar. Because of its hilly position there were multiple terraces on several levels, from which you could view the mountains and, in the other direction, the town below. Rosalie had a good eye and there were elegant statues, rugs and artwork all over the house. Of course they had a hi-tech kitchen with all the best Italian appliances but my Auntie didn't do any of the cooking: there was a cook for that. Outside there was a swimming pool surrounded by vibrant flowers and beyond that, a garden that seemed to go on forever. I was so spoiled, always staying in the 'pink' room with its matching en-suite, waited on by an army of maids who would bring me drinks by the pool, make me lunch and continuously make me feel like the princess I wanted to be. I loved staying there, well who wouldn't, and Rosalie herself was as grand as the house she lived in. Tall, slim, tanned with immaculate grooming, laden with jewels and a wardrobe of designer clothes straight from her regular visits to the Milan collections, she was the epitome of the stylish Italian woman.

And that wasn't all. Aside from the splendour within, there was the excitement of the accompanying social aspect. The boys... My uncle had lots of nephews, most slightly older than me, a few younger but there was one in particular who caught my eye, as he did all the girls. Fortunately, I caught his too. Much younger than him I was nervous but excited.

Thursday 12 July 1990.
Finalmente I have a pen.
Here I am at the Excelsior, with Rosalie! As if staying in their beautiful home wasn't enough, they've brought me to the beach to this amazing hotel! Of course it's the best one here!

MAJOR NEWS!

It's four a.m. and have just got back to the room!

Wow Riccardo arrived today, Mario's nephew. He is GORGEOUS. He's cool, very cool, extremely cool, not your typical Italian; he's fair skinned (but tanned), blond hair, recently cut from long to short, twinkling blue eyes, great body, typical bright preppie clothes and that lethal Italian swagger.

We all went for pizza earlier and he was constantly stroking my leg under the table, so passionately I kept jumping, having to give him the 'stop' eye. I mean everyone else was there... I literally kept gasping!
We've just got back from KINGS nightclub. What a night. The place was packed with gorgeous guys. I've been having an amazingly incredible time here. They're taking me to all the best clubs, and I'm clearly way younger than everyone else, it's so cool – makes me feel... well... privileged.

Life is for living!

Sunday 15 July 1990.

Sadly was our last day... spent entire time with Riccardo. We walked to the car arm in arm and have basically been inseparable since he got here. He's so loving and affectionate! – It's just amazing. In the car on the way back he kept looking round and touching. Bless 'im! Then he put his seat right back, stretched his arms back and pulled my hands towards him. I tried to get them back, but he kept one and played with it, sucking my fingers, licking them up and down and biting them in a really sensual way. He is seriously amazing; I've never been in something so toxic! Think I'm really falling for him.

Think I'd prefer him with a ponytail though – said he had one until recently 'cos his hair was long.

I couldn't believe he liked me as in 'like'... 'cause he asked Rosalie if after when we got back to Vicenza, just him and me could go for a drive; she said no. She also told me he only goes for older girls... looks like he's made an exception.

Sunday 29 July 1990.

Has been a brilliant trip. Stayed with Renata and co. last few days, love her! She's more like a sister than a cousin (think 'cos our grandmothers are so close, we have that extra something); still saw Riccardo too.

Last night before dropping me off, we were sat in his red convertible golf and he took my head in his hands fixing on my eyes. It was romantic!... There was nothing around us but the sound of crickets and warmth of the air.

"It's written in the Bible," he said. "If you lived here, we would be together."

My heart was pounding and I boiled up, hope my mega tan hid it.

"You are the light of my life," he whispered, then kissed me. Couldn't believe it. My first real taste of Italian romance! Don't want to let it go.

I HAVE TO LIVE IN ITALY!

In Italy, the days just unfolded and they always seemed to bring fun. In years to come I would wonder if I'd been a little unfair on my home country and city. But if London was my husband, then Italy was my lover – exciting, brimming with possibilities and fun. Even my friends there didn't have the kind of attitude that oozed out of every Italian pore. Was I making too much of it back then I wonder? Perhaps. But our memories are all we have, so I resist questioning them too much. Those days were idyllic, regardless of the type of lens I was viewing them through.

Even the stationery in Italy was special. Little leather-bound books of handmade paper, made with so much care and attention. Colourful *agende* with artfully designed pages and characters. I used to love being taken to these shops. Amongst an array of spectacular boutiques, these were by far my favourites, Cartolerie; magical caves, isles filled with books, diaries, journals, pens, pencil cases, satchels, packed to the brim with countless great gift ideas, never mind Hello Kitty, there were thousands of characters and every brand, every designer had a collection, Armani, Benetton... I'd wander around picking up notebooks that seemed so perfect as they were with no words in them. To me they were pure objects of beauty. I had to have one and that's how I ended up starting to write a diary at thirteen years old. Thoughts, feelings, events, dreams, it all went in... I've filled many notebooks since that first one, my childish wittering at times embarrassing and more revealing than I remember.

Easter came and went quickly but there was always summer to come and summer in Italy was the only one that mattered, especially since summer in the UK didn't really count as you could never rely on the weather. Jesolo on the Adriatic coast was the first resort I remember, a place my parents took me to and one that I returned to for years to follow. This was where northern Italians came in great numbers, many to their second homes or regular hotels, where they would take up position in the sun surrounding themselves with all the accoutrements needed in order to maintain their beach posture throughout the day. And then they would begin the serious stuff, the suntan ritual, turning over throughout the day as if on a rotisserie in search of the perfect tan. They liked to go very, very dark and unfortunately I liked to copy them with the result that I now know I have overdone it in terms of sun exposure but if this was what the beautiful people did then why should I be different? I wanted to be one of them.

I was in a lift one day, in our regular hotel 'Monaco and Quisisana' when the door opened and in walked this girl with mischief in her face and a giant inflatable cigarette under her arm.

"Hello," I said without thinking what language she spoke. She was skinny with freckles and dark, tight curly hair. She pretended to take a drag on the cigarette and offered me some.

"Hi. I'm Sam."

"I'm Natalie. I like your cigarette."

"Me too!"

She laughed, her blue eyes sparkling. Sam immediately looked like someone I would have fun with. She was English, in fact she lived around the corner from me in North London but it was my perfect brother that she was really interested in at the time.

"Who's that guy I've seen with you with?" she asked warily as women do when they're sizing each other up.

"Guy, what guy?" I mean I was on holiday with my parents and there were no guys, well not in close proximity where my parents could see them. At fifteen I was in that no woman, no girl zone. Not quite able to begin a fully-fledged pursuit of boys but past the stage of supervision.

"That guy with the dark hair, tanned, hot, chiselled face, little eyes or should I just say Ralph Macchio? The cute one you were with at breakfast. I've seen you."

"Oh God, you don't mean my brother... Christopher (Crispi). Mr Bloody Perfect?"

"He's your brother. Wow. He's hot... Does he have a—"

"Girlfriend?"

"Yep."

"No. I don't think so. Least not that I know of... I mean he might not even know if he did."

My brother is the bane of my life. He's a lovely guy but honestly you'd think he was a child prodigy or the Dalai Lama the way my parents carried on sometimes. He's a good looking man and clever; academically it always came easy to him though he always maintained to me that because of his track record he had more pressure to get straight A's while I didn't have to worry about anything as everyone would be swinging from the chandeliers if I got a C+, since they didn't expect me to amount to much beyond a nice job somewhere, if that. I wasn't quite Winnie The Pooh of Very Little Brain – I had a good brain – but it wasn't as academic and since I was convinced that was what my parents valued, regardless of how much they assured me otherwise, I often felt like I didn't quite cut it. Anyway thanks to him, my friendship with Sam flourished on that holiday and continued to do so thereafter. As for their romance, it wasn't going to happen since my brother was being pursued by everyone and would end up with no one. Better. This left her free to drag me off to Papaya, the nightspot where it all went down. The place was brilliant: a small entrance, hidden in a back street guarded by very sexy, young doormen, leading to an interior world of neon lights, split levelled dance floors, cocktail bars and a huge outdoor space made up of further dance floors, more bars all surrounded by palm trees glistening with tree lights. Fortunately, on the man front she and I went for totally different types. I was unwisely partial to the classic Italian gigolo while Sam liked her men with a rock 'n' roll façade, Guns N' Roses being her reference point. It was therefore far easier for me to amuse myself as the place swarmed with smarm. There was also a group of regular guys we'd befriended, the neat trio of Roby, Luca and Marco in their ankle length jeans, Timberlands, El Charro belts and bright freshly laundered T-shirts. These three were safe and a bit older than us so they were our entrée past some doors that we might otherwise have not known existed.

Coming back to the UK I did so with mixed feelings especially as I got older and my London friendships matured. I actually began to look forward to seeing them again and sometimes before going on holidays; I'd almost wish I were staying. But maybe that's how we are when we have too many choices.

Wednesday 12 September 1990.

People are telling me since going away this summer, I've changed a lot. I've become a lot maturer without losing the immaturity! Well I had a deep conversation with Kim about it. I think it's mainly 'cos I'd gone around with people a lot older. People are saying I've become a lot more adult but am still as stupid as I was when I want to be. I really do have some great friends here and coming back after hols makes me realise how lovely they are. I know I don't write it much any more but I guess that's because I take it for granted. Kim wrote me this:

I don't need words to express…
I don't need tears to shed…
I don't need to ask for a smile…
Or a hand to hold me…
All I need is

To be your friend, forever!
(Unknown)

My friends meant everything to me. The only person who meant more in terms of the effect on my life was my grandmother who in many ways was probably more responsible for my affection for Italy than anything or anyone else. She was such an incredible lady, a mother, a housewife, an adventurer and a war heroine. Wise, down to earth, tolerant, amused and at times appeared almost regal. She was tall, straight, cuddly, beautifully dressed, had deep brown shiny eyes and wore bright warm lipstick, always. Her name was Laura and it seemed to me she embodied not just the wisdom of the world but all of its curiosity and beauty as well. She was born on 29 December 1917 in Arzignano, Vicenza, the daughter of a wine merchant and one of nine siblings. She loved the mountains and their siren song was irresistible to her. If you've ever marvelled at the splendour and the terror of the craggy peaks of the Dolomites you'll understand what I mean. Grandma was born to rule the mountains and it seemed that she spent most of her childhood alfresco. She became a founder member of the Alpine Association and was an expert skier. When the war broke out in 1939, she was twenty-two and engaged. He died at Tobruk and for her love was finished: she would never give herself again that way, or so she thought. Instead she devoted herself to the resistance. With Northern Italy under Nazi rule in 1943, the resistance united workers and peasants against a common enemy.

The war needed people like Grandma who knew the mountains and could find a way through without leaving a trace of their whereabouts. She learned how to pick people's pockets, how to tweeze information out of people. She carried grenades in her suitcase and smuggled passes and weapons to those who needed them. Her whole family lived those years on high alert, especially since they chose to shelter a family of South African Jews in their loft – while entertaining the occupying forces downstairs. On one occasion she was tipped off by a friendly German soldier and that exchange meant her life was saved. She'd missed a firing squad by five minutes. At the end of 1944, General Alexander's decision to suspend operations for the winter allowed the Nazis to unleash terror against the resistance and 40,000 people died. But Italy was soon free and thankfully so was Grandma.

War has always produced great love stories out of seemingly coincidental moments, the kind of things they make films about. Grandma's life was about to enter a new phase. Standing outside with her cousin at the end of the war, they wanted a photograph of the two of them.

Seeing two British soldiers, they cheekily called out: "Take a picture of us please." With one snap left on the roll, Grandma photographed the soldiers in return and told them where to collect it. One of those soldiers, a man called Alec Cunningham, returned to collect the picture a few days later. And Grandma. He had fallen in love. Neither spoke the other's language but they managed a courtship before he had received notice to return to England. My grandmother, wary of putting her heart on the table again, told him to leave even though he asked to marry her.

"Go back to the girls you knew before all this chaos and madness," she told him. "See if it is the same and if it is you stay there. If you still feel you want to be with me after six months then you will let me know." Of course he never forgot her and they wrote back and forth until the letters could contain their love no more and they were married in Italy. My grandmother left her life of wealth and comfort and travelled back to London to begin a new life amidst austerity and rations in suburban Fulham, a long, long way from the colour and joy of her native Italy. But she was a woman who found joy wherever she went. She carried herself like a duchess and never complained.

She epitomised the love and strength that means family. Her life with Grandad and their unequivocal love for each other resonated with me. In my young chaotic life and later in my slightly older, just as chaotic life, I think it was her story that helped me keep the faith. One day my prince would come and it would be for life.

CHAPTER 3
A Milestone

If you live in the present moment the future is just around the corner. If you live for the future the future will never come.
(Unknown)

Monday 7 January 1991.

Getting really pissed off with Charlie. I mean I really like him, we get on and have such good times when we're together and that's A LOT, really fun and natural but whenever I have a laugh with Bunny or Tobias or any other bloke for that matter he gets jealous. Like we were all out the other night and Bunny was there but every time I got to speak to him, Charlie would fly over and stick his nose in. I guess it's predictable, I've heard he likes me from so many people. Ravi says he's besotted — which I'm sure is a SLIGHT exaggeration. Found out Bunny's going out with Tobias' sister. So unfair!! Of course she's really pretty and he's not interested in me at all. I could cry. I like him so much, mainly 'cos I can't have him! That's my problem!

PS: Got 4/29 for my Economics exam. 14%

"Anyone that shows an interest in you, you don't want."

"That's not true. Not all the time."

We were at Kim's house just hanging out on Saturday afternoon after a big night out with Charlie and a whole bunch of other people at the local, the Hare and Hounds. As the school year drew to a close we were accelerating into major party mode. Not that we hadn't been having fun all year but the brakes were now off, our exams were over and we could unleash the tension and hormones that had been building up all year. I had drawn an uneasy truce with Tanya really for the sake of the greater good but it was painful. She'd spent the whole of the year seemingly making it her mission to cut me off from anything that I wanted. She did it with anything and everyone literally. Somehow she would manage to cut me out at a house party, the pub or wherever and make me feel worthless. Her final act was to try and take Charlie away from me. She started calling him for a 'chat' every night, meeting up and stuff, telling him that I mustn't know. She knew we were part of the same after school gang, that we got on well and she was doing all she could to split us up. What was she telling him about me? It was so upsetting. He was the one thing that was kind of mine, we'd become really good friends and it was like we had something no one else did. Fortunately, unlike a lot of teenagers who do enjoy those power games and ego boosts, Charlie wasn't the type to betray a friend. He told me. In a way that suggested insight, that he really understood what she was doing he said, "Don't worry, Natalie, your friendship matters way more to me than anything Tanya says." I was relieved.

"Stop playing sulky Natalie. You've said it yourself. If a guy treats you well, you run a mile. Look at you and Charlie. He adores you. And Anthony or John... Seriously!"

"Charlie adores me as a friend and as for Anthony or John... let's not even go there."

The Charlie thing had become a bit of a recurrent theme with my girlfriends and frankly I didn't want to hear it any more. We did have good times and we had great fun, with him always treating me to the theatre, drinks, meals... everything. At barely eighteen he was showing me the finer things in life. He took me to the best restaurants of the time, San Lorenzo, Daphne's, the top shows, Phantom, Les Mis and coolest bars of the moment and never once let me put my hand in my pocket. But he just didn't do it for me in that way. I loved spending time with him and with the other boys for that matter. It was just easier. Boys make you feel special, they make you feel protected and treat you better, with slightly more respect (generally) particularly when they have a soft spot for you. Plus there was no competitiveness; something I was never interested in though inevitably got partially sucked into regardless. And what two girls would go out to all those places together anyway? At that age? Precisely...

Kim wasn't totally right. I didn't run away from a relationship with him because he treated me well: I had others on my mind, Riccardo and people that really got me going. I just didn't think of him THAT way. Each time I thought of us kissing, it just didn't work. But when I thought about kissing Brandon, or Bunny for example, well that definitely worked.

"He just likes me as a friend. He told Richard the other day that we have a brother/sister type relationship so there is nothing there. I don't fancy him and he knows that."

Despite what he was saying to his friends, Charlie had told me at a party the week before that he really liked me. Just the fact that he said it so easily unnerved me. What kind of a guy says that? After you tell him that you like him as a friend? I actually think he was really mature; there are men I know now who wouldn't be able to lay that on the table. And while the idea of someone being able to say they liked me was something I wanted with each passing year, at this point it was, well, unnecessary. He was just too damn sure of himself and his cockiness annoyed me. Particularly when there were other guys around he just changed and became really arrogant, typical rugby boy style.

It was tricky. Whilst he was adoring and yes, on the surface appeared the perfect gentlemen and boyfriend, particularly to my parents, on the other hand there were setbacks. The demonstration of interest and verification of our close friendship was restrictive. I felt cramped. At parties, I'd be having fun, chatting, mingling with everyone and he'd just keep dragging me away. It didn't make me feel loved or anything; just like he was being overpowering and possessive, too possessive.

Kim lay back on her pink quilted bed, wearing old pyjama bottoms and a grey Levis T-shirt eyeing me up while tossing an old, chewed up teddy in the air. My feelings for Charlie fluctuated on a daily basis, sometimes hourly. I questioned whether it might be different with him, because we were friends, that maybe I wouldn't get fed up. But my mind couldn't conceive it.

"I mean he's good looking and he wears greats clothes and knows so many cool people…"

"And…"

"And the thought of getting off with him doesn't do it for me."

"Ha. It would if he didn't like you."

"No it wouldn't. It doesn't work like that. He's just not my type."

Saturday 16 March 1991.

Really good night: loads of us went out for pizza and then back to Charlie's house. He was so nice to me, bit flirty with innuendos 'n stuff but really listens to me. We had a few drinks, mucked about doing stupid things, listening to cool music. We were all slouched in Charlie's room listening to mellow music with the lights dimmed when Charlie and I who were lying on the bed (no strings attached of course) decided to have a huge play fight; we keep doing that lately. Obviously he won – but it was fun. I know we have our differences at times but he's really nice. So brown since skiing! Wow.

After much internal debate, encouragement from friends and considerable persistence from Charlie, I decided to give it a go. What the hell I thought, nothing ventured nothing gained. I tried to be open-minded. I gave it a chance and put some effort in, albeit minimal; these things have to come from within after all, not pushed upon you. It didn't work, just didn't feel right... it was... well it wasn't romantic. And all it did was make me seek out the mysterious, the bad, the wayward, the Lotharios. And of course the unattainable.

Saturday 20 April 1991.
Finished it with Charlie.

Relationships will fall apart if only one person is trying to hold it together.
(Sonya Parker)

48

Perhaps she was right. I was aware that I had a tendency to chase what was obtuse, difficult or downright unattainable. I seemed to think that happiness lay in capturing whoever it was that didn't want to be captured, not in a forever way but in a now way. Achieving the apparently impossible. That warped idea was to stay with me for a long time. The list of dysfunctionals, unattainables, bad boys and players would get longer and longer as the years went on, rendering me the perfect contradiction: the girl who wanted Prince Charming but insisted on looking in all the wrong places.

Wednesday 19 June 1991.
Just to say it's really annoying not being in love with anyone and no one being in love with me. I guess I'll just have to be patient.

I had officially decided my life was going to be fun, until Mr Amazing came into my life. I had a plan. In fact I'd worked out exactly what I'd do when I got my A levels. I would go to university in Italy, get a degree in Italian and get a cool job on Italian TV. Despite the growing uncertainty within me, and my increasingly flimsy self-confidence that seemed to fluctuate according to the amount of compliments I was getting at any given time – and who was giving them, more to the point – I wasn't shy about putting myself forward for things. The idea of working on TV in Italy seemed perfectly reasonable to me and did not seem like a big ask at all. Far from it. Unfortunately however, and somewhat predictably, my A levels were not up to scratch. This was not helped by Andrea, one of Riccardo's wild crew, now also a good friend of mine, dying of an accidental overdose. Naturally the importance of an exam paper paled into relative insignificance by comparison. The grades I achieved, or (didn't) would not get me into Royal Holloway, my dream university, which threw a rather large spanner in the works. 'Bugger it,' I thought. 'I'll just go and au pair somewhere.' So I bought the deliciously old-fashioned *Lady* magazine and searched for a wealthy family in a desirable location (maybe even Italy!) My parents were not entirely in tune with this plan to say the least and felt it would be better if I stuck to my original goal of studying. A flurry of activity ensued and I managed to get a clearing place to study languages at Anglia Poly in Cambridge. The only slight hitch being I'd have to study French too, not pure Italian. I wasn't disappointed at all and actually began looking forward to it.

But first there was an Italian treat to be had. I'd organised for five us to go to Jesolo for the summer holidays which turned out to be just the riot I'd expected, if not more. And this would be the summer where I lost something that I'd never get back. An event I'd planned with meticulous precision, well OK, not exactly but I'd certainly thought about it, dreamt about it, about how best I'd like it to happen. I was determined from the outset that it would not be with someone where it would be hugely embarrassing (on my doorstep) but in an idyllic scenario so that I would look back on it and admire it as a thing of beauty. My knight in Italian labels for this occasion would be Chicco 'Baci' who I'd known from a few years of going to Papaya. He offered security, familiarity, charm and definitely filled the shoes of my imaginary Mr Perfect, or *perfetto* as the case may be. We'd got to know each other and had what I considered to be a good friendship, which occasionally expanded to include a kiss.

Monday 12 August 1991. (A day to be remembered.)

Can't believe I've done it. Knew this was going to be the night, just knew it. Woo hoo!! Especially when we got to Papaya and Chicco ushered us all in free, winking at me. His eyes were so bright tonight – probably the tan, he squeezed me tight, kissed me hello and ran his fingers through my hair. I dunno something seemed different... just something, I felt it in the air. Plus, clock was ticking, I'd vowed myself to pass this obstacle by my eighteenth birthday and time was running out, I had roughly twenty-six hours. I lost Sam, thought she'd hooked up with Dennis, Axel Rose look-alike DJ, had no clue where the others were, except Kim who was holed up in a corner with some bloke, so just did my own thing. Chicco appeared! He grabbed me from behind and pulled me in, was nearly closing and he said, "Mi aspetti?" (Wait). Shit. We went back to his place, was just as I'd imagined, pretty bare with the odd bloke thing. I was so nervous... (Thank God for all those brandy Alexander's!!) We fell on to his bed bit awkwardly... Guess it didn't quite go to plan... not like you see in the movies or anything. Was quite messy; avoiding too much information, bit clumsy but regardless, a total SUCCESS. (Apart from staining Sam's skirt! Eek) Yayyyyyyyyy! I've crossed the boundary!

Chicco fitted my vision perfectly of the ideal romantic 'first-time' situation. And even if the act itself wasn't quite as perfect as I'd envisaged, I'd done it with a guy who was charming, romantic and blindingly gorgeous plus Italian, in one of my favourite places on earth. And I scored his club T-shirt in the bargain. Job done!

The whole trip was a blast. I knew it would be and I knew I would enjoy it but I was a little concerned that the other girls would have just as good a time. I suppose because it was the place I returned from year after year and raved about I wanted them to see what I did. I needn't have worried. They had a blast. When Lucy told me how much she loved it, I was chuffed.

"Oh Luce you mean it. I'm so happy. I just wanted all of us to have the best time we could before university."

"Nats this holiday has been EXACTLY what I needed and WILD I tell you. WILD. And you know what. I'm so going to miss the way everyone just walks in and starts talking to you. It doesn't matter if they're hot or grossos, they're so friendly and not like anything at home."

"Told you Italy was cool!" I smiled to myself. They'd got my point.

I was so pleased. It was like it proved a part of me, a cool part; they perhaps didn't quite get in the UK. When they saw me there, how I was, how everyone was with me, the fun they had being a part of it, was like me shouting out 'See' without needing to say anything at all. There I had control, it was my place, and I led the way. I couldn't do that back home, it wasn't the same, everything was out of my hands, I had no control. And that state of things would continue for a while.

CHAPTER 4
Moving out... Moving on! Off to University...

Monday 28 September 1992.

Faith is being sure of what we hope
for and certain of what we don't see.
(Hebrews 11:1)

Friday 9 October 1992.

First night alone in my room — have had Daniela stay almost every night as it's hard for her to get home (she didn't get halls and her place is miles away, somewhere down the end of Mill Lane) — Julie stayed too the other night, and last night there were four of us as Sam was here too... going to enjoy some 'me' time tonight.

Things are getting better... I've been enjoying it much more. It's all the little things that people say that keep you going. Spoke to Mum yesterday; she's going to come up and visit. Also, got a lovely little letter from Grandma and Grandad, with a parcel of stamps in it, so sweet. Still not heard from Emilia, but I did get a nice letter from Charlie — was just lovely.

Starting university was a slightly daunting thought for me. Though I'd spent loads of time in Italy away from family, this was my first proper period away from home with a group of other people my age and absolutely no one to answer to. I've always thought that it's funny how we leave home to recreate our homes elsewhere, flowers, photos, soft toys, memories, we do it at our desks, at university and the strangest thing is doing it on holiday after announcing we're going 'to get away from it all'. Maybe we don't really want to get away from all of it, what we actually seem to want – maybe even need – is something of our home with us. I certainly did but not everyone shared this view. There were a lot of people around me whose rooms looked exactly like they did the day they walked in. It was as if they ran in, dumped their bag and went "Yippee, I am so going to have fun. See ya." But I was a bit more pensive than that. Before I had my fun, in typical Natalie fashion, I would, as usual, be a little more organised. I covered the walls of my little room, floor to ceiling with magazine cuttings, *Vogue* covers and loads of photos, plus various other random things people had given me and my otherwise dull floor was covered with a brightly coloured Mexican style rug, (actually from Habitat), a gift from home.

Prior to leaving home, I'd been having a few angst-ridden moments about how I'd be perceived. While I'd finished school on a good note and made up with Tanya, albeit in fragile fashion, the bitchiness and isolation I'd felt as a result of being on the wrong end of her manipulative takeover antics, had left emotional welts on me. I had told myself repeatedly that this would be different. A new phase. "This is about being grown up and grown-ups don't act like kids at school." But how wrong I was to be about that throughout my life!

Before actually embarking on this new journey, my parents were keen for me to be in the best possibly shape to confront it. They were encouraging and enthusiastic. But Mum was concerned about a few things, particularly the apparent disappearance of my menstrual cycle over the past year or so, convinced it was due to my equally disappearing waistline. Worried that it could spiral into the much talked about eating disorders, she took me to see Dr Amir, a specialist in the subject to see if he could help me. Our parents always remain parents, no matter how old we are or how independent we become and they try to protect us from what might happen, which was exactly what she was trying to do. I felt so bad for all the worry I'd caused, that now she had to do this. I also thought there was nothing wrong with me, I was just trying to look good. But I knew she was upset and just wanted to try and help, so I went along with it.

It was a tough experience, being scrutinised in every way, what I ate, what I weighed, what I did, how I exercised; anyone would have thought I was running for President or something. Mum and I didn't talk about it much, something was being done and that was what mattered. I was marginally concerned myself as to the disappearance of Aunt Flo, although I chose not to voice it. The visits, which became quite regular, made me feel increasingly fragile and regardless of not wanting to discuss it, I never wanted Mum to leave my side as we left the oppressive UCH building.

"You'll have to take the tablets."

"I will, Mum."

"And eat properly. Promise?"

"I promise!"

"It's important, for your future, for a family, you know… you have to eat."

"I know, I will, I know what I'm doing, I don't want to talk about it, I've listened to Dr Amir and taken it in – that's enough."

I just wanted the whole thing to go way.

Issues addressed and set aside, albeit awkwardly, I set off feeling rather positive, with just the expected reservations. Fortunately, there were a couple of girls from my school who would be at the same university so I wouldn't be totally alone. Although we hadn't been part of the same crew at school, Daniela and I were sort of friends already; she was half Spanish, so we related on that Mediterranean level and had hung out from time to time. The really good thing for me was that somehow I'd managed to wangle myself a place in halls – so I was bang on campus! Excellent! In theory these rooms were supposed to be reserved for those from outside of London and further afield, abroad, or with some kind of special requirement, but not so surprisingly there was a pretty large group of Londoners; people who had no real reason to merit those rooms, other than being savvy, pushy, and frankly a bit cheeky.

My block was interesting enough; pretty bland in appearance, modern, whitewashed walls, that kind of grey blue rough industrial carpet, hanging lights that rarely worked and a string of heavy duty, red, sprung doors. But it was behind those almost prison like doors that things livened up. Initially we didn't venture much further than our hall; we were a good group and got on. There was an eclectic mix of people. Victoria, pretty, petite, fair, slightly up herself English rose, parents lived in Hong Kong on one side. Stacey, Welsh girl, well off, with a massive limp. Karen and Jane, mid-country blondes, sweet but relatively boring, polar opposite to the hoity-toities and Brady bunch Penny from Newcastle. On the other, Dean, immense Indian 'special' policeman from south London who failed to grasp that his work ended when he left the station, Abi, half Chinese, too cool for school, 'don't mess with me' Peckam girl, Barri, Welsh apparently uber affluent farming heir and Russ, half Italian north Londoner, Joe Bloggs jeans type. Then upstairs, Ben and Jason, can't remember exactly where from, South... both blond, blue eyes, hot, smoked spliffs constantly and rooms were like Camden market, total grunges.

Monday 12 October 1992.

Have had such a laugh so far! We cooked a great roast last night — and have been out every other night. I'm knackered. Tomorrow night we're going to Cindy's (club) should be a laugh, student night — half price drinks. Must thank God for things having got so good, am having so much fun lately — although must add I wasn't too pleased about having Russ (actually quite good-looking as it happens), Jason and a hundred other of their loud-mouthed friends invading my room last night or people nicking all my stuff for that matter (i.e. bread), but I guess you just have to put up with a few things!

Abi keeps telling her friends how lovely I am — that's cool, isn't it? I also couldn't believe Victoria was really nice to me before too — went to the Anchor with them all the other night where I got my palm read by some pratt who probably didn't know what he was on about at all — anyway was a laugh at the time. Tried to get into Trinity but couldn't. Victoria actually said I had a really good figure and that she really liked my jeans. RESULT coming from her as she's super, super cool and has an amazing figure herself!

Saturday 17 October 1992.

Am supposed to be doing some work today and tidying room, before we go shopping yet again! I've seen so many gorgeous things, especially in Jigsaw (not exactly the cheapest shop on the high street... far cry from Sue Ryder!). I really can't get a hold on this student budget business... well on the way to an overdraft already!

You can never have enough casual clothes.

Oh — I got a gorgeous letter from Charlie; really nice, saying he misses ringing me and always having someone to talk to! Tanya wrote to me too finally, on a Postman Pat postcard... weird!

Sunday 18 October 1992.

I'm SO worried, I'm looking after Maude, Stacey's goldfish whilst she's gone to London for the weekend, it's 11.40 a.m., and she still hasn't woken up. I've shaken the bowl and bashed it. I don't know if it's dead or just asleep? Ahhh. So frustrating! I'm gonna have to buy another one if it doesn't surface! Oh dear.

She'll prob never know.

PS: Last night was feeling a little pissed off. I came in here, washed my face, in my tiny corner sink and there was a knock at the door. Who was it? Crispi, my adorable brother. Such a brilliant surprise. Went to the Anchor again, and no, Jason wasn't there.

A note to my sister,

Always put relaxation alongside work and never do anything that you know you'd be happier not doing. Having fun and keeping smiling seems to be what life's all about. Work hard for what you want but never for anyone else. Most of all, always remember, don't worry about things, after all they're only things!

My love for always,

Your brother.

Friday 23 October 1992.

Friday night and I'm back at home in my own bed. At first it was so weird walking into my room, like a fairy-tale, almost like I was looking down on everything. Well, it was a really nice evening and trip back here. Couldn't believe Jason came back too — we got the same train! Real fluke and am supposed to be going back with him on Monday. (Gulp) So, Mum and I had a lovely chat when I got in, then Dad and Christopher got back from Oxford; we had gorgeous dinner and watched good film, in true Savvides style. Message from movie:

We build too many walls and not enough bridges.
(Isaac Newton)

Saturday — completely excellent day!

Didn't do any work at all. Went shopping with Mum — bought some gorgeous things and got on really well. Think some space has made her treat me more as an equal. Saw Charlie in the eve, went for drinks then to Big Easy on Kings Rd, Amazing lobster! He got them to make me a cocktail with all the things I love — gorge!!! Was real giggle...!

Wednesday 28 October 1992 (back at Uni).

Baked beans! The food of university! God knows I've had more of them than I know what to do with — they're coming out of my ears! Or should I say arse perhaps. Good high fibre food (... that provokes wind!).

Looking at my food diary notes, it's literally all I've been eating... a wonder I haven't gassed the place.

On a more serious note must cut down on All Bran and Raisins, can't live off that.

Saturday 31 October 1992.

Mum was up today, and Charlie left this morning... Is now Saturday night, nearly three a.m. I'm all ready for bed, and am sitting at my desk, with a really dim light on and the radio playing quietly. It's so weird to think this is all mine now — this is the life I live. I do exactly what I want and get cosy in my little room here with my posters and my rug. It's so nice.

We all got in from Queens (again) — quite late — Victoria, Stacey, and others. I had tea with Stacey. It's disgusting though. I can't stand it (Assam or something) then toast and gorgeous marmalade, which I've now just dropped all over the floor. I haven't seen Jason in ages, hopefully will do soon. Have heard of a couple of people who are supposed to like me, which is a real compliment, confidence boost! Don't know why I don't believe in myself more... I'm gonna really try and always make an effort. Just waiting for this stupid front bit of my hair to sort itself out!

Sunday 1 November 1992.

Can't believe how time's flying... Slept in this morning, then Mark turned up (Charlie's friend from school, totally forgot he was even up here — he's at Downing, just across the park). I'm seeing him again on Thursday — actually a really nice bloke! Going to church with Abi in a minute — being good girls. She's v. sweet, gets on my nerves a bit sometimes, but she's nice... kind of streetwise.

Twelve thirty a.m.

Spent whole night with Abi — was fun, had massive pizza meal deal thing (compensating for excessive clothing expenditure) then watched tons of fashion videos in her room — brilliant, all the models and stuff, so cool! Love it!

You have to suffer to be beautiful.

Wednesday 4 November 1992.
Off to Oxford...
Here I am on the back of the coach, all my stuff sprawled everywhere and my huge baseball jacket over the seat in front. They're playing 'that's what friends are for'. Dionne Warwick and I'm on way to see ol' Crispi, mon frère. (Love that we get on.) It's a really nice day, and other than the fact that I've had a huge choc flapjack, I'm feeling pretty good about myself. Last night at Cindy's was excellent. We had such a wicked time. Absolutely everybody was there, except Jason of course, and everyone was being especially friendly; was lovely. Russ kept picking me up and dancing; a whole bunch of us came back and went straight to Fat Gits for greasy kebab and chips, then had hysterics about Gersh. Daniela stayed with me, and this morning we watched string of morning programmes together with endless cups of tea.

Thursday 5 November 1992.
Never got to fortune-tellers. Will reschedule.

Friday 6 November 1992.
Not feeling too well, touch o' flu (as Grandma would say) I fear. Think I'm a bit run down.

As much as everyone was nice enough and we had fun, at times I just felt uneasy, something that was becoming quite a regular occurrence, particularly in groups. I was having trouble with the concept of sorting out the right people from the wrong ones, something that can still trouble me at times. University life brought with it a wave of new acquaintances and at first it all seemed really exciting, all these possibilities and options but it wasn't always so straightforward. Even if I was in the middle of a crowd having fun, I felt strangely disconnected. Like I didn't belong or that everyone was really just pretending. I wished there was some way of knowing who really liked you, properly, like for 'you' and who didn't so you didn't waste time or get hurt. Imagine if we could have a Real Friend Detector that would save us time and heartache figuring out if someone cared or they were just in it for what they could get. Fortunately the phone was never too far away, just at the end of my corridor. There were always people to speak to and whether they understood or not, they helped. I spoke to my mother about it.

"I don't know, Mum, no one's really like me, like how I'd want sort of thing."

"You can't expect everyone to be the same as you and be a best friend. You're always going to come across people that are different."

"I just feel like I don't really fit, feel kind of confused?"

"You just have to be yourself and take people for what they are, darling. Use them for what they're good for; some may be good for you in some ways and some in others."

"That's a bit callous isn't it? I'm not like that, it's not me."

"I know it sounds mercenary but you can just get on with everyone and let them believe whatever they want to believe, and if someone turns out to be a really good friend, then great and if not, so be it.

"That's the way of the world how people are so you shouldn't get upset by it, just don't think that everyone who's nice and you get on with is going to end up your best friend. In other words be a bit wary."

I would be careful who I got close to and confided in. I was going to try and be more relaxed about it whilst remaining vigilant at the same time.

Friday 13 November 1992 (back home for weekend)... not at all bad for a Friday 13th.

Had really good chat with M&D about everything, feel very independent — is great. Decided I really like Cambridge too and I'm going to have the odd cigarette there and here. I don't care — it really doesn't matter! Well, I'm feeling quite tired now, well — more restless 'cos I'm thinking about my legs! I've put on a bit of weight to be honest. I just hope I never look... like... 'big'. God Forbid! (Discovered Fybogel — should hopefully keep weight down!)

Saturday tomorrow, not quite sure what I'm doing exactly, think I'm seeing Charlie in the evening!

Saturday 14 November 1992.

Great day with M, great night with Charlie.

Had such an excellent time. I wore those black/blue tight jeans and that white body I got last time I came down and pink jacket. Ate in a gorgeous quaint nouvelle cuisine restaurant down a backstreet in

Hampstead. French with a huge white grand piano and pianist. Waiter, manager was so lovely, kept saying how nice I was. Food was gorgeous. We always go to such cool places. Had mega conversations again as well — drugs smoking, people, love, everything and a real laugh. Then went to this private party at Beluga Club on Finchley Road. Excellent, there were famous models there. Record producers and Samantha Fox! Couldn't believe — real film stars' party!

Well on the way... to film star fame!

Karl and Ravi were there, both sweet and friendly. Kissed me hello and said I looked really nice!

Sunday went to church with Mum... bit boring but had a good singsong. Scrummy dinner at G&G's. Dad drove me and Abigail back up here after the clothes show. Abi was embarrassing in the car; she's so bloody loud!

Monday 16 November 1992.

Sometimes it's tough changing back into the university me — after such easy, fun times at home. Lovely that people are so welcoming, saying they missed me n' stuff, but still... Am feeling a bit pissed off... bit down. I don't know — I think it's mainly 'cos everyone smokes or at least smokes 'shit' n stuff. They make you feel like you can't have fun without it, really annoying! I've considered just smoking to be done with it, to fit in... but it's stupid to just give in.

Gonna see what's on TV now. Might do some of my history — seriously doubt it though!

Tuesday...

Feeling a lot better today, although am a bit too spotty for my liking. Crispi rang last night around midnight; felt so much better after speaking to him, said he'd been through it too. Peer pressure, everyone gets it and that's exactly what it is 'pressure' — just gotta be strong:

Don't change so people will like you.
Be yourself and the right people will love you.
(Unknown)

...*Should be doing my history now. It's so crazy — I really never do the work, it's terrible. Hope I get by.*

Thursday 19 November 1992.

I'm so pissed off. Absolutely everything's annoying me. I really could cry. Got a letter from Luce; she's smoking like a chimney — it really pisses me off. I mean I can smoke on my own, but I just don't ever want to in front of other people. It's so unfair. I can't seem to win. Life can seem so easy sometimes at this age, but it can also seem so hard. Why can't I sort something out? I just want to cry so much it's not fair. Don't know what to do. I mean M&D both smoke, so them saying not to isn't really much to go by.

Abigail got off with Barri last night. She's so weird, never likes anyone talking to him when she's not there. It's always like — what were you talking to him about? Why? So it's just not worth it, so much hassle when she's around. She just dives in if she thinks you may speak to them! God — what's she worried about? So much for leaving all this behind at school!

Really should do some reading now, I'm so behind. But am also supposed to go to the bar to meet Rob — guy I met in Cindy's! Not in a musicy, smokingey mood though. More of a pensive, sort of sad filmy mood. I did once read somewhere though, that if you're feeling a little sad/low, don't wallow in it, watch miserable films n' stuff — just SNAP OUT OF IT!

Thank God, I've got my diary to write in — don't know what I'd do without it!

The biggest freedom is to accept yourself.
(Unknown)

Saturday 21 November 1992.

It's three a.m. and I'm in love with life. I'm completely pissed, can't believe I'm writing this and I've just got in from a party. Cocktails are the answer — or snake bite n' black! Went to bar tonight after M, Lizzie and Crispi were here, had a giggle then went to a huge party at 44 Besche Road. Was pretty good. Everyone was there, so cool. I must sleep now as going to Downing tomorrow for brunch with Mark.

PS: Went to Kings last night was OK — quite good, met this guy Simon, Rich's friend, went to his room, was OK — quite fun. Smoked joint!

Sunday morning.

One p.m. (just gone) so... seriously missed brunch with Mark. Hope he doesn't mind, will definitely go next time.

NB: I'm running out of toilet roll big time — mainly cos everyone's nicking it!

Wednesday 25 November 1992.

Jason is so sweet, can't believe how much he talks to me now, keeps saying how I just know everybody. So nice to hear things like that... He's funny, always goes on about it! Could be a slight exaggeration but nice all the same.

66

"Scusa" a soft voice addressed the teacher, as the door swung open and a distinctly Italian-looking girl stumbled through, almost tripping over herself.

It was winter. We were sat in Italian history, the lecture hall dark and heavy and my eyes were on their usual protest – I was battling to keep them open. The disruption startled me from my daze and I pulled myself up. This pretty girl, angelic, dressed all in black, tight jeans, polo and boots with an arm full of files and bag hanging wide open over her shoulder made her way clumsily across to the empty seat beside me.

"Is this free?"

"Sure – go for it!"

She sat down and whilst her papers ended up halfway across my knees as her bag fell open between her feet, I realised she was probably about as scatty as me. I knew we'd get along. The giggles started right there. Our first few words were reserved and serious, yet kind but before we knew it we were giggling about something it seemed only we found amusing.

So it wasn't long until I did make a real friend, one that I really could be myself with. And I knew she would be as soon as I met her. It was like a Sam moment all over again. Valeria was great. From that day she toppled in a bit late, making a spectacular entrance. She reminded me of Monica Belucci or something, her curvaceous figure, long black hair, large puppy eyes and pronounced features. She made an impact. Valeria was transparent and our friendship was easy. She lived with a single mother opting against the full immersion student lifestyle and this instilled a different kind of calm in her, something I never found in others. We became friends and by the time we reached the much-awaited year abroad, she'd taken a place up there next to Sam as what would now be called a proper bestie. Later we would end up in the same town on our year abroad and that would cement our friendship forever.

CHAPTER 5
Control

Tuesday 1 December 1992.

Well this book 'The Unbearable Lightness of Being' is so odd. Not odd like that but odd because it's sad and true. I don't know, it's so deep, makes you think a lot — yeah like I need any help doing that — can't quite believe I'm actually reading it. Perhaps sometimes I feel that I'm maybe moving, leaning towards the next stage in my life a deeper, more sharing and personal stage, not sure. Who knows?

PS: Mitch should be coming over later — the personal trainer — super hot. Not sure if he is — hope so!

Yep, Mitch's coming over tonight.

Cambridge was definitely a great place to be a student. Unlike Oxford where its university elite would never have socialised outside their hallowed halls, in Cambridge it was different: there didn't seem to be any real divide between the University and the Poly. We hung out together in all the same local haunts and relations were cordial even to the point of being very friendly indeed. Mitch was one of those people who belonged neither to the university or college but was playing basketball on a scholarship. I can't remember who tripped over whom at first; that bit's a blur, but he certainly isn't. He fitted my fantasies of all those seminal American College movies that I loved, like *Some Kind of Wonderful* or *Say Anything*, where I was simply in awe of every aspect of the film from beginning to end, particularly the college boys. In their bright coloured baseball jackets, these gorgeous beefy high school boys with their combed hair, white teeth on golden skin, walking tall in groups eyeing up the cheerleaders giggling amongst themselves, just drove me wild.

After my obsession with the grunge-ridden dark side of Camden, Mitch was like coming out into the light, a muscular, clean cut, open-faced boy with spiky blond hair, bright blue eyes, gleaming teeth and a tan which could only be artificial but who cares, it worked. His only downfall was that he wasn't quite as tall as he should be. He had somehow managed to acquire an American accent; in fact I think he actually thought he was American, which, strangely, I didn't think odd at all. I suppose I was so caught up in acquiring my fantasy that I accepted it along with everything else. And that 'everything' happened to include an entire basketball team of equally fit and fun-loving boys: basketball was Mitch's life so I inherited his friends as well. And I was not complaining. I didn't care that when we all went out, they crashed my room and partied until the early hours. My prince had come. I felt swept away in the dream world I'd so often envisaged watching movies. It was exciting, unreal almost. Whether he would stay around was something opposing teams in my head discussed on a regular basis. But it was about the now. Towards the end of term, panic set in as I began to fear that when I wasn't there he would forget me and it would all disappear. I spent a lot of time preoccupied, worrying about him not being there which, when you think about it, is very self-defeating but in the circumstances, it was hard not to. I often wondered if this was part of being a girl and, as I got older, and those feelings of potential abandonment by a boyfriend continued to play in my mind, I was just so happy to have someone around that I could talk to AND be physical with. I tried to live for the moment. While I really liked Mitch, for the obvious reasons, there was something bothering me. I began to wonder how he would fit into my life outside of Cambridge. The idea of him coming down to London for example, made me anxious; I just couldn't see how I could fit him into the jigsaw of my life at home, But I was to find out soon enough... In mid-December, the phone call I wanted, but dreaded, came.

"Hey, Nats, I'm coming to London."

"Wow cool." Oh God. "When are you coming?"

"Tuesday. I can't wait to see you. I need to talk to you."

I froze. Tomorrow. Was he breaking up with me? No of course not. He'd just said he was coming to see me. Guys don't come and see you when they're breaking up with you. Well no, actually they do.

And then he said it. IT. "Natalie, I think I'm falling in love with you."

What? Run that by me again? Did he say 'falling in love'? Hang on he said he 'thinks' which means he's hedging his bets. Still this was the kind of news you'd hold a girlfriend summit to discuss especially since last time we spoke – a week ago – we were, in his words, 'sort of going out'. How had we gone from 'sort of' to 'in love'? I wanted to believe him so desperately but I didn't want to feel like a fool, even at the tender age of nineteen, I'd been caught out enough times; it wasn't going to happen again.

"Anyway, Nats, got to go. I'll see you tomorrow night."

It was a strange sort of London reunion. For a start we weren't in London actually. We drove to Heathrow to see his friend off and mucked about there a lot (great night out – not!). He wanted me to drive his car but I refused – I just do not do that. I drive my car and that's bad enough; then we headed back late, along the motorway to Cambridge, or highway as he called it, getting back about four in the morning. In line with his persona, our rendezvous had essentially been a road trip. We went back to his and he gave me his room. It was weird; he lived with his mum who was kind of young and pretty and very un-mum like – like one of those people who gets pregnant really young, father doesn't stick around, mum takes care of kid (probably with Grandmum), child and mum eventually become much like mates. So the room resembled a slight progression from that of your average teenager. Single bed (even I'd managed to wangle a double), pale blue duvet with similar colour papered walls, grey carpet with mags all over it – fortunately not the type you're envisaging or at least I didn't see those; most of its contents were quite predictably to do with basketball! Large poster on wall, hoop, various other memorabilia plus of course unrelated token overfull laundry basket. Anyway, I had my space, which was considerate of him and he slept on the sofa. He'd been a gentleman; just as well as I was by no means ready to venture to the next level after a date of scooting around terminal 4.

Friday 18 December 1992. (Home for the holidays!)

Oh my God, I should be seeing Mitch right now, supposed to be meeting him at Leyton tube station (??) but M&D didn't let me go. Oh dear, tried to ring and say I couldn't make it but he'd already left. Ended up staying here, watching a movie and having a giggle. When I finally spoke to him I said I wanted to take things a bit easier, not feel so tied etc. hate that. (I mean he'd hardly given me a choice for tonight). Not sure how he took it. To be honest, I'm not sure exactly what I want but I can't really fit him in here, into London. Plus I want Christmas to be a real family thing. He said so you basically want two lives, one here and one in Cambridge. I said, "Nooooo – of course not! That's not what I mean at all." But he'd hit the nail on the head (that was exactly what I meant!). I told him it was the same life but I needed time for different things. And then it all got a bit out of control. In truth we're from different backgrounds. I mean he smokes spliffs with his mum who calls his friends things like Dickweed!

It feels much better now he's out of the way for Christmas! M agrees. I don't think she really likes him but she hasn't said anything obvious. I'm sure him turning up last time in his stretched whatever estate car it is, seat reclined so far back it was almost vertical with 'Everyday People' blaring out the open windows didn't help much.

Charlie turned up today, full of fun as usual and we had a great afternoon shopping in Brent Cross, then looking at stupidly expensive houses for sale in St John's Wood. He gave me a white dove. You have to know 'Home Alone 2' to understand...

Christmas came and went in whirl of outings, meals and parties. Mitch had briefly made me feel I'd attained something special (even if he was a poor imitation of the All American Boy) and in doing so had given me the validation I'd always been so desperate for. What I didn't recognise was that you need to have that validation already inside you and that it's not going to come from anyone else... and stay. You have to be true to what you really want but I was a long way from that and so I'd launched my hopes and dreams at Mitch and then retracted them abruptly. It was my overwhelming need for a boyfriend who fitted my ideal that resulted in someone I really had no interest in. How often, I wondered, does this happen to people? You work yourself up into a frenzy, devoting every waking moment to hoping someone really likes you and wants you, only to then find that you can't wait to get rid of them, have them out of your life. In fact in some cases they repel you almost as soon as you get to know them. At least if you find out then though, you haven't hurt them too much. It's not like you strung them along for a year or anything is it?

I'd wanted a boyfriend so much I wasn't able to actually figure out exactly what I wanted in a boyfriend so instead projected my vision onto them. When, like Mitch, they didn't turn out to be what I visualised, I couldn't find the exit fast enough. It seemed sad that all that time and effort of wanting frequently ended up like this. Putting people way up high on that glistening pedestal only to have them come crashing down minutes later. I was convinced that love in all its splendour would make my life complete and that to be loved and cared about by someone I desired would really throw a golden glow over everything. Sadly though, I was constantly frustrated that my choices of boys never quite seemed to yield the romantic results I fantasised about. I'd try to rationalise my way through it, telling myself that there must be a motive for it all, everything happens for a reason and all that, it must be God who was putting me through this for a purpose, as it was all decided by Him anyway. I gave God quite a lot of responsibility, particularly in situations like these, probably a bit too much!

I decided I had to tell Mitch that it wouldn't work between us before term got under way properly. I finally managed to do it a few weeks later in January. "But I'll do anything for you, what do you want? Anything... I'll give up basketball for you," he said. He

74

spent the next couple of nights finding possibly the world's lamest excuses to see me of which "I've got your scrunchie" has to be the worst. He also went through a phase of throwing stones at my window back at college, whilst I was asleep yelling, "Nat, Nat, Nat." All very romantic you could say, but I'd made my mind up; I wasn't interested so I ignored him until he eventually went away.

Sunday 3 January 1993. (Private note to self.)

I'm in my room, no music, dim lights and a cup of tea. I'm really trying to get over this eating thing a bit more this year. I intend to stay in shape but also not let eating restrictions control my life. I'm counting on God for this one as I do for most things hopefully. I'm thinking about and talking to God a lot lately. I've experienced feelings − are they feelings? Not sure... signs maybe? − that this special being really is there to help and guide us on our way. Just sometimes it's not so easy to let yourself go, hand over your problems, burdens etc. and truly believe they will be sorted out. But that's what faith's all about. Right?! The easier option is not to let go. It's hard to have such strong faith, trust and belief in something or someone who is not that immediately apparent. Got to give it a shot though, I can't see a better alternative. Am wondering what this New Year will bring us. I doubt anything hugely exciting will happen but I'm really trying to believe that it will. Should sleep now... am tired. Got bit of a cold annoyingly, right before I go back to Cambridge. As I stop writing now, I hope and pray to God for a lovely, successful, profitable, prosperous, healthy, fun, enjoyable, rewarding and deserving New Year for all of us and for everyone else around to help make the world a happier more harmonious place. Please, Jesus, God, answer my prayers. Amen.

While God was tasked with sorting out most of my life I didn't totally leave it up to him and had taken to consulting various clairvoyants and fortune-tellers too. Both Luce and Sam were into fortune-telling and Sam had been doing the cards for a long time. I figured I needed all the help I could get in life, so for me, there was no problem reconciling a bit of black magic, as we called it, with asking for help from God. Don't put all your eggs in one basket so they say. I'd seen a clairvoyant on New Year's Eve who'd told me a job would come through and wondered if she meant modelling? I'd had some shots taken by a photographer following a lot of encouragement from friends and family after he picked me out at an event and was hoping I could get into something: maybe face modelling if my body wasn't perfect enough. But I couldn't stand the way I had to look so damn serious, verging on miserable, it irritated me – that wasn't who I was. I waited and hoped, always striving for something above and beyond the norm. I had to prove myself.

Monday 15 February 1993.

Yippee – got four Valentine cards. Yeah! Shame they were a day late. But at least they came. Better late than never but annoyed why I had to go through all the torment and agony and wait a whole day! Perhaps it's the snow? Am reading Joan Collins' 'Secrets'. Great book. She is smart. Have gained a lot from it:

- Eat clean, you are what you eat
- Take care of yourself, work out, be well
- Avoid smoking
- Always look your best! Others will value you if you value yourself

- *Whatever you feel about yourself you mirror to the world*
- *Pamper yourself — you deserve it!*
- *Love what you love and who you love, with all your heart*
- *Laugh freely and often*
- *Be aware of the immense beauty around us*
- *Know who you want to be in life — what you want to become and work hard to achieve it*
- *Smile*

My obsession with being perfect never really got a rest: it only lasted as long as others showered me with compliments and propped up my roller-coaster self-esteem. I did my best to override the issue, trying to gain as much control as I could but it ended up a vicious circle. My parents noticed though mostly stayed behind an invisible force field, keeping their thoughts to themselves. Though my father, normally reticent on the subject, chose to bring it up one day during my second year at university, obviously unable to hold it in any longer. Grandad sadly had taken ill, which affected us all and I'm not sure if that was the fuel for D's intervention that took the form of a story, which I think he thought was terribly covert but of course it wasn't.

"You know there's a woman I work with, Maria, whose stepdaughter has an eating disorder and it's very serious. She's so worried about her."

"What's wrong with her?" I knew already he was trying to get to me but as far as I was concerned I had no such disorder. I was just disciplined.

"Well she's a very pretty girl, slim, twenty-three years old, has everything going for her but she's barely eating." He shook his head thoughtfully as if he was deeply thinking about it. "You know she became a vegetarian and cut out everything else and she's just had a stroke. Can you believe it?"

"Whoa, Dad, hang on there. Isn't that a bit dramatic? I mean she must have had something wrong with her anyway."

"Well Maria says she was perfectly healthy. Just like you."

He'd barely disguised his 'story' and even if it was real I was sure it didn't apply to me in any way at all. I wish he could have just been honest about it and not gone about things in such a righteous, clumsy way. Anyway, that seemed to set my mother off and the whole thing descended into one almighty family row where nobody was sure what they were even arguing about any more. There were lots of tears but really they were misplaced. I had no interest in entering a conversation about this, particularly not in the way that it had arisen.

Grandad had become seriously ill. He'd been having seizure issues plus had a fluid problem in his legs, which was causing him a lot of trouble poor thing. He'd sit there in his big green armchair and if anyone so much as brushed past him he'd be in agony. Seeing us, and having his single piece of Cadbury's dairy milk chocolate each night were his only remaining pleasures; everything else had become unreachable. He was taken to hospital. He'd been there for a few days and nobody was really sure what was going on. One of those incredibly frustrating situations, where there are a sea of questions and next to no answers. I visited him in hospital daily, we all did, an environment that despite kind, smiling nurses radiating as much positivity as they could muster, just said 'death' to me each time I walked in. Grandma however, was not so cowed apparently and took to bringing him whisky, beer, gin and vermouth — anything she could, disguised in an inconspicuous coffee flask. She would not be dissuaded from her humanitarian mission and though he clearly shouldn't have touched it, she continued her deliveries of hard liquor to his ward, possibly in the hope that it would rouse him and he would get better. The decision was eventually made to operate and fortunately he came through just as I was about to head off for my year in France.

CHAPTER 6
Besançon

While my Italian language skills were already highly accomplished, my French was lagging a long way behind. From the beginning I'd wanted to do a pure Italian course and had deliberately never really paid attention to anything to do with France or its language. To say I'd left it behind in a messy state at school would be kind. Prior to second year of university, I informed my parents that in order to even remotely progress in French, I would need to attend an intensive six-week summer course and that course could only really take place in Nice, (party capital of the French Riviera). I had thoughtfully already done the research for them and pointed out I would get a proficiency certificate that would also put me in an excellent position upon my return to Cambridge. Happily they agreed and I began to contemplate not what I was about to learn, but how I would invest in the necessary chic to fit into the French lifestyle. France failed to captivate me in the same way Italy's lifestyle and spirit had done over the years. I didn't like the French. It appeared the feeling was mutual. Of course I'd decided up front that I didn't like them, so no matter what they did, that wasn't going to change. They weren't Italian so how could I? It just so happened that there were loads of Italians who spoke the local lingo as badly as I did so I spent most of my time hanging around with them and living *la dolce vita* in Nice. But that was only six weeks. My year abroad was approaching during which I'd spend a lifetime, well actually, six months in France. Six months, decidedly inland in Besançon, so not even a sniff of the Mediterranean. A place I'd never heard of and neither had anyone else it seemed. It would be cold too. At least there would be loads of foreign students, hopefully some Italians. If I could just get France and the French, out of the way and get on with the rest of my life, my happiness would probably increase in leaps and bounds.

Wednesday 12 October 1994.

So here I am in France. I've been with M&D for the past couple of days, and it's been really nice, even though perhaps I've been a bit offish, just kind of anxious to get on with it. We've had a good time though and they took Valeria and me out for dinner last night, though I drank a wee bit too much. V's apartment's, two floors above mine, seems to have nice girls in it. Mine's full of Germans. We don't really talk much but at night I can hear them banging away with their boyfriends. Well at least one of them does! Valeria and I figured out there's an easy train to Milan. Yeahhhh! So that's next weekend sorted. We're gonna stay with her friend Marco, in centre. Can't wait!

It's a pretty enough town here, we had a quick look around the centre earlier, typical kind of greyish French town with uneven paving, tiny shops, boutiques and lots of very serious looking people hurrying around. There's a big pedestrianised bit which is nice — still grey, but nice and there seem to be quite a few little bars, or more like café's where people are clearly drinking tiny glasses of wine. (Small ones but definitely wine... Promising!) There's a huge river, which is nice, in fact it's all pretty nice. It's not Italy, polar opposite, but it's nice. Not something I can say about where we're living, which in fact is probably the most horrible concrete

jungle I've ever seen. We're living in and amongst a bunch of council flats,
full of immigrants and then us — foreign students. Hey ho...

Some of my initial fears, the ones about being killed by copious amounts of cheese-laden cuisine — I was convinced they put cheese in everything — and bored to death proved unfounded. Our particular area appeared to be largely populated by boisterous American boys with atrocious French accents. Finding comfort in our shared mother tongue, we partied with them while unsuccessfully trying to follow our tutor's directions to 'absorb a little culture'. As much as I was in a different country, my beliefs helped me to feel at home wherever I was, sort of, and religion was always a useful catalyst for meeting people so Valeria and I decided to go to church. It was a rather beautiful old church in the centre of the town, in a square unsurprisingly called, Place de l'Eglise. It was a tall, grey, imposing building, that clearly held its reign over the town and relatively simple on the outside; its beauty was within and the priest was very friendly indeed — we even ended up having lunch with him some days. After the church, the pub seemed like the logical, old-fashioned way to meet a local. A cute pub at the edge of the bridge stuck in the middle of a town that seemed a lot like a set from the movie *Chocolat*. It was a tacky English pub, Pub de l'Etoile, with heavily advertised karaoke but it did its job. There we met a small crowd who seemed to be slightly alternative and they introduced us to new places in town, which of course was great. One of these was Pierre — pronounced Pierrgh followed by some kind of rough vomit sound — and we figured that he would be as good a place as any to start befriending locals. He was a sweet kind of guy, smallish, well probably our height, (without heels) and dark, olive skin, black hair, dark eyes and quite a chiselled look actually. It was one of those friendships that Mum had advised could be 'beneficial'. Pierre was generally OK, until he invited us to watch his drama class one evening. Valeria and I went along, I wouldn't say eagerly, we'd have far rather been at the pub screeching out some '80s lyrics but it seemed cultural and as far from touristy as you could get so worth accepting. We should have read between the lines when he said 'experimental' for that is exactly what it was. A group of amateurs, grunting, moaning, shouting, jumping around and occasionally throwing out an impersonation of a monkey... It was hard to take it seriously, let alone as seriously as Pierre and his colleagues took it, so we spent most of the performance looking at each other, wondering what on earth we were doing there and bursting into hysterics. Intense Pierre made it clear he did not appreciate our lack of culture and appeared to lack any humour at all. However, that said, he did have one redeeming quality: his cousin, Léonard – mandatory pronounciation Leiyyyonargh - whom we'd met briefly, liked, then didn't see again for some time which naturally made me more interested in him. I soon found myself looking out for him wherever we went. The town was not huge; we were bound to run into him sooner or later.

Sunday 20 November 1994.

Finally, I did see Léonard, at Pub de l'Etoile. Of course he came really late – seems to like to make an entrance. Quite the lad. Was great, he's great to talk to albeit it's a bit tough to understand each other sometimes! I really, really like him but he spends half his time talking to everyone else. Well, gee, let's face it; if he only spoke to me the whole time, I'd get pissed off with that too! Hmmm — we'll see... he is a bit of a star though. Would like to think he did like me. Not think low of me or anything or get bored when my French is rubbish.

Must stop eating so much when I drink... Ahhhhhhh!

He was clearly a semi-bad boy. I think he would have liked to think he was a bad boy proper but he affected much of it. Still it appeared to have the required effect on most women including me. He was good-looking, tall, immensely so by Pierre's standards, tanned, soft fluffy hair, squinty eyes and very kissable bee stung lips. He wasn't thin but cuddly and wore old jeans snug where it counts and the short metallic green bomber jacket that anyone who was anyone had at the time, his hands permanently glued in its pockets. And he had a very husky voice; undoubtedly enhanced by the endless packets of Marlboro lights he smoked to complete the image. There was something intensely familiar about being around him and I'd realised that in many ways he represented all those North London cool boys that I'd spent so much time with, though never dated, probably because I wasn't Jewish. One thing mastered, now I had the chance to conquer that too. On top of that he was French so it was all rather exotic, in fact much more so than any of my Italian dalliances had been. Whilst there were all these stars in my eyes, on the other hand there were cultural barriers and they went deeper than my mispronunciations of French. One night he came over to dinner, the first time I'd rather nervously invited him over to our territory. Like a lot of French seemed to do, he enjoyed taking the opposing view and showing you how much he knows about something, which of course I was in awe of, he stood his ground firmly. He was effortlessly cooler than the other guys that Brigitta or Geraldine, my flatmates, had ever brought back, usually older Algerian, or some other non-French figure laden with couscous. Léonard listened a lot too and that really mattered to me; he looked at me intently when I spoke. And responded accordingly. The problem came when it got late and as I would with my English friends – male and female – I asked him to stay over. Well of course he took it another way. I never really liked jumping into bed with guys straight away, no matter how much I wanted them; I just couldn't do it. I had to feel safe with them, to trust that they really liked me – or at least I felt they did which might be a different thing. Aside from anything, from not being immediately 'ready', I was petrified they'd have their candy and run and that would be it. But you never know I think quite often in these situations you're damned if you do and damned if you don't.

Wednesday 23 November 1994.

It's so hard trying to second-guess a guy and what he wants! Practically impossible – though I guess a part of it's pretty obvious. At the end of the day, I think you just have to trust your instincts, follow your gut, do what you want to do... that way if it doesn't work out or have the desired effect, at least you know you were true to yourself. Does that make sense? Think so!

Trust your instinct to the end, though you can render no reason
(Ralph Waldo Emerson)

After endless Thanksgiving celebrations, meals, parties and whatnot with the Americans (was hard to believe we were in France at times), we rolled on into the festive season, that I actually understood, with just a few weeks remaining before a trip back home. The beginning of December signalled frantic study for exams, pre-Christmas festivities and a definite ramping up of my relationship with Léonard. Whilst learning French I did what I do with everything: I begin to idealise the world I'm in and so felt it appropriate to watch tons of French films by directors who seemed to get inside the heads and souls of young people, particularly Eric Rohmer. I'd discovered them back in Cambridge and now sought them out with intensity. I loved the settings and lost myself in the dreaminess and romance of it all. Amongst the arty, chicness of the Parisian or Riviera setting, there was always an apartment in a narrow, cobbled street into which the camera would probe through the aged shutters and there would be a couple – him equally as pretty as her, lying on white sheets – smoking after making tender, imploring and passionate love. There was often nothing joyous in these so-called romantic French films. I always felt an exquisite undercurrent of tension as if something was going to go wrong and it often did usually betrayal with a best friend or some awful hidden secret. Or something would happen like someone would wake up one day and announce they had to go hundreds of miles away and just leave and that would be it. But those scenes left their mark, crystal clear in my mind. I came to think of this as very French as it didn't tally with anything I'd experienced either on film or in real life so far. I wanted to live that moment, I dreamed of it being me held in the arms of someone special, on that significant bed laid in that significant room. I forgot about the ending that was irrelevant; it was that moment I was after. And I did. I did get to wake up in a simple white bed, with plain bed linen, a largely bare room, tall window before us with long linen fabric floating around and pale green shutters open to hear church bells chiming, birds singing and the early morning breeze caressing our bodies. I smiled to myself; I was living yet another of my dreams.

Thursday 15 December 1994.

On train home...

So exciting, sitting on TGV on way to Paris to catch plane home for Noel! It's a total jumble of mixed feelings. Looking forward to seeing everyone though will miss here too. Has been such a laugh lately. So great that Leo called yesterday – just made my day and year! Hope he feels what I do. Which is a lot!

Only thing is his friends are kind of dark. I just don't really like them, I mean they're OK, friendly n stuff but they're kind of depressing, heavy... serious... like super cool but in a dark way! They all smoke drugs... and are obsessed with Jim Morrison and the Doors who I happen to hate. (Thought I'd left that behind with Dominic and his morose crew.) Hate that depressive shit. They're all so close though. I sort of I feel a bit on the outside when they're all together. Room filled with smoke, everyone sprawled around listening to some droney, miserable bloke and a ton of background rock noise! Total headache! (They even asked me if I wanted to watch porn the other day!) I mean whattttt??

Hope I get to see more of him on his own after Christmas. Still feeling incredibly hung-over from last nights party – so am gonna sit back and enjoy the comfort of this rather luxurious train xx

Léonard was really my first relationship. The Italian ones I'd been too youthful for, they were really just going with the moment not actually getting involved consciously. The ones in London, well they were not much to write home about. In fact they were barely existent, rarely lasting more than five minutes. I had been good at making male friends, like Charlie and Karl, but not so great at the boyfriend thing. I mean look at Dominic and Mitch for starters. What was I thinking? This was the first time I felt the intensity of involvement and with it the need for a certain kind of resilience. The deeper you get into something, the more rewarding it can be but it also becomes riskier the more there is to lose. For all the moments I awoke and sailed into school with a huge 'I've just been rolling around on white bed linen' smile on my face, there were times with Léonard where I just felt inferior. Quite the opposite of the plan, where amongst other things, he was supposed to be giving recognition, making me feel good. In addition, he could be painfully critical. Having worked so hard for my skinny figure and achieved it, it seemed he didn't share my delight and instead insisted I needed bigger boobs.

We'd be in bed, usually my rickety old council flat bed, albeit with nice sheets, where the idyllic romantic scene definitely required some effort and he'd splurt out in a husky whisper:

"You sood take ze pil" like a great bundle of birds' shit falling on us.

"Why?"

"Vill make you bubs biggeur."

"It won't."

"Qui?"

"Non, this is how I am."

He suggested, no actually he insisted, I go on the pill, as it would increase their size. I pointed out that nobody in my family had big boobs and it wasn't going to happen. Should a boyfriend make you feel bad about yourself? No. Definitely not, however at the time, I had no idea quite how out of order he was. And I was vulnerable. My grandfather had taken ill again and the news was that it was quite bad. It broke my heart, but I felt helpless, I didn't know what I could do where I was or at home for that matter. Being so far away made it harder for me to manage though, without the family circle around me, I guess it was like just dealing with it all on your own. Fortunately, Valeria and I had fitted landlines so that we could call each other instead of having to traipse up and downstairs all the time, which was now coming in very useful to call home and Grandma of course. Léonard was there for me and I needed him. As I landed at Heathrow for Christmas, expectant of the usual euphoric family grins I was greeted by the whole family heavy with half smiles, and a solemnness. Grandma was there too. My heart sank as I imagined what must have happened yet I was confused at the same time. As Mum walked towards me, held out her hands and tilted her head in silence, I burst into tears. The journey home was quiet; I held Grandma's hand. When Grandad passed away I knew I could not let go of Léonard, no matter what I thought of him. I needed something to fill the void.

Thursday 22 December 1994.
Grandad's funeral.

Lots of dark colours — all very sad. God bless his soul. Rushing around the house, everyone collecting people from all over the place, the Italian relatives are here... and we're all running a bit late, typical.

Incredibly tough thing to go through. To see the poor coffin — could hardly look at it etc. and then the cremation. Very difficult and touching, though went smoothly, tons of people — Grandad couldn't have had it or wanted it any better.

It is not death that a man should fear, but he should fear never beginning to live.
(Marcus Aurelius)

Grandad was afraid of dying... very afraid. But I think now he's realised he didn't need to be.

Perhaps it was my faith however a feeling gradually came over me that Grandad was OK wherever he was. There was peace for him now and he was making it easier for me, us, to accept what had happened.

I was standing at the kitchen sink with my mother, the day of the funeral. Everyone else was in the lounge, drinking and eating. It felt unexpectedly upbeat.

"It's strange. I don't feel as bad as I thought. I mean I feel sad he's not here with us any more but I feel like I can accept it and that Grandad wants us to be at peace."

She put her arm around me. "I feel exactly the same way."

"It's as if he's helping us. Doesn't want us to feel miserable or mourn... I mean after all that's what he was all about, in his good days..."

"I know, darling. I think you're right."

Wednesday 4 January 1995.

Back to Besançon! Would love to see Leo this weekend. Not sure how possible that is. Let's hope the journey back goes OK for now. And let's just hope it's an excellent New Year for all of us... that we are happy, healthy and tanned!

Life is a roller coaster! Full of ups and downs.
(Unknown)

New Year Resolutions.

1. *Enjoy myself and have a good time — without drinking too much!*
2. *Stop scoffing: no more scoffing my or anyone else's food when coming in late etc. No more from fridge in my room or anything. No scoffing after big piss-ups (which incidentally shouldn't be happening anyway. See point 1.)*
3. *Not to miss too much college. Make a super huge effort to learn loads of French.*

Besançon was covered in snow and looked picture perfect pretty. Seeing the snow-capped trees from the train, the little têtes des maisons and the flashes of green popping through the landscape in gleaming sunlight warmed my spirits. I was so happy to meet up with friends and predictably I totally broke each one of my resolutions, before they'd had time to set. The night I arrived I drank wine, a whole bunch of Kirs, had dinner at Petit Polonais then more wine and more Kir and then came home and pigged out on anything I could find in the fridge, mainly Brigitta's cheese. And I missed the first day of college due to a massive hangover.

Sunday 7 January 1995.
New Year Resolutions Begin Tomorrow!

We were due to leave France at the end of February and take up residence in Siena for the Italian part of our year abroad. I was still seeing Léonard but it didn't seem the same. It was apparent to me that my interest in him had become far greater than his in me, no matter how many sweet things he said – I was probably just another foreign student, but I had to see it through. The relationship was feeling strained and he seemed to be stepping back a little but at the same time was happy to drag it out until the end.

"Les sentiments, sont les sentiments, l'amour, c'est l'amour, et le business c'est le business," is what he said one day. Though oblivious to it at the time, this was and is the way of someone who simply compartmentalises everything according to his own agenda and always has an excuse up his sleeve for not being present. After all, there was always 'business' and it was always more important than anything else. He was preparing the escape tunnel. For my last weekend in France Charlie had suggested coming to meet me and spending a couple of days in Paris. He was still seeing Karen, the German girl he'd been with for a while but we'd kept in touch and he wanted to celebrate my departure (and see Paris). Despite Léonard's reticence, I was still wrapped up in him, clinging like a limpet to those last moments and so when Charlie eventually couldn't make it, I spent that last weekend with Léonard, savouring every tiny moment. I had not conquered France, nor had it conquered me. One thing I had done though, most certainly due to my relationship with my French beau as opposed to any form of lesson was, I'd managed to learn very good French. In fact I was practically fluent and very proud of it but that significant achievement was momentarily clouded over by what I thought were inconsolable feelings for Léonard. That final weekend was emotional. I was in pieces. He didn't promise anything, other than to keep in touch, and nor did I expect him to, though of course I hoped that he would be thinking of me and we'd see each other again. I am not exactly sure what I really expected. Did I want him to come after me? Would we live happily ever after? All I knew is that I didn't want to let go. I couldn't. There is a complexity to relationships made abroad because they force you to ask certain questions that the relationship may not be ready for. The urgency of meeting someone when you're travelling can be exciting but in some ways it's a bit false, predicated on a certain scenario.

As Valeria and I struggled to the station with a ridiculous amount of luggage, I was in no mood for a fun trip. I felt sorry for her having to put up with that but as usual she was wonderful. What should have been the crescendo of the year and indeed the only part I'd wanted to do originally, now felt like a right old trudge.

CHAPTER 7
Siena

France had not turned out to be a poor second cousin to Italy after all. We'd learned to ski, met some brilliant people, learned French, discovered Christmas markets, *vin chaud* and yes, there was of course Léonard. Leaving for Siena, I was pretty much a bundle of misery but Valeria did her best to lighten the load. Our transit was pure comedy, which also distracted me from my woes. We took the sleeper train to Italy, a first time experience for us both. Our couchette was already full of sleeping Italians, who we were soon to discover were also extremely grumpy as we lugged our oversized suitcases into the cabin. They didn't appreciate our cases or our noise or us it seemed. It took a long time for us to figure out where things went, most importantly how on earth we got into our lower bunks once the cases had taken up all the space. We left no room in the carriage, woke everyone up and gave ourselves a fit of the giggles.

Once I'd waved Valeria off at Pisa and changed trains for Siena, the rot set in again. When I left France, Léonard had seemed determined to intellectualise the state of our relationship. "Well it is what it is," he said with indecipherable candour and his attitude was completely devoid of any emotion. I was so upset that he was acting as if I was just another one of the gang at the pub. It was crushing; whilst I hadn't thought I was the love of his life I had thought I'd meant more than this. But he seemed to be going out of his way to make me think that nothing special had happened. On the other hand there was the possibility that he was being strong for me, as one of my friends had said, but in truth I knew that wasn't Leo: he was too selfish for that. Léonard was all about Léonard.

I had to face the fact that what I'd had was really a quintessential travel romance. The kind of connection predicated on nothing more than me being there and up for a party. I pondered whether it would have happened in the UK. Would I have been interested in him if he was local? I doubted it. The mere fact of being in France set me free just like it did in Italy. Yet I hadn't taken any of the Italian 'romances' to heart, apart from Riccardo I suppose, which seemed trivial now, so why was I pining so much about this one? I guess I never actually slept with Riccardo, so as much as I adored him, he never quite held such a place in my heart. I was also annoyed because I'd let Léonard criticise the way I looked in a way I wouldn't take from a guy back home in London, so there was an element of feeling stupid because he didn't want me after all, at least not for 'me' as I was. This was probably my first set of 'grown-up' feelings about a man: the realisation that yes they could be bastards and they could do it intentionally. I cried all the way to Siena, much to the dismay of the other people on the train, fortunately nicer than the previous ones I'd encountered, who offered, tissues, drinks and sweets.

Friday 10 March 1995.

Back in London for Miserable Weekend!

Have been thinking a lot of Léonard lately. Have rung so many times and never managed to speak to him. Think I'm really just going to have to forget that one. I've been feeling total crap, really weak and run down so had to come home, back to UK for the weekend. I really needed these few days at home. I've got conjunctivitis — great, blocked nose and am literally so so sad. Now Crispi's put on a song from 'Lion King' and that's seriously the last straw. I'm sat here crying my eyes out. I'm having a mini break down! Had to have proper chat with family about it all, about Léonard — it felt good just to let it out. Went for dinner with family and Grandma who is so wise and funny; she always takes the edge off, sat with her air of wisdom and harmony. We giggled a lot and had fun. It's a hard time for me at the moment, not really 100 per cent with not seeing Léonard, even though I guess I know it's over. Very confused, weak and emotional. Feel like I've been hit by a bus. I just can't seem to pull myself together like I usually do.

Note: Strength is not a measure of the body; it's a measure of the soul.
(Unknown)

According to my stars, tomorrow supposed to be a lucky day for me.

My arrival in the beautiful Italian town of Siena was made more welcoming by the presence of an old friend of my mother's, Sandra. Sandra lived close by in the beautiful town of Lucca, a town heavily populated by Brits living the Tuscan dream and home to Prince Charles's favourite Pasticceria. Sandra was crazy, my mum's childhood friend, wild and eccentric. A strong woman, not slight, short blonde hair and spoke well-learned Italian albeit with a strong English accent. She was lovely, taking me under her wing, helping me with all the administration I needed, of which there was tons and even helping out Crazy Penny, my Brady Bunch friend from Cambridge. Penny and I had been neighbours in halls, then we shared infamous 'Herbert house', and now we'd be in the same flat in Siena. Penny was petrified of Italy, the reverse of me as we embarked on this adventurous year; she loved France and French and panicked with all things Italian. Her language was indeed appalling, and when she did get something right, it was simply masked under an unfathomable Geordie accent. She was the kind of accident-prone person who could be guaranteed to trip over empty space. On this occasion her arrival was pretty spectacular. She'd seen me outside the flat with Sandra, whilst passing in a taxi, opened the door while it was still moving and hit a motorcyclist who'd gone flying over the top. Luckily nobody was hurt and Sandra was there to help with the smoothing over. And that was just the start. To say we settled into our new lodgings easily would not be accurate. The place was chaos. You cannot settle into a flat with eight other girls from around the world, raring to go, ready for new experiences. And some with rather ridiculous expectations:

"Ciao! Benvenuti – sono Erica."

"Ciao Grazie, sono Natalie, e Penny."

"Inglesi?"

"Si voi?"

"Americani."

"Ah so we can speak English then?"

"No no no no no – solo Itaiano!"

"What? But we all speak English, it's our language."

"No! In questa casa solo Italiano."

"That's just weird!"

Penny looked mortified, like she wanted to keel over and cry, I looked at her stunned with a, 'are these people for real look and ushered her into my room. 'She'll be damned if she thinks I'll speak Italian to her' 'don't worry!' Erica looked like Trunchbull... definitely not one to mess with.

Moreover you can hardly settle when you discover that your flat is opposite an Italian military academy filled with local testosterone, wrapped in swagger and crisp new uniforms.

Can't deny it wasn't immensely fun living directly opposite the local military base! Lots of hot young males doing their obligatory service, Italian style: with a huge air of fun. Who can resist a man in uniform anyway, let alone a whole troop of them! Hanging out of their windows, khaki uniforms open, sleeves rolled up, yelling "Ue Bella... Bellissima!" Somehow leagues more charming than the butt-crack-showing builders you might get hollering at you back in England. Needless to say our adrenalin was regularly pumping – as was theirs no doubt with the amount of topless prancing around going on, clearly visible through open windows, soon progressing to similarly half naked sunbathing on the balcony until dramatically called to a halt by the local police. If they'd had any personal choice in the matter, I'm sure they'd have probably encouraged it by the look on their faces. Anyway... the military boys became quite a part of our 'apartment life'. Of the ten girls from around the globe, at least half of us I'd say had a dalliance of sorts with a military man. They had their curfews, their strict routines, which we knew pretty much as well as they did – and if any one of them was missing, our place was always their first point of call. Genario was the one after me. Genario? Who calls their child Genario? Well, he was from the south, so very dark, well built; this was something that ran through the group and their uniforms did nothing but accentuate it. Genario was sweet, quite persistent which was flattering but he wasn't for me... hello – another friendship! Regardless of the countless love letters that appeared at my door and hot as he was, for me he was a friend. That's something that had never changed in me – I either liked you in that way or I didn't. And if I didn't – you might as well forget it as you won't get a look in. (No pun intended.)

Perhaps unwisely, I had planned a week back in Besançon during one of our breaks. Actually the whole time in Siena was a break really: we only had school for half days, which left plenty of time for drinking prosecco, eating pizza, sunbathing and partying. As the week away approached, I wasn't sure whether to go but I decided I would: I told myself it wasn't about Léonard and that I would be staying with one of the friends I'd made there so whether I saw him or not didn't matter since I'd have fun anyway. That is what I told myself. And while I did have a blast during that week, visiting old haunts and meeting up with the old gang. It was really good to see everyone and in some ways it made me realise Besançon was not just about Léonard but so much more. Nonetheless I was disappointed, as he hadn't appeared. Then finally, at the end of the week on my last day, we met at the pub. "To talk," he'd said.

I was relieved. No matter how hard I tried, I still hadn't managed to get him out of my head. I had to see it through to the end, read that all-important last page! Nuts really – I rarely read the last page of any book, lucky if I got past the first half... but in life – well, that was a different ballgame. I couldn't let anything go; it was never over until it was over.

You know how people tell you when you meet up with a guy you should be absolutely calm and on top of things? I wasn't. I wanted to be but I was seriously angry with him, though not that angry that I hadn't left a little trapdoor open of the 'innocent until proven guilty' kind of thing. If Léonard had known how to do it, he could have pushed that open in a millisecond but of course he didn't. Or maybe he didn't want to. He did manage to soften me up enough to stay and chat and we ended up going to his cousin's flat in a reasonably friendly manner. At this point I was feeling OK about things, open-minded. So we finally got to Lioneeeeel's place, supposedly for some quiet away from the pub... away from all the new students living our life. I was looking forward to this new step, away from the tourist trap, into real life Besançon to talk with my... Whatever he was. So we get there, he drops down the bed and I swing round the chair from the desk right by him and sit on it. I wait for him to speak. He pulls my hand towards him.

"Vien, vien."

I move on to the bed and he pounces, his hand halfway down my jeans before I know it.

"No."

"Wot? Wot you wont?"

"I don't want to just sleep with you... I mean..."

"But zats wot piple do in relationship"

"Yeah and they also keep in touch!"

That was it for me, gave me the clarity I needed! I was done. I was hurt but at least I knew where I stood, it confirmed my view that was all I ever really was to him. End of play. Read my final page. It wasn't a happy ending, but it was an ending and I guess the one I'd predicted. Time to move on.

Back in Siena our little temporary family was weaving itself together. Flatmates, military passers-by from across the road and a few others, including the mysterious Italian twins, Marco and Massimo were all part of our somewhat irregular circle. Marco and Massimo were very good-looking boys, aged mid-twenties who hailed from Bari. From the beginning there was something mystical about them, slightly sinister. I'd been somewhat drawn to Marco, classic mix of ambiguity and good looks that set me off. We spent time together and the flirting increased. Emma, another Erasmus student I'd befriended, had taken up with his twin Massimo and was insistent I gave Marco a chance. I had my reservations but as time went on and we got closer our relationship likened itself far more to that of Emma and Massimo until we were sort of seeing each other. We all spent a ton of time together, in their flat cooking pasta; well, they cooked it, convinced we wouldn't have a clue how to do it. Tomato pasta, simple but exquisite, abundant with chilli, the smell filled the air. I often felt a sense of Grandma when I was in there, almost making me aware to guard myself. I don't know what it was, almost a 'be careful', a warning. Anyway she wasn't there – maybe it was just my mind playing games. But there was something that held me back. Not least their odd friendship with an eccentric Tuscan count, who was more than twice their age and was frankly quite peculiar. He was a large man, overweight, immaculately dressed, quite the old school Italian aristocrat. He'd buy us all drinks, be friendly but never give anything away. He was very close to the twins, extremely so. Everyone knew but no one really got it. One day, with drama and tension clearly in the air, he met us on 'Piazza del Campo' and suggested I should come back to his house with the twins. I wondered why as it hadn't been a fun afternoon but I couldn't deny myself the curiosity of seeing where he lived. He inhabited a grand Palazzo that had obviously been in the family for years. It dripped with fine art, vintage furniture, precious ceramics and exquisite rugs. The entrance was signposted grandly with an extravagant yet beautiful and obviously old, crystal chandelier. Below this was an equally impressive grand staircase lined with thick red carpet that swirled its way to the upper floors. *Meraviglioso!*

I was in the kitchen, when I heard shouts.

"What! How dare you."

"I can't... not any more..."

"After all I've done for you? All I do? You'd be nothing..."

I heard doors slam, and saw Massimo almost fall into the garden. Where was Marco? It appeared in the bathroom with Armando but I daren't check. The plate of mozzarella, tomato and basil laid out on the kitchen table lay untouched. Through the glass doors, I tried to catch Massimo's attention but no joy. My heart began to race, I felt quite lost, in what was clearly a serious issue.

"Natalie, Natalie, come this way." I was being ushered along the corridor by Marco.

He pushed me into a room and the next thing I knew he had shut the door and I heard a key turn in the lock.

"Ehi! Let me out."

The shouting continued for some time while I demanded they open the door and let me out.

Helpless, I sat on the floor in this beautiful room, antique cream and gold tapestry sofas like something out of Buckingham Palace, frescos on the sky high walls, worn rug centrepiece with a story woven through it, that had to be hundreds of years old and almost floor to ceiling windows looking out onto what appeared to be endless landscaped gardens. I wondered how I'd ended up in this mess. I knew they wouldn't hurt me. In some ways they were too crazy, too stupid but I still panicked and hated being locked in, I was slightly claustrophobic at the best of times.

Suddenly there was a click and the door opened. I pushed past Armando and made for the door. At that moment there were shouts of phone, phone, Natalie, Mama.

Marco's mother wanted to talk to me. What the hell did she want?

"No I just want to go home."

"Please, please, she wants to talk to you," said Massimo.

"You must stick with Marco and not leave him in the house, Natalie. Please."

"Why?"

"You are important to him. You are the only one he will listen to and only you can persuade him not to see the Conte."

What was she talking about? Why was it my responsibility to be part of their little games?

I gave the phone back and announced I was going.

"It is not as bad as you think," said Marco with puppy dog, yet reserved eyes.

"I don't care. I'm sick of you all. And locking me in like that. Get out of my way; I'm going home."

It was a couple of days until Marco and I made up. We talked a lot but I was wary – one day he kept insisting he wanted to make love to me… in that all Italian passionate way. I said, "I only want to make love to you if you love me, which you don't…" I was kind of playing along though still not sure whether I would or wouldn't.

He said, "I love you." Really? He said, "I do today, but tomorrow is another day. I'm not saying I will love you forever, I'm saying that I love you now." What bullshit. Then he forced himself on me – with pressure. I fought against and he held me down. He was unbuttoned, hard and ready and cleverly getting under my clothes.

"Basta!" I yelled at him and swore I'd scream if he didn't stop. He put his hand over my mouth. I bit it.

"What the hell are you doing?" I said as he backed off. He had tears in eyes.

"You don't understand… I need you. You're different, I need you I do."

"But you're not open with me – how can I be close to you?"

A few days later I managed to get the truth from Marco. And just as I'd imagined, it turned out, they were on the dodgy side. The twins came from a very poor family and the Conte was exceptionally rich – and gay. This paid their education. Urgh.

Sunday 9 April 1995.

Yayyy Sam's here – we've had such a fun time as always… love having her here. Fab day yesterday in Florence, went round the Uffizi and drank prosecco on the rooftop bar overlooking the city having meaningful chats! Incredibile. We just get each other, SUCH a good time, loads of chats, laughs and mucking about.

A best friend isn't someone who's just always there for you. It's someone who understands you a bit more than you understand yourself.

(Unknown)

Letter from Sam

Cara la mia Natalie

Hello darling Duckie.... Hope everything is jubbly, it's 11 April and the end of my beautiful holiday, I've had a lovely time and will be sad to leave this wonderful country but more than anything I will miss you and your constant chatting of yoghurt. Goodbye Gennaro. Goodbye Barone Rosso. Goodbye your balcony in the sunshine. It's not good-bye for us as we'll be 'insieme' very soon; we'll celebrate with a bottle of Spumante. We always have an excellent time together and lets hope that when we're ninety we'll be in Italy bombing around and drinking Pina Colada together. Have fun, I'll think of you and wish you the best of luck with the ninja turtle (Léonard) and Fabrizio. When we're apart we're together in spirit – if you're feeling lonely just shout out Albatross and I'll be there. Thanks 4 having me.

Love forever, your chicken, Sam xx

Léonard was by now a distant memory and with the slight hiccup of Marco put to one side in a friendly truce. I was well and truly back in the arms of Italy and the Italian stallion that was Fabrizio. Fabrizio was one of those men you think are out of your league when you meet them. He was beautiful, had an angelic face, the poise of a model and ticked every box. OK I know I've said

105

that before but he really did. I saw him standing at the bar in Barone Rosso, where we'd pile in nightly to sing along with the live band whilst drowning in a wealth of cocktails. I'll never forget that night. I'm going to marry him I told myself. His floppy dirty blond hair falling in his crystal blue eyes and brown leather bomber jacket collar half shielding his face, he stood out. I tried to catch his eye – subtly. Surely this was the one. He was studying business at the time, which I thought was a strange choice for him, as he just seemed to be more the creative type. We hung out a lot, sharing drinks, jokes and a mutual love of sunbeds.

EASTER 1995 VICENZA HURRAH.

Wow, I got to Vicenza after a pretty awful journey. Had to sit on my bag the whole way there was literally no space, totally packed. Carlo, the driver was there to collect me and I immediately felt totally special. Love it! So great to see everyone. Predictably they're stuffing me with food, whatever they can get their hands on, or at least they're trying. Just can't eat like this all the time. We've come to Sirmione, on the lake, it's amazing. I have the most gorgeous suite in the most gorgeous hotel... Wait for it. Obviously the best here! It's one of THE top three suites in the whole hotel! Room service all the time. Call 408 for breakfast in bed. TV, ciggies in room. Proprio la vita di una stella (a movie star life). Have thought lots about Fabrizio and obviously told everyone about him! They all want to meet him now, so hopefully we'll get to that at some point. Sure it will go down the drain now I've probably jinxed it. Rosalie booked me sunbed (like I needed it) and then we had huge Easter Sunday lunch and lovely walk around town. Got back and dinner! Four more courses. Crazy, always the same. Food. More Food and more Food. Like let's see how much we can stuff ourselves with in the shortest time. Geez. Well it's so lovely here but am kind of sick of eating. Rosalie choked on a piece of steak last night (total drama) I mean, slow down guys! Look forward to heading back to Siena but want to see Grandma first. It must be hard for her. Pasquetta. Monday.

Seeing Grandma at the airport, standing there all stick straight was very moving. She had tears in her eyes, which almost made me cry. I sat next to her in the car on the way back. We chatted all the way home and when we got there too. Then I had to leave.

The journey back was about as much of a disaster as the one there. My uncle clearly told me the train would arrive on the platform where he dropped me, which was pleasing as I've always been a disaster at getting around. So as soon as it pulled in, I lugged my case on and sat down, relaxed and excited to get back to see Fabrizio... things had been hotting up lately but we still hadn't sealed the deal so to speak. I hadn't felt ready. The train was stopping lots though I didn't recognise any of the towns we were passing through. I asked a normal looking guy next to me where we were and it turned out we were going to Bologna! Great. Bang went my pocket money from Rosalie – had to spend all two hundred euros on a taxi back to Siena! But I did meet a nice boy – Giacomo.

Back in Siena we were gearing up for one of our infamous parties. Our terrace spanned the entire width of the building and round a corner so it offered the perfect space. As it filled up, the door opened yet again. Standing there, posing, one arm leant high on the door frame, the other on his hip, wearing a black Dolce and Gabbana suit and white open shirt was of course Fabrizio. Over dressed, yes – did it work, yes.

"Ciao, Stella." He squeezed me tight.

"Ciao Fabri, vieni vieni…'

I led him in and no sooner had I done so he was gone. He spent the whole night ogling the six-foot Norwegian girls, flirting and flicking his hair. After just a day before, he'd had me squashed up against my bathroom wall, insisting we took things to that next step, whilst I could hardly breathe. What is it with these aggressive men? I was amazed at the gall of his behaviour. Sure enough he was back, his tail between legs at the end of the night – but seriously – no.

I had my fun though. Danger free. Well, in the emotional sense. I'd kept contact with Giacomo, my train guide, and he'd been asking me to visit him on Isola d'Elba where his family ran a holiday park. I took him up. I needed some fun yet everything around me was complicated and false. He met me at the port – we sailed across to the island on the ferry, sat upstairs, holding hands, basking in the sunshine. It would be a weekend of detached harmless fun, where there would be no heartache or competition. And so it was. He treated me like a queen, showed me the island and his home and we dined by candlelight by the sea. He was gentle, kind and affectionate. I felt loved and appreciated that night and even though he would have wanted more this was all I needed. I returned happy and satisfied. Far more satisfactory than the dramatic love triangles of Siena.

The year out was drawing to a close. I had managed to stretch it out until the absolute last moment, extending my lease to add on the entire summer. In these few months, I'd started to feel I had changed. It was the first time I felt properly grown up in my life. I can't really pinpoint how or when it happened but something big had shifted inside me. Perhaps it was the time with Léonard and the way he'd treated me that had set it off. Maybe it was just something that happened organically. I felt I had to mark this progress in some way. And so I took my beautiful, long sun-kissed hair to the hairdresser's and did the most grown-up thing I could think of: I cut it all off. When my mother turned up to the flat to collect me, she didn't recognise me. Mission accomplished.

CHAPTER 8
Back to Blighty

Monday 18 September 1995.

Monday... Ahhh... Back to College... Can't believe it, yet another change — 'tis difficult keep switching environments also fun I guess, have to say though, I had such an excellent, excellent summer this year just made it even tougher! I mean totally Excellent!

PS: Really don't want to lose tan.

PPS: Alcohol=brilliant but false friend. You have great time etc. but often end up doing things you don't really want to.... hence the regret and guilt. Urgh!

Must stop pigging out and drinking so much. Went out and had sick and disgusting kebab which I didn't want or need at all! So stupid, Then came home and pigged out on stuff from fridge. Which I also didn't want! — and it all boils down to the drink! Just read women should consume fourteen units PER WEEK. I DO THAT PER DAY!

You make a mistake, you pay for it.
(Unknown)

News: Marco wants to visit. Can't quite believe it! Not a good idea. Massimo's been speaking to Emma about it too apparently. Penny's been really sweet but will always be type to gossip a lot and talk behind your back. She's been whispering loads lately with Nikki (new addition in house — grunge type from Bristol). Thought she wouldn't do it to me after how close we've been and all I did for her in Italy, but if you gossip, you gossip; she talks about everyone so she's obviously talking about me too. I know they talk about my food and drink habits. But I'm no way as bad as Amy was. I mean she actually ended up leaving the house and Uni for it. I mean I admit I have weird habits regarding these, don't deny it, so many girls do anyway. Think it's far easier to be open about it. Guess Penny will be how she will be. Gossiping is her way of assuming a friendship with another person, getting close to them quickly. Not going to let it get in way of our friendship though... may not be my principles; just the way she is.

Treat people as if they were what they ought to be and you help them to become what they are capable of being.
(Johann Wolfgang von Goethe)

Makes me think of something Dad said once. People who have no faith, no religion, are just out for themselves and only think about themselves.

Anyway hope I get my job back at Benetton and they haven't forgotten about me. I just have to spend so much money. (Wish I could just be famous or something.)

**For those that think, the world is comedy.
For those that feel, the world is tragedy.**
(Horace Walpole)

Some people hang on to university, not wanting to let go and move on. As much as I loved the people I'd met, I was ready for new things. Coming back from Italy I had no desire to stretch out my final year. I wanted to finish the work, do exams and get it over

111

with. Something had changed in me and while I still enjoyed the house, the parties and the fun, deep down I knew this wasn't what I wanted the rest of my life to be. I enjoyed the people around me but I hadn't planned on carrying them with me eternally. I certainly didn't want to be defined by who I was there and by those people and I was aware that could happen. It was too easy, too safe to stay in this bubble. I just couldn't see myself being happy like that and the idea of marrying someone from college terrified me. It was all too convenient this life and I was sure there was something more, something better! My desire to Do Something had already seen me get modelling shots but nothing had come of those. Then there had been the *Cosmopolitan* competition but that hadn't proved fruitful either. Not to worry though, I had another idea. I would become a television presenter and separate myself from the rest of the pack. The thought of this excited me; the idea that I could be hosting *The Big Breakfast* or something. It wasn't impossible.

Thursday 28 September 1995.

Horrible day at Benetton. Got lovely letter from Sam though, all her news. She's on good form, gave me all the goss from the weekend.

Belated birthday night out night. Was a scream... So much fun. Spumante and G&Ts at our house, then out on the town, to Zac's bring your own wine – Mexican. Whole load of us. Val got me Baileys and two glasses, which is now practically gone.

Also went to Toni and Guy earlier and had hair cut again! All pretty short – Exactly what I wanted. Will probably grow it out again now.

Note from Penny 29/9/95.

Dearest Nats.

You're so cool and I'm pleased I'm living with you once again. Yet another year has passed us by and now we are here at the end of our course. Almost! It's going to be a toughie but we'll get through by drinking plenty of Pina Coladas and spumante, nice food and good chats.

Cin Cin jolly friend

Love Always

You're the best

Penny

Penny wasn't the only one to notice I had a problem with food and I knew it didn't look good to others. People often remarked that I looked thin or unwell. In my bid to take some control of the situation and de-emphasise my focus on what I was eating or not as it happened, I decided an exercise programme was in order and discovered the joy of aerobics, the forerunner to pretty much every exercise class going today. A group of us joined, so it was the social thing as well as immensely beneficial. We'd cycle there and back, usually risking our lives but reaping maximum rewards. I was delighted to feel my body moving and it had the effect of making me feel positive, indeed I began to evangelise about it. Sometimes I ask myself where this intense desire for control came from. I knew the regime I set myself – and broke on a regular basis – was not a totally healthy way of living but it gave me some power, not just over my body but over my mind and hence seemingly put me in control of my life. I wonder now if my early days at school, the spite and nastiness I felt from Tanya and others at such a critical stage had something to do with it. On the other hand there was the possibility that I was kind of messed up but it baffled me. My parents had never asked for perfection or put an emphasis on such things and for them looks were not the end game. They always encouraged me to develop my character and brain. I had a strong, loving family, friends who embraced food happily so I couldn't excuse myself on the grounds that my peers were influencing me. As for the era we lived in, well it was no different to any other era. Sure there were women's magazines but if you think back to the twenties when women went mad over the skinny flapper look, there were no celebrities in magazines like today – or on Instagram. The funny thing was that even if I achieved some control on a daily basis it didn't make me particularly happy. The achievement itself wasn't worth the agony I put myself through. I was also drinking too much and I wasn't really enjoying it. The two were definitely connected. It's funny but for someone who wanted to be in control I really wasn't and the fact that I would sneakily drink before I went out and sneakily eat when I came back in, was symptomatic of something I was sure. Perhaps it was just that big, yearning, gap of emotion that exists in all of us and that we all try to push away.

New Year's Day 1996.
NEW YEAR!
A new year and certain changes have to be made. Had an excellent time last night until two o'clock of course, when the alcohol caught up with me! Pigged out then fell ridiculously asleep in a chair. Everyone was really good to me though it can't happen again. Ever. Not like that. Am going to stop sneakily drinking before going out and generally all afternoon. NO AFTERNOON DRINKING! And just drink socially when out and not too

much (not obsessively). Also stop obsessing over what I eat. (Stop taking laxatives!) Generally try to relax more, be less fanatical and maybe that way stay slim or even lose a few pounds. If I don't think about it, it will happen sort of thing. I shall also aim to find and nurture some sort of direction in my life, which is definitely lacking. Plus, I wouldn't mind a GREAT GUY and perhaps for once have something a little more serious or profound than previous experiences.

Generally hope I can stay relaxed and happy and not change at all (i.e. physically! Unless slimmer of course).

God helps those who help themselves.
(Benjamin Franklin)

Why Léonard turned up to stay in Golders Green I'll never know. Anyway I wasn't particularly fussed about it; shocked but not fussed. I agreed to see him anyway and all it did was put me in a bad mood. His self-assuredness and nerve wound me up. He irritated me. I don't think a girl has to be around a man who rejected her. I'd had my exams and was a bit worried about them and my drinking was becoming more of an issue. Albeit disguised as partying, it was too much. In a bid to conquer both food and drink challenges I'd created, I decided not to eat, just to drink in the mistaken belief that it would prevent me putting on weight. It also made me less hyperactive or so I thought. I was often anxious but had no idea what about. Drinking calmed me down and helped me forget. I wasn't bothered about Léonard though; in fact I was more bothered about not being bothered. It hit me again that whenever I worshipped people abroad, thinking how amazing and special they are, it just doesn't work when they come to my territory. Of course it baffles them: Léonard couldn't understand how I'd gone from needy girl to blowing him off with barely a phone conversation. I'd done what I always do, in fact it's what lots of people do on holiday or when they're away and meet someone: you idolise them and their surroundings and it all seems to glitter in a way that whatever you left behind cannot possibly compete with. It's new, different and exciting. But it's also easily disposable as I came to find, time and time again. I was getting bored with disposable men and an impermanent life. I wanted something real. I wasn't going to get it at university and that's why I was probably so impatient to get out of there. By May, the restlessness had well and truly overtaken me and I was looking for methods of missing lessons and lectures to head back to London. If I could have just sat in a room for a few days and done it all then walked off I would have. I realised I was in the minority; everyone else was enjoying what they saw as halcyon days, even bemoaning the end of exams because it would signal the move that many of them didn't want to make into the big, wide world and they would have to get a life instead of just tagging on to whatever was going on at the time. Though, if I'd thought of just sneaking out of there I was wrong, very wrong. There was drama – it seemed the tutors didn't believe I was capable of the level of work I'd produced in my dissertation and I was accused of plagiarism. It was a complete falsehood, based on their value judgements about me. People just never give me enough credit. So I had to present myself in front of an insanely pompous, exaggerated 'university court' and argue my case. I won and graduated. Thank God, I could get on with the rest of my life.

Back in London I hit a wall and found myself just staying in bed a lot. If I wasn't going out I had no motivation and could foresee the boredom setting in. I decided I had to get a job and naturally my parents thought it was a good idea. Given my experience at Benetton, it seemed natural to apply to them and with family encouraging me I went off and dropped my resume in and the new shop in Oxford Circus. I was quite excited as it was supposed to be their flagship store in London and the biggest in the world. Plus I wanted and needed money, badly. They gave me a job and for a while it felt good being in central London, knowing I could meet old friends after work and just cruise from bar to restaurant. It felt good to have Sam in such close proximity again. Distance had not dulled our friendship: like Valeria, Sam was someone I counted as a true best friend. There was still the whole usual crowd we'd been hanging out with most weekends, mix of Crispi's friends and mine, and then there was Alex. At least once in your life something is put in front of you that you haven't got a hope in hell of having but it doesn't stop you toying with it. We were in Hard Rock Café for cocktails and burgers (or salad in my case). Sam had warned me about Alex, that a) she knew I'd like him and b) he was trouble. So in he struts, (literally), this amazingly attractive, gigolo type, open dark suit with partially unbuttoned white shirt, no tie. His squinty eyes assessed the room and landed on me, he knew who I was, his eyes fixed for a second, my heart sank and mouth watered. With expected post boarding school slaps on the back, the boys saluted each other and then it was my turn.

"Hi... Alex," he offered, in a deep surprisingly un-boarding school accent, then again none of them had that, more North London than anything.

117

"Natalie."

He gently pulled me in for a kiss on each cheek.

"So! What are we drinking?" He was waving down the waiter in an efficacious 'listen to me' way. Alex was cool and flash.

Benetton soon became less of a novelty and more of a chore and through a friend I'd met in Siena, now a pretty solid part of our crew, I got a job in PR. Well that all sounds rather more glamorous than it actually was, something you can safely say about PR in general. Like most jobs that involve offices, PR boiled down to mostly, average people with minimal talent trying to make their presence felt. The realities of the working world hit me in the face with a huge whack during one of London's uncharacteristic summers and all I wanted to do was leave. I'd already figured this job thing involved a lot of game playing and couldn't wait to get away the minute the clock struck five thirty p.m. And this was a habit that was to continue through my working life: every minute spent inside after my specified finish time was met with aggressive resentment.

Sunday 8 June 1996.

Much discussion whether to go to Carwash or Cuba tonight... we went for Carwash! Funky evening. Wore some hideous clothes — hilarious... Sam's lot turned up, her cousins, Matt and usual cute, rich, North London boys. All just went mad and.... Can't believe I met this guy Adrian. Shame about the name I know, but he was so cute; I had my eye on him the minute I walked in. Half Italian. Looked like Fabrizio, sort of. Kind of got together with him, lots of kissy kissy etc. was nice! I like him, he's better looking further away but then again that's not so important, also a bit worried he

118

sounds kinda 'awright mate'… hope not. You can't always expect
perfection-like speech, clothes, background, ambition etc. (I do, but I know
I can't.)

Be Curious not judgemental
(Walt Whitman)

I hadn't stopped thinking about Fabrizio. We were in touch.
He was the one I felt I wasn't good enough for. It still annoyed me
that he found Josie and did things with her I wish he'd done with
me. And I failed to see what she had that I didn't, apart from him
of course. I didn't want to be the heartbroken one, the one who
didn't get what her heart wanted. It hadn't occurred to me that I
didn't know what I wanted, beyond desperately wanting
something called a boyfriend. I'd foreseen Fabrizio in my home,
hanging out with my brother, having dinner at Grandma's – the
works, a part of the family, but isn't this just what we do… a big
film in our head the second we meet someone? Didn't seem to be
happening. Adrian was a mystery. Things moved very slowly with
him and he never seemed to want to go out, a definite red light.
Men who just want to come round to your house or have you go
round to their place are bad news but there are a lot of them.
Adrian annoyed me not just because of his behaviour but also
because he was another in a long line of 'not really normal' guys I
kept getting involved with. It was like I had radar flashing 'if you're
weird come to me'. Stress, confusion and ambiguity appeared to
be the hallmarks of my relationships. It wasn't until later on I
found out Adrian had told one of our mutual acquaintances I was
OK 'to see once a week'. It didn't stop me wondering though.

Sometimes I wondered what it would take for me to be completely put off by someone and stop thinking about them. I seemed to waste a lot of time on men who did not or would not give anything back. I may as well have just gone out and thrown my emotions on a burning pile. Why was this happening? What was I doing wrong? Was I drinking too much, did I seem 'not serious' – the girl you date but don't marry? Not that marriage was what I was after but some sincerity – yes please!

Saturday 10 August 1996.

Kartouche – champagne – singing – dancing (Alex's birthday)

What a night! Took Crispi to airport to go to Philippines, (is going for few months for work), then got ready to go out! . . . Postponed any concrete decisions for ages as was waiting for Adrian to call, which of course he didn't. I guess there's little more to say on the matter.

Kartouche . . . soon got back into the mood. Gorgeous Alex was just continually supplying champagne bottle after bottle, music was super cool – commercial so we knew it all, danced on tables, great – love it! Sam and her 'summer squeeze' Matt, and the rest of the gang were there, plus some I didn't know. Alex's such a big shot, hotshot type of guy . . . literally owns the room! Brilliant night, drinking so much champagne, dancing and hanging out with everyone, was really cool. Alex actually asked about Adrian. Weird. Then he told me lots of his friends had hots for me! Very good to hear! SNOGGED ALEX LOTS! Ended up going back to his place, very cool flat in Kensington. Nice evening. So nice to sleep next to and wake up with someone sweet right by your side, in your arms, so lovely. He seemed really keen, said we'd see each other in the week and he's coming down Wed. for my birthday. Only thing is we established again that I'm not Jewish, not sure if that changes anything, (think so though – he's a pretty religious guy), so annoying. He's so perfect but the Jewish thing means a lot to him, and I suppose I feel a little pushed out, like he's not really ever all that interested in what I have to say or in knowing me in any depth at all... Who knows? Came home feeling v confused − with his tartan RL shirt!!

Went to Grandma's on Sunday. Ate lots. She got annoyed again... 'cos I turned down some cake. For crying out loud − I don't know what happened to the freedom of choice but whenever I turn anything down, it's like world war's about to break out! Charlie turned up in evening. Nice to see him. Went for drinks and he told me about this girl he's sleeping with (She's thirty-two!). Well...

Newsflash: WE'RE GOING TO THE CARIBBEAN! Yeaaahh. Just found out M&D got an offer and said I could take a friend as Crispi's away! So Valeria's coming! Yeahhh Rasta man, ship, coconuts, Pina Coladas, beach... here we come.

My parents had generously decided to treat me and Valeria to a Caribbean cruise; fortunately, having a travel business meant good perks. The trip came at a good time, boy-wise, not that there's ever not a good time for a holiday in my view, but this was needed. Adrian was not really there and Alex appeared to have me on some sort of restricted timetable so I really only saw him when it was convenient for him. I also hated the PR company and realised the working world was fraught with uncertainty, quite the opposite of what I'd thought it would be. I applied for a few jobs before we went and decided I had to get my life in order. Everyone was reading a book called *The Celestine Prophecy,* so with much encouragement from my mystical guru Sam, I decided to read it.

I felt I needed some sort of guidance and though I already had God, the Tarot Cards and even Joan Collins's words of wisdom, I needed self-help. In retrospect I don't think it helped me all that much, though at the time it seemed like a gospel, kept me positive and believing that there was a meaning in everything. My vision of being calm and mindful in the Caribbean evaporated at the first sighting of an eligible boy, in this case someone called Blake, blond, preppy chap from Manchester and I spent my days looking forward to the evenings when I could sneak off and be with him. After each of these episodes, where I put boys at the top of my list, I felt pathetic. I knew I was much more than that: I knew I should be getting on with my life and that the right man would come along but I was impatient and perhaps like many women, a bit needy as well. I didn't see it as a big need but somehow the men I'd got involved with made it seem like I was asking for a lot. Why was that? All I wanted was someone to put their arms around me and hug me and be there for me. Was that too much to ask? Or was there something about me that meant it wouldn't happen? I was seriously beginning to question this. The summer had been one huge bonfire of fun, games, alcohol, excess and unfulfilled hope. And an introduction into the world of work that felt like a sharp slap.

Saturday 12 October 1996.

Well this is a big one. So today I have something important to say. This is the first day of the rest of my life and I mean it! The rest of my life without drinking! Not not drinking at all, but no more than the normal person, i.e.; pre-dinner aperitif – perhaps a glass of wine at dinner or perhaps not. No extra ones any more. No excess. So much has to change and that's it from today on. It had to happen someday and it's today. In a sense is probably easier to cut alcohol out altogether but unrealistic and antisocial. This way I guess it's a bit harder 'cos obviously the entire problem is keeping it moderate. But now that's it, time for change or I'll never move on in life. I don't particularly want to talk about it but before a definitive change is made it needs to be aired. Anyway that's why I'm writing it here. I don't know who I'm speaking to... myself? God? Whoever? It's going to be tough. But if I can do it, I can do ANYTHING! On the surface it's great to have a drink. Very Ab Fab. I like that. But know it's not good to overdo it and not right. It's just me trying to cover up for all the other things... niggly feelings, confusion, sadness, sorrow, anger, insecurity... I have to face up to my feelings. There's too many reasons to stop. Hurting my parents for a start. I can't do that. Embarrassing them or making them worry so much. They don't deserve it after all they've done. I have to have more respect for them and for myself and for my body, which I am so abusing. Respect for others and for myself. I need to stop and think a bit more. Got to grow up. Here is where it starts!

Now.

CHAPTER 9
Working Girl

Wednesday 23 October 1996, Evening.

There's so much I could write at the moment, so much playing round in my head. Usual things I guess... I don't talk to ANYONE about a lot of this stuff, just try and solve it myself. I need some tenderness, someone who really falls in love with me, makes me feel special like I'm the only one for them. That would make me feel a hell of a lot better and hopefully clear up the problems with everything. I worry though that I can't get in touch with myself, accept and face up to things, so how am I going to get past the first few steps of getting to know someone else, properly?... Will be really hard. You have to love yourself first they say! I was kind of hoping that someone else would help me learn to love myself.

Goodnight! Life's getting confusing.

I'd emerged from university, battling to take control of my issues with food and alcohol, and I was growing weary of it all. The thought that I was wasting my potential annoyed me and so it became a vicious circle. I began to question myself when I was out, wondering how long it would be before these 'normal' people would discover what I was really like. A job would fix it I'd told myself, especially if it was my dream job as a fashion buyer. I'd applied for one of London's largest Department Store's graduate training scheme but unfortunately I missed out. I ended up accepting their offer of a job on the sales floor as a starting point, with the aim of eventually working my way into the buying department. There was a fair bit of HR type stuff to get through; I had to do a medical and briefly panicked when they asked me about my alcohol intake. I lied and then thought 'Oh what if they take a blood test?' but they didn't. The job didn't live down to my lowest expectations, which was something I suppose. It in fact turned out to be a lot of fun, largely because I hung around with a good crowd who, like me, were searching for that special something to do in their lives and had either missed out, had no clue, were being unrealistic or, quite often all of the above. We were all in the same boat and, as we had no idea where we were headed, we were going to have a good time doing it. The job itself was dull but we embellished and gilded it with our breaks, our lunches, the nightly gatherings after work and a general sense of camaraderie.

My typical pattern of fixating on boys who were not interested in me continued to manifest itself and almost immediately I had my new object of unrequited desire. He worked in the department next to mine, stationery, however in all the time I was at the Store he pretty much ignored me and was not remotely interested in being part of our social group. I knew he was a lost cause almost immediately but that didn't stop me wanting to look my best for him, you know, just in case. There was also one really nice guy, Gregory – known simply as Greg. He worked in the Hugo Boss concession but knew all the girls on my floor and we soon became good pals. He was generally next to me at coffee, lunch, the pub or wherever we were. He wasn't dreamy looking but there was definitely something about him, probably his genuine niceness and contagious smile. He had a lovely physique, down to a past basketball obsession, fair skin and thought himself very much one of the lads. I guess he was. He was fun, had good teeth, always a bonus, so much more pleasing on the eye and pretty smiley blue eyes. Hair was sparse but he joked about that and his hands were welcoming. Greg was always up for a laugh, he'd rarely say no to anything, if there was a drink happening he'd be there, a cigarette moment he'd be there, spliff... whatever. I guess that was one thing I didn't really like but who was I to criticise, hardly miss perfection and like we said, each to their own. There was always a giggle ready to bounce out of him, a listening ear and a friendly touch, he really was a warm and happy guy and I should have felt privileged, the amount of time he gave me. 'Babe', I was always babe to him. He wasn't the sharpest tool in the box but he was kind and he knew his stuff. He knew what he knew. He was streetwise.

The one constant in my life was Grandma. Dear Grandma. She was always the one to talk to, always the one who understood what I meant even if I had no idea and always the one who knew how to give life that 'it doesn't matter' kind of shrug. I told her I didn't like work and that I was worried if I stayed there I would never find anything else.

"No problem," she said. "If you don't like it, just leave." She'd said the same about college. "You don't like, just pack your bags and leave. Come home." And even though I hadn't planned on walking out of the job – my parents would not have been pleased – I felt good knowing that somebody understood exactly how I felt and that I had a choice.

Tuesday 5 November 1996.

... Life is changing, for the better, it seems and I hope. Think am going through transformation period, sort of... Reading explanation to Celestine Prophecy is helping clarify everything. So inspiring and uplifting, I love it. MUST retain faith and trust in myself... Grandma says the same, as do M&D for that matter. Believe in myself, in my abilities, strengths and energies, then all will flourish! The book is good, about accepting self, the present and forgetting the past and future! Have to acknowledge, accept, and be open about all personal facts (negative ones too), then get rid of them. I could be much more frank and honest about all this but don't want everything written down 'cos a) then it's real and b) for fear of someone reading it. Though I really ought to have nothing to worry about, as the times I've prayed for a problem to be solved or an obsession to go away and have trusted in God for it to happen, it always has! It's worked! I really have got to trust in myself too, know that through faith my prayers will be answered.

Besides... Why can't I do what I want without other people commenting all the time? At twenty-two I should be able to do as I please. I mean as long as everyone's happy and no one's getting hurt, what is there to worry about? Live and let live! Accept, understand and respect everyone's view and let them get on with it — me included. Don't know why all this stuff gets to me so much.

For now will leave it to God as HE knows best.

I really need to give a bit more credit to God. I've always believed, never really questioned, even when I did go through those moments of trying to get my head around the world, universe and what on earth came after that. With God, I've never pondered the question for more than thirty seconds. He just is. I've been to church since the year dot — not that in itself it means much but it's in my blood. I believe, it's just hard to actually

127

*relinquish control sometimes. Heaven knows I want to. I pray every night,
and morning! A lovely feeling knowing that I'm handing over all my
concerns to someone with the power to fix them, it's reassuring but then…
my hands come apart, eyes open, I bounce up and half an hour later the
anxiety kicks back in!*

*Need to take a page out of Dad's book — he literally doesn't worry
about anything. And Grandma, what would Grandma do without her faith
now? Since Grandad's gone, even before, church was part of her life even
if it wasn't part of his. Apart from us it's her faith that's kept her going…
when we're not there, it's her beliefs, her love of God, her chats with the
priest, her little pearl rosary in its velvet pouch — that's what keeps her
going.*

As much as I wanted to believe in God making things right, I
also wanted to help it along, do what I could to improve things,
God helps those who help themselves and all that. *The Celestine
Prophecy* which had become the self-help book of the moment, was
definitely helping me understand more about the cosmic world,
how to manage it and how it can affect us in all sorts of ways, plus
I was also reading *The Way Of The Peaceful Warrior*, which Sam had
given me. Basically it was *The Celestine Prophecy* reworked as many
of these books are. You know someone writes one and then a
whole lot of copycat books follow and they make a load of money
out of them. Whether anyone actually changes their life because
of reading a self-help book is another matter I guess. Who's to
know, it might not have happened anyway. What if you just had
to wait for your time to come or your luck to change? But if they
bring hope and feel good, then all for it and when you're twenty-
two, looking for something and you have no idea what it is except

that other people seem to have it, then you latch on to whatever you can, be it God, self-help or fortune-tellers. The basic message of all of these things is pretty simple though: BELIEVE. And that is one of the hardest things to do, which is why perhaps so many books are devoted to it.

Wednesday 11 December 1996.

Why is fun not fun? What's a problem often is being in a group etc., and not really being interested in what anyone's saying. Hate feeling like this but it happens, quite often. Like the other night, I'm sitting with, Jen, Rich, Raj... same old crew having a chat and a giggle but just didn't feel it. Like I was there, but not there. There's no real reason to feel like that — it's so unpleasant when I do. Sometimes I'll be fine and others like yesterday and today, I'm there but don't really know why. I talk but am not really with it, it's like I'm kind of outside myself looking in... I think it can be sensed by others too — hope not! Thank God for Valeria, she came tonight and we had a good chat before joining the others. I didn't go into too much detail though as I don't even really know what I'm feeling myself — too complicated. I just want to be HAPPY. There's no reason why I shouldn't be able to just relax and put this accepting and letting go thing into practice. So frustrating.

I really hope this just passes, and quickly. Maybe I should purify myself, revitalise, detox, be pure, healthy, strong, less alcohol, ciggies etc. more water and good stuff. Maybe that will give a new slant to things. Think the whole Greg issue has a lot to do with this too. Especially after Saturday... I was so looking forward to seeing him, so pleased when they got into the club, thought about him all Sunday and talked to Val and Raj about it, i.e. he's not really my type, not good-looking, but is so so nice, thoughtful, deep, kind, considerate, reflective. Majorly fun too. Thought

I really like him and it's like... I don't know... he's just another one who isn't my type!

It's so confusing, everyone says he's into me, wants more and with all his pro's I really should give him a chance but every time I build myself up to it, it suddenly just doesn't feel right, he's not who I see myself with.

When will this end? I try to make an effort to pull it all together but half the time I just can't be bothered, would rather be at home or get completely wrecked. Maybe should see doctor... energy levels must be out or something? Don't know, or could be hormones maybe?

Am trying to eat normally but must get rid of spare tyre around my waist. Are Martinis fattening?? Don't think so. Must stop thinking about my body so much too! And just enjoy!

I think I would have found life even more confusing if I didn't have the few special friends, especially Sam and that crowd in London with me, and Valeria of course. Much of it was superficial, in the sense that we just went out for a fun night and I was able to forget the boredom of work and where it was going which was pretty much nowhere as I saw it. At times it all felt really shallow and I'd feel guilty that all I looked forward to was partying, the next night out, the next new bar, the next object of my desire. If it wasn't the work crew, or the school crew there were the people I was at Uni with and assorted others who'd been in Siena with me. It never occurred to me that I might be depressed but I suspect if I went to somebody now and said, 'I take absolutely no pleasure in anything I'm doing', that's what they would tell me. In 1996, the concept of talking about how lost and unfulfilled you are feeling was not well known. It seems amazing to think it now, barely twenty years later but words like 'depression' were dark and forbidding and you never really mentioned them. As a result a lot of people who were really depressed couldn't acknowledge it and had to just muddle on or worse, get very ill.

Happiness is the meaning and the purpose of life, the whole aim and end of human existence
(Aristotle)

What made things worse was that occasionally someone would pop up to remind me that I had somehow got this life thing wrong. They didn't do it intentionally but when Emma, who I'd met in Siena, turned up in London to catch up, it unsettled me. I was envious of her. She'd stayed in Italy, and was driving around all day doing a kind of non-job, job where you show tourists to their villas. Sure she was out in the middle of nowhere and working weekends but she was in Italy and seemed to be having a good time. She was bright, smiley and clearly happy. It just made me think back to all those good times in Vicenza and Jesolo and yes, Siena, when everything seemed so much simpler. Nowhere is perfect but in one respect Italy made life easier: people didn't spend all their time thinking about the future or advancement or the next new thing. They sat around, eating, chatting, staying close to family and friends and generally being in the moment. It was the thing I was struggling most to do and while I could try and live like that in London, it wasn't easy when everyone else was racing ahead. And then Mystic Alex as I called him, popped up again. He was friends with Sam's cousins so it was inevitable he would resurface. He seemed to be showing an interest in me and though I knew he was not for life (or even for Christmas since he was

Jewish after all) he was a charmer and for me, irresistible. I decided he'd be worth knowing as he might change his playboy ways, you never know, apparently my dad did. In retrospect I didn't have a hope in hell. It wasn't long before he joined the work crew on a night out and afterwards he took me for a meal. It shouldn't have happened but it did: I ended up at his house and when I should have been enjoying the moment of being with this beautiful boy, the most salient thought was that I must not pin my hopes on him or get too attached. Enjoyment, with big glaring price tags.

They were all coming out of the woodwork. Fabrizio came over and was still trying to sleep with me but meanwhile was constantly on the phone to other girls, which was hugely sobering. Then he announced he was off to Brussels.

"But Fabri I've planned this massive weekend."

"Soooo sorry, Natalie, but I go see Josie."

He was off to see another girl. Basically he'd flown to London to crash with me for two weeks so he could get the Eurostar across the channel at the weekend to see his latest squeeze.

"I've invited a bunch of people to come out with us, made reservations and everything, we're going to a brilliant club. Are you sure?"

He could see I was upset, as much as I was trying to hide it. His tone became more conciliatory.

"Maybe I refund ticket OK? I go later."

"Do you think so...? I mean if you can... Oh I don't know – do what you want." I wasn't going to beg.

He couldn't. Or he didn't. Anyway he went to Brussels and I spent the whole weekend crying. Grandma just shook her head.

"Exactly what you expect from someone from the South," she said, nodding.

I actually called him when he was on the train there to tell him how it had upset me. Not a great move since I don't think it registered with him: guys like that have their own agenda and don't see anyone else on their radar. After I'd called him I then spent the whole time worrying that I'd ruined everything. The fact that there was nothing to ruin had not occurred to me. In the event, he returned from his rendezvous and, true to form, yet again tried to sleep with me. I could forgive and yes we had a good time for the last few days but I cannot forget. I already felt so degraded by the episode; there was no way I'd give in to him. I sometimes think that's my way of protecting my self-esteem when all is lost. Unlike many of my friends – and I'm not judging anyone – I never had sex with guys that easily. Sure I got huge crushes but the idea of having sex before I thought I was ready never occurred to me. I was thankful for that and continued to be as I got older. I think it protected me from further heartbreak. He invited me back to Italy but I wanted and needed to stay in my comfort zone. After all he'd have probably left me with his mother for the weekend whilst he went off to be with someone else.

Sunday 9 March 1997 (Mother's Day).

Visited Grandma in hospital. She's such an example to follow. A happy life. She's a star that continues to shine brightly no matter what. Mum's another star and so is Greg. V v nice bloke. That time of the month again so maybe that is why I have a spare tyre!

Sunday 13 April 1997.

New healthy eating regime to provoke wellbeing and happiness, whilst curing chronic stomach acid caused by overindulgence, alcohol and exercising too soon after a meal.

Rules:

> *Eat small meals regularly / whole foods, rice, grains, cereals*
> *Fruit and veg*
> *No processed, preservatives or spices*
> *Don't exercise immediately after eating*
> *Pray to god I don't put on any weight this way...*
> *I'm trying it!*

Monday 21 April 1997.

I'm debating whether to continue writing a diary basically because I think it is making me more insular and that's not good. Keeping a diary might not be good idea as it reminds me of what I haven't done. All the things I write down and rules I make and then break. I remember Grandma saying once how she doesn't believe in writing diaries. (I didn't listen at the time as didn't want to burst my bubble.) Grandma tends to be right, very right on these things and living for the moment is not what you do if you write a diary, is it? But to let go of it now would be weird. I mean after ten years. Where am I going to put those thoughts I can't speak out loud? How am I going to make a plan for myself? Not writing would leave a huge gap.

PS: I wish I didn't have such a bloated stomach.

CHAPTER 10
Change and Chances

Sunday 31 August 1997.

Sunday morning. Wake up early due to rubbish alcohol induced semi sleep after fun evening with Val at Al frescos (love that place!) only to hear that... Shock horror, Lady Diana died tragically last night in a car crash with Dodi. Talk about rock the nation. Nobody could believe it. Incredible. The nation if not the world's idol dead — gone. In fact for twenty-four hours, the whole country has been at a standstill, TV, radio people, cars, everyone and everything. It's been all we've talked about all day. There's a strange stillness in the air inside and out that I've never ever experienced before... It's almost as if time has stopped.

Bless Grandma, she said she woke up early and put the radio on; she said she heard a story about a princess and a car crash, thought it was a fairy tale — then realised it was all true! I can just imagine her laying there in here little bed, thinking that... the innocence of a child that somehow seems to creep back in at old age.

Since I'd started at the Department Store, a few things had shifted: some of the crew I'd begun with had moved on, bosses had changed and I had been picked off the floor to become the personal assistant to the buyer of ladies' shoes. The buyer's name was Megan and to say she was a bitch was really only scratching the surface. Apparently she'd been watching me on the floor and decided I should be her personal assistant. When she approached me with the job, I was kind of speechless but realised this was one of those fate moments you don't turn down. I had to tell her that I didn't think I was equipped to be an assistant: I had no secretarial or computer experience, having cunningly avoided anything remotely related to computers the whole way through Uni due to total PC phobia. Being a woman who would not be dissuaded from her goal... ever, she offered to put me on a secretarial and computer course on the condition that I stayed with her for at least a year after it was completed. Megan wasn't someone you could like but that wasn't the point. This was an opportunity and it would enable me to get closer to a real buyer and therefore open the door to me actually becoming one.

I thought I could cope with her personality and so dutifully ignored the warnings. I completed the course, which after initial pandemonium, I actually enjoyed and began the role enthusiastically, but as the year wore on, she became unbearable. She was short, wore flat shoes, always. She was all about the practicalities. She had very short dark red hair, pale complexion and freckles, lots of them – in fact she was covered. She came from a big US chain, which naturally implied she meant business and she did. Anyone who's come from there does. Our Store was on the up, going through a creative phase but there was a remarkable soberness to her and all from her background who had been recruited for their apparent expertise. She was simply hard. It was the South African accent that put the fear of God in me, and the big mouth – it was powerful. Lips always nude or if anything with that cold, frosted pinkish mauve ice queen lipstick. Her steps were deliberate and her eyes huge and focused – you know the types where you can see the whites the whole way around the pupils as if they were little islands.

In hindsight she was a normal woman trying to do her job – to bring some heavy experience from a successful background and enforce a little order. She had kids and switched persona when she spoke to them and her husband was cool. Young and good-looking – though clearly also very successful. All that indicated she must have had a nice side but did I ever see it? Or any of us for that matter – no.

At least I had the gang on the shop floor to bitch and moan to; her office where I was based was a few steps up from where I'd been working so I still had 'my team' and 'support group' close by. Plus I was getting on really well with Greg; more and more so; he was fun, seemed to lighten the load of everything and was always there for me. I still couldn't see him as my type of guy but we were having a great time in the lovely way that boy/girl friendships do.

We'd taken to hanging out at La Rueda in Fulham Road, amongst other places but that was definitely one of the faves along with Chapel Lafayette, where we'd pass many a night drinking and dancing 'til the early hours. We'd become a strong crowd; me, Crispi and his friends, who were by now both of ours, Sam and the boys, then the Store lot, the group kept growing. Randomly having not seen him for ages, although apparently sill living around the corner, I bumped into Brandon down there one night. I was right outside Chapel Lafayette as we were walking along in the drizzle and I thought I saw him at a traffic light, was sure it was him. Both from the other side of town it was quite unexpected and provided the perfect opportunity to say 'hi'. I distinctly remember tottering over in my heels as he was rolling down the window having spotted me too.

"Hiya." I was all done up for a night out and not yet pissed, so spoke confidently. Quite the opposite to my usual ducking and diving at home avoiding him when barefaced.

"Hey – what you doing down here?"

"Going to Lafayette – You?"

"Oh some house party round the corner… maybe we'll drop by there later."

"Yeah do!" Perfectly handled, I spun on my heel as the lights turned, miraculously not killing myself and skipped back to the others. Well played.

Couldn't believe he was driving? How did you go out and have a good time… whilst driving… and to a party of all places? We never actually met up beyond that fleeting traffic light moment, but I did of course question it… It's not often you bump into people you know in London, particularly when they come from a totally different part. And as the deep books I'd been reading had taught me, nothing is by chance. There is no such thing as coincidence. One thing it did confirm to me was that every time I saw him it simply reminded me how much I liked him. Timeless. But it seemed I had to put him down to a childhood dream that would remain just that – a dream.

Back to reality, One night in November, one of the sales assistants was having her birthday and had organised a night out at Carwash to celebrate. We loved a dress up and that place was a guaranteed riot. We started off with pre-club drinks at Greg's place in West Hampstead: which he shared with his extremely hot brother, Ant, then we headed off to the club. Greg and I had become pretty close by this point but were still purely friends regardless of the amount of time we spent together. Everyone was up for a good night, dressed in our '70s gear, Afro wigs, platforms, glitter, shot skirts, flares, the works. Carwash was always a blast, don't think it exists anymore which is a shame as the '70s vibe always seems to bring out the friendliness in people, plus the music was fun and easy to dance to. I remember feeling more relaxed than I had in a long time, chugging down round after round of drinks, drifting into a joyful fog where I liked myself and everyone else too. Greg and I were almost permanently side-by-side, dancing a lot together, trying to outdo each other throwing shapes on the dance floor and then all of a sudden, something happened, the moment caught up with us I guess. We kissed.

Back at work he came to find me nervously, with a face like he'd committed a crime or something. "Natalie, can I speak to you for a moment?"

I could tell something was bothering him.

"Sure. What's wrong?"

"I want to apologise for the other night."

I was mystified.

"I really shouldn't have kissed you, taken advantage like that. I really like you, Natalie, and I don't want anything to spoil our friendship. I just hope I haven't ruined anything."

"Ruined what?"

"I don't want to mess things up between us."

"Greg. You haven't messed things up at all." I'd been thinking about this a lot, playing it over and over in my head. "I liked kissing you. In fact I actually think we should give it a go." His cheeky face lit up and his contagious smile had us both going. It felt nice. Good. Honest.

Saturday 22 November 1997.

Can't believe I'm in a relationship, sort of. Early days... So different from anyone in the past though — Léonard, Fabrizio, Alex, they all seemed to just want you when you're around but Greg's different. I actually have a boyfriend! Not counting chickens though... I'm not even sure how I feel about it, it's weird having someone you do everything with and everyone sees you as not two people any more but one.

Anyway now we're going to the Christmas Ball (whole Store one) together. Wasn't going to go but it was like 'Shall we, shan't we, shall we, shan't we?' everyone was edging us to go; there were some tickets left, so that was that. Cinderella is going to the ball.

Still haven't handed in my application form for Grad Training Scheme but am getting things together slowly but surely! Still have a few more things to sort out. Decided during my fresh and positive thinking during the early hours of the morning that I am not going to put on any weight; in fact, I shall lose a bit and keep very toned, by just behaving normally, in a totally normal manner.

Thursday 4 December 1997 — Store Christmas Ball.

Such a fantastic day — one of the best days of the year. Managed to faff my way through work until five fifteen, time to get ready. All girls got ready in the loos, me, Victoria, Raj, Jen, etc. then headed to Dome for pre-ball bevvies. Dome was packed with everyone. All had a few drinks then Greg and the rest came. Got on coach and headed down to Battersea. Great night, ate, drank, and danced. It was cool, Greg always there for a hug! Lovely! We all had such a good night, plus didn't get too wrecked so stayed all night till the end, – then cab back to Greg's. Woke up in Greg's arms, after much-needed long sleep, lovely. Thank heavens, I took the Thursday off! Wow – needed it. Stayed in bed till late, then I was so hungry. Greg got dressed and went out and bought a warm baguette and orange juice, sat in bed, and ate that; then slept again, whilst he read the paper. When we eventually got up – we went off for a cool day in Hampstead shopping for a pressie for Sam's b'day!

I wonder sometimes exactly what's going on with Greg, about what he really and truly thinks and feels about me. I know of things he's said in the past to Raj and to others of what he's thought of me, but that was all before he really, really knew me. One thing we have said is that whatever happens, we'll always be 'mates'! Now though, he kind of knows me, beyond the surface image that I have, other than the 'Nat' that everyone knows and loves, I hasten to add (he-he). He kind of knows a lot more of the real me now. Wonder what he thinks of the whole package?

Greg and I were getting on well, much like before but with added affection and I spent pretty much all my time at his place in West Hampstead. We had a lot of fun there, and fortunately, his gorgeous brother Ant was also very welcoming. The mornings of fresh baguettes and orange juice became a regular occurrence and I was enjoying being doted on for once. It had been a while. The last time I'd experienced anything close to such adoration was Charlie back at school but that was then and it never got to the morning after treatment so this really was an entirely new experience and entirely enjoyed. After all the arseholes I'd pined for, it was as refreshing as the juice he brought me. However, despite all of his enamoured behaviour, I still wasn't entirely sure about Greg. He really was the good guy and I'd consciously decided that I should see that as a purely good thing. After all, the guys I'd chosen so far had landed me on love's scrap heap. All the charm, mystery and intrigue I'd been captivated by had so far got me nowhere and as they say you shouldn't make the same mistake over and over again. I had to give it a chance.

We had some really good times together and it was great to finally feel secure in a relationship, in a way that I simply hadn't before. I could pretty much get away with anything with Greg, which was nice and made things easy. At times, I worried if I was pushing it a bit but on the other hand he never seemed to comment, it was always just 'Babe' this 'Babe' that, 'my little bubble'... (the Greek thing), whatever, it was pure affection. There were endless meals in La Brocca, our local red checked table-clothed Italian, where I'd devour their delicious sun-dried tomato and artichoke antipasti followed by huge seafood salads and he'd have pizza, we drank wine and went for post dinner cocktails before stumbling down West End Lane to his huge mansion block flat. It was a good life, slightly Mediterranean almost with everything on the doorstep and a young, carefree vibe. I loved this type of thing and for a while even forgot about Italy. Aside from his good points he'd always had the spliff tendency that I didn't like, he knew that so tended to minimise it around me and what I did see I just accepted... after all Sam and the boys did it too. It wasn't new. It appeared to be just me that didn't. No problem of course as there was always a glass of wine to hand. And so I found myself in a relationship that I'd never expected to be in and was feeling quite comfortable though not quite visualising marriage I'd say. You may think it's way too early for that but frankly, I visualised myself walking down the aisle with almost whoever I went out with.

As time drifted on, I was niggled by a strange feeling, like now that I had the real boyfriend, a proper Nice Guy, I wasn't sure if he was really what I wanted. Why it all became so confusing, I don't know? Maybe I'd been kidding myself? We always want what we don't have? But there was definitely something missing for me and I wasn't sure if what we had was enough to compensate for it. I'm not talking about the bad boy charm not being there – though yes I might have missed some of that Alex or Léonard factor – but while he was lovely, caring and would definitely never be intentionally nasty, there was a real lack of ambition and drive about him. And for a girl who was always dreaming of bigger and brighter things, this was not ideal. It was almost as if the hand brake was left slightly on. I wanted desperately for this not to matter because I'd wanted a real boyfriend for so long, someone I could take home to my parents, who could join us in our family meals, who I could rely on, be myself with… but regardless of him being all of that, it did matter. I had big plans and even if they were just dreams I wanted someone to dream big with me, I needed it. That's what ultimately got me over my personal hurdles of food, alcohol and wondering if I was ever good enough – the fact that I would one day make my mark and none of that would matter, as it would all disappear.

Other than that niggling factor that I struggled to see beyond, the straw that broke the camels back, almost… that was the biggest strain on the relationship was when he'd decided he'd had enough of work. Great. I tried to convince him to wait 'til he found another job, as it would be so much easier to find one whilst already in one, but this concept made no sense to him.

Wednesday 10 December 1997.

Greg meant to pop over for dinner or something as M&D were out all evening. Anyway, he'd had the day off and spent it playing on the Nintendo and smoking. He was basically so messed up that he couldn't even talk coherently on the phone! I was a bit peed off! I don't like that about him. I mean on a day off, a guy should be doing other stuff or nothing but not that — but then who am I to judge? Anyway — I was pretty pissed off, but as a result, I had numerous good chats with the girls on the phone!

He quit. Wonderful, a jobless boyfriend. Perfect step towards my glamorous future! I supported his decision once he'd made it, no point doing otherwise. I just got on with finding him a new job, which proved to be the ultimate mission impossible, as nothing seemed to please. The spliffs multiplied and the cash diminished. I ended up funding his empty days sat puffing away with his partner in crime Dave and trying to pull him out of what appeared to be nothing short of depression. The happy-go-lucky days, I'd signed up for were fast slipping away.

How could I pursue my goals with a guy who wasn't ambitious? He would have been happy staying home slouched over on his futon with PlayStation and a spliff for an eternity had I not exercised my best efforts to remind him there was far more to life. I hate forcing people to do things, in fact it's entirely out of character; you either want to do it or we won't. This was tough. Even when he'd volunteer going out, I knew it was just for me, and the second I was gone he'd be back to his toys. Sure I wasn't exactly toxin free myself but since the senseless resignation, he rarely wanted to do anything different and I started to feel he was holding me back.

So the months passed and despite my misgivings and general lack of passion for Greg, we were still very much together. I was giving it a go, making sure I'd given it a 360 degree check before calling it quits – through thick and thin and all that. At the same time I was spending a lot more time with my trusty Sam, her brother and her cousins 'the boys'. That also meant Alex would be there from time to time. I knew he was wrong, I'd had endless proof of that but hey, lots of things are wrong and you still want them.

Thursday 8 January 1998 (letter from Sam).
Dearest Duckie,

OK, my little cherub, we're sat in a bar in London drinking cocktails and imagining we're somewhere warmer and more Italian. Christ, seven and three quarter years haven't changed us much.

We've both given relationships a chance and gone out with English blokes whilst dreaming of a steamy Italian romance. We still dance in our bedrooms, we still shout when we sing, we still write in each other's diaries. Have many stories to tell...

What's changed – we carry mobiles, wear work clothes, we're a little more computer literate. Have degrees, have parents asking for rent money, we're no longer virgins, we drive.

Life's whizzing by and our best friendship is stronger than ever. We thrive in sun and summer. We love clubbing and still wear little dresses – not our regular little black dresses of the '80s though. I love you loads, and

145

we're both gonna be successful and happy, but who cares about that with friends like us! You'll always be my precious Duckie, from a movie star to a successful businesswoman. Through thick and thin, we've seen wrinkles develop, boyfriends come and go, many changes…

The soul would have no rainbows if the eyes would have no tears.

Eviva Duckie & Chicken, all my love always,

Sam.

Fortunately my clever, wonderful brother, he of the First from Oxford and the banking job, seemed to see something in me that few others did, least of all me. He encouraged me to apply to another Department Store for the following year, a much bigger one, one of the biggest in the country, suggesting I could get onto their buying and merchandising graduate training scheme. I laughed as frankly that really was the only reaction possible, if I couldn't get on to the one where I was, how on earth would I get on that one – a far better company?

"Just go for it! Why not?"

"I won't get on…"

"You will. Try – it's a great company, seriously. What's there to lose?"

This Graduate Scheme was one of the most sought after in the UK and my competition was likely to be better qualified than I was with many of them coming from top universities, graduated in fashion or similar. After I'd picked myself up off the floor I could see that he really meant it and to prove it he helped me fill in the application. To my absolute amazement, I actually got an interview. In fact I got through all the interviews.

Greg had finally landed a job behind the scenes at a major Sports store and he was happy. He was at the point, we both were, where he needed to do something. He would be based down the street from me whichever store I ended up in, so we could pick up where we left off. There were some serious chats about bucking up to give the relationship the chance it deserved and before embarking on this new start I treated him to a holiday. Miraculously I'd won a trip to the Gran Bahia del Duque, an amazing luxury resort in Tenerife, via a travel event I attended with my parents. With no one else able to make it, I decided to take Greg. After all, holidays are supposed to bring a lot of truth to the surface in a relationship so it seemed the perfect thing after recent dilemmas and the hardship. We set off like two school kids and were blown away upon arrival at what appeared to be the glitziest, grandest hotel I'd ever seen, like something you'd expect to see in a mafia movie. We were shown to our room, a top suite, bigger and more beautiful than I could have imagined. There was a palm tree in the bathroom! I knew this would reveal.

One blistering afternoon by the pool a receptionist approached with an envelope, a note from my parents saying they had a letter at home from the infamous store I'd applied to. An immediate phone call and I discovered I'd been offered a position. I couldn't believe it. My analysis of our relationship had now gone firmly out the window as I was thinking of one thing and one thing only – my fabulous new buying career. I was proud of my current role but Megan was becoming too much for me. Well she was probably too much for anyone but a year with her was going to be more than enough. I'd learnt to touch type and for that I will be eternally grateful. I was glad to have found a plausible exit and as I'd envisaged, taking her up on her original offer had led me to bigger and better things. I'd learned a great deal and become a very good assistant in the process but I needed a move, not just because this was a plum job but also to give myself a boost and also my poor parents who were worried about my health. Working with such a psychopath, together with the effect barely eating had on my nervous system, was doing me no good. Many of my childhood twitches, continuously sniffing, clearing my throat and generally being anxious, that had plagued my late teens had begun to resurface. I did a good job of hiding them mostly, or so I thought but it was draining. I needed a new change. I needed to feel good.

Tuesday 3 March 1998.

Just watched programme about anorexics. So sad I just cried and listened and cried and listened. Thank God I've never been as bad as the girls on there but certain things hit me, really hit home. One thing it did do, is make me very aware of how much Mum has always been there for me. (Yes she's driven me mad and upset me lots talking about it all too.) But every time I've had to go to the doctor — Edgeware, Russell Square, Harley St, UCH with Dr Amir, Mum has come with me no matter what.

It's awful though, I do think things are a lot better than they were. I think I eat a LOT, often I think more than others just in different ways. I'd obviously love to always be completely skinny forever, that's just how I feel best — although it may not necessarily be best. Dr Amir and I talked about it and he asked me why I think like that. Who knows why I do? I just do? I told him maybe it's because most of the desirable women in the world are skinny, aren't they? And as I've learnt from the wonderful Kate Moss no food will ever give you the same pleasure that being thin does!

Donna. We'd met on the training course and hit it off immediately. Thank God we were in the same department, because the job didn't really do it for me. Merchandising sounds like something creative and interesting, but actually it's just all figures. Donna had a far more fun and interesting role as she'd got on the buying team. In the same way that people try to make brussel sprouts more appealing by putting them with chestnuts or bacon, I think merchandising was put with buying because it really was incredibly boring and they wanted to make it sound like fun. My role was all numbers and spreadsheets, monitoring sales and reporting back, not to mention the early Red Bull fuelled Monday mornings where I'd have to be in before the world woke up to prepare the weekend's figures. I couldn't see where it would get me. But at least it was stability and I think it gave me a kind of taster of the self-esteem I'd been looking for. The idea that I was working for this big brand was good for me and I was determined to make the best of it. My parents were delighted of course, even prouder than me, happy that I'd done all that they kept telling me I could do and at last I felt I could give them something other than worry. They deserved it really.

Wednesday 22 July 1998.

OK, so I haven't written in ages, basically 'cos everything / life's been very busy and chaotic, out partying, drinking lots, working hard, changing jobs, and analysing my feelings with Greg constantly. Plus I haven't had the time to write at work, as I've no longer been in an empty office! Boo.

Recap.

Well, I guess from the beginning things with Greg were really great; he's such a loving, wonderful person, and we had the most amount of fun

*together, out, talking, laughing, singing, pubs, bars, restaurants: all of it.
Even just in the flat, we spent so much time together and there most
definitely was a time when I strongly believed that I was in love with him.
OK, so I've never really liked the spliffing side of things, lack of money and
job (when he quit), but underneath it all, I still loved him, and still now I
do love him immensely! But I'm just not sure what sort of love it is any
more. I guess things began to go a bit sour a while ago, when he had not a
cent to his name and wanted a Nintendo. The 'f' ing and blinding and
bitterness that was spurting out all over the place, I really thought 'sh*t,
I don't like this!' Then I kind of started questioning things a bit more. I
guess I stuck with it 'cos I just didn't want to lose all the constant love and
affection, the independence of the lifestyle that I've had with him, and
most importantly, what we had together. I've just carried on with it, and
what with me asking myself more and more is this right? I've not seen
clearly and eventually (now) got to the point where I think I need out! I
was debating it way too much. I'd often debated the prospect of a future
with Greg but never whether to end it right now, but perhaps it was time.
I guess it didn't help that a certain 'Alex' out of all people decided to spring
back up on the scene after such a long time. Now he's let me down many a
time before, twice in fact, two years running and then not spoken to me in
ages, but the fact that he rang mid-August (as per usual) and left his new
mobile number and then called again, I felt I had to see him. First of all,
I was concerned about the feelings I had when I heard he'd rung. I
shouldn't have those feelings (surely?) if I was in love with Greg. Then
what with all that was going on with Greg, having no money to go out,
and Alex being the complete opposite, I thought I'll go for a drink and see
him. So, feeling completely ridden with guilt, I went. We met in
Kensington, my heart pounding as I went up the escalators. Then I saw
him, and he looked gorgeous. We went for a couple of drinks (the whole*

night on him of course), then for a lovely meal in a smart Italian restaurant. Was all lovely, then on to a bar to meet his pals and to a club. Now the evening was great. I do like him a lot, but of course couldn't think straight 'cos of all that was going on in my head, Greg back at home, completely different but that I love (not sure how?) plus Alex's extremely poor track record with me and girls in general. As a result the whole night was great, but there was a certain, obvious, unspoken something and strong vibe between us that was as if making two magnets repel. More than likely mainly my fault, partly the guilt and confusion and partly that I just found it impossible to be completely open and friendly with him as I have no clue what he's seriously thinking or what he wants from me... or what he's going to feel the next day. Anyway, this whole thing put a huge question mark in my head about my feelings for Greg. I plodded along with Greg and saw Alex the following Friday night – he met me from work; we went for a meal and got quite wrecked. Again, there was a similar untouchable distance between us, which I feel will completely turn him off me anyway, as I seem cold and withdrawn. Surprisingly, he sat there at dinner and attempted to in fact open his heart and confess a bit as to what he was feeling, something I've never seen in Alex before. He tried, and to cut a long story short, asked for another chance. I basically said that I couldn't trust him and that unless I could really see he wanted ME, I couldn't open up sufficiently to build any sort of relationship. The end result was that we should get to know each other properly, better, as we don't enough yet – so we're supposedly doing that! Saw him the next day with Sam too. On the Friday, much as there was that sort of slight distance between us (combination of guilt and fear of being toyed with), we did end up kissing, which I will add was lovely! Similarly, Saturday night out, we had a few drinks and then stayed at his friend's flat in Kensington, had a cuddle at night and a couple of little kisses, all feeling a bit cheeky and wrong! Came home Sunday morning — all feeling rather thrilling but wrong at the same time.

When Greg wasn't around, all was confusing but exciting too. When he was there, I just didn't know what to do, how to feel, or how to react. It became such a headache.

I probably shouldn't be so pessimistic, but the chances of something working out with Alex are, let's say, rather minimal. Maybe I'm wrong, let's hope so! But the one thing this has taught me is that I cannot be in love with Greg. As a result of all this, when I see Greg, much as I want to hug, squeeze, cuddle, and be with him, I don't really want to kiss him, let alone anything else. Plus I can't seem to get Alex out of my head — which makes it worse for both of us.

Options:
1.   Give it a shot with Alex and then see what happens with Greg?
2.   Ignore and forget Alex and make a huge concerted effort with what's gone/going wrong with Greg and me and work on that, dismissing Alex?
3.   End it with Greg and give Alex a shot?

I figured that if I had all these feelings for Alex, just ignoring them and concentrating on Greg wouldn't be right a) 'cos I couldn't possibly concentrate on Greg without getting Alex out of my system completely or I'd think about it and probably begin to resent Greg for the whole thing — totally not fair; b) because if I've felt it once, then it's more than likely I'll feel it again probably with someone else at some point.

The first option of seeing them both proved impossible as a) I'm not mentally or emotionally able to switch from one to the other offering one

100 per cent of me, and b) 'cos of the amount of time I was spending with Greg, i.e. six out of seven nights a week.

So... bad as it may seem, I kind of had to end it with Greg, in the attempt to clear my mind as best possible. And as a result if I don't even end up carrying the Alex thing any further, it had to be done anyway to find out exactly how I really do feel about Greg! Hopefully we'll both be able to see more clearly now, exactly what's going on and how to deal with it. As we've always said, right from day one, we will always be friends and we'll stick to that. Just hope now that I've decided that, I can relax more with each of them. Alex issue being far less important but I still want to be able to feel comfortable, be myself, and offer a 100 per cent relaxed me around him and more to the point I want to be me again with Greg, even if it means no physicality for a while or rarely or whatever.

Clearly the 'break' didn't quite function as planned, as months down the line, I was still in the exact same position.

CHAPTER 11
The Noise in My Head

Email from Sam
Friday 8 January 1999

Subject: Quack Quack

Duckie,

Please read this before anyone else, seeing as I will mention your extramarital affair with Alex more than once. Thanks for your email. I knew you would eventually be the one who contacts him. You can't get him out of your head, you think you've been really controlled and left it for ages, don't you, ducks? But it seems like years since you made any contact, and it's been eating away at you. Your attraction to him is consuming your thoughts; how are you coping with this duplicity? How brutal was that and how dramatic can I make it all sound? How depressing and reflecting is what I have just written? The thing is this drama will only occur now, it is something you will look back on and giggle about on a dull, rainy day some time in your forties, and just the thought of now will make you burn from head to toe in secret delight. Or maybe it will all be immortalised and I'll surprise you by including Laura Anastasia and Israel's affair in a chapter of my third bestseller. It will be the only time I will dip into writing romance, but this romance has consequences for me; it will make me dosh when I write about it, and for you, it will drive you mad unless you resolve it. You know the consequences, I don't need to tell you, but somehow you have to work this all out of your system. Only time will answer this one, but as you know, I'm here for you, if only to aid you in tearing yourself up or make you over-reflective.

On another note though, I've done my good deed for the day, because the very sad, ginger, and unemployable Bonnie Langford telephoned. It is a usual occurrence as this company represents her. I hear she can't get work and she's broke, probably because she is highly annoying. In the name of charity and failed actress, I told her that she was more than tolerable in panto this year. I told her she was very good. She asked me why I didn't say hello after the show. I had no answer. The conversation ended. Bonnie smiles a showbiz smile. Sam feels quite nauseous at even having said a word to the queen of trashy entertainment; end of my story. I am sure there are easier ways to make me feel like a decent individual. Next time I'll just buy a big issue and be done with it.

What are you up to this weekend? I'd love to see your duckie face. I hope you are as intuitive as I would wish you to be. They may have found my phone; if it does turn out to be mine, I will be giving you a big, fat, psychic, and hopeful hug. I must work now but write soon.

Lots of love,
Your best friend
Chicken xxx

Horoscope:

While you're unlikely to have had a chance to explore the full range of developments that accompanied last week's lunar eclipse in Leo, one thing is clear and that is that life will never be the same again. Some changes come as no surprise and could well be a relief. But others, particularly those that involve those closest to you, whether in business or romantic relationships, are less clear-cut. You may as well relax, because it won't be until after next Tuesday's solar eclipse that anyone knows what's what. In the meantime, consider your options. These are intriguing now, but become even more interesting after Saturday's move by the expansive Jupiter into Aries, the sign of initiative, which accents ways you could broaden your horizons. What's good just gets better. But it's the unexpected – what simply never occurred to you – that could change your life.

How is it that we are constantly so sucked in by our horoscope? They give an amazing sense of clarity that suddenly puts everything into perspective – but this has to apply to a tenth – or whatever it may be of the population. How can it be that every single Leo is going through a type of situation that this horoscope can identify and shed light on? Yet we continue to read them obsessively, treating the advice as gospel! There has to be something wrong here – yet I have to say it is still the first (and generally only) thing I read in the Sunday papers. At this stage in my life neither horoscope, God, *Celestine Prophecy* or handy tips from *Cosmopolitan* magazine looked like they could save me. Confusion had settled on me like a heavy, dusty blanket and I was struggling to fight my way out. Here I was trying to cement a new job – OK well kind of fix it to the ground in stable fashion – while wondering whether to extract myself from a relationship that felt like it was going sour, and juggling my various phobias, health issues and indulgences. I couldn't handle it and in a period, which should have signalled the stability I needed, I was splattering my emotions and energy all over the place. It was all too much and I'm not sure whether it was the weight of expectation. Theoretically, I had all the things a girl should want. I had a boyfriend, a really good job, money to spend and an overflowing social life. What could be wrong with me? How was this not enough? Why is it that you get what you're supposed to have and then it doesn't make you happy? Or in my case it just makes you ask even more questions? Was I ever going to be like a normal person and just accept and get on with it? I could understand why my parents despaired. I was beginning to despair of me myself and yet if this, all this, wasn't enough for me, was there anything that ever would make me content and stop me putting myself through ridiculous hoops both emotionally and physically to reach this euphoric, yet undefined goal? This was madness. I was sure of it but I didn't know what to do. I really didn't.

Yet again I decided it was time to set myself a few parameters. It occurred to me that my drinking was an indication of my general inability to inject the merest amount of discipline into my lifestyle. I decided I would not drink alone and while I would drink with my parents in a civilised way in the evening, that would be all. I wondered why I found this very simple behaviour so hard when so many people around me could just decide to do something and stick with it. But then I was a girl who wasn't happy when I had the things that most girls would have killed for.

Tuesday 19 January 1999.

Waiting for Greg to collect me to go to Bushey — we're house-sitting for the rest of the week for his parents. Still longingly thinking of Alex, although am desperately trying to not let it get in the way as it has before, as I fear it could all be a lost cause for the third or fourth time (I've lost count)! I must say I've put on a few pounds much to my disappointment and will not be able to exercise at all this week — grrrrr! Hopefully all will go well and they'll drop off.

Wednesday 27 January 1999.

So much for the joys and wonders of having Alex back on the scene! Some people never change. Our little rendezvous planned, confirmed, and supposedly guaranteed was yet again abandoned due to a bout of tiredness and excess office work! (Which I must add, I do actually believe — maybe wrong — but I believe it.) It is however once too often that this should occur! I did enjoy a very pleasurable three days off with Greg though and thus an unexpected Saturday night together too! Better fly now — Brent Cross calls, screams, shouts (store placement — can't stand it!). Being honest about the whole thing, I can't say I remotely enjoy it — especially when I can never find my car afterwards. Anyway — shall have to press on with it if I can't cut it short (which it seems I can't — did ask — plus don't like to be a cop out) — I shall just hopefully appreciate Baker St (head office) so much more. Must go!

The attempts at self-discipline were faltering and I honestly wasn't sure if I'd manage it, which was a bad way to start. I liked going out too much. January's deadline came and went and, needless to say, was not successful. I was annoyed with myself. I wasn't sure if I was cross because I couldn't stick to my own rules or whether it was the fact that I had to have these rules to live by. With February whizzing by I decided I had to set a new deadline for cutting back my drinking. My experiences of life since, both my own and those of others, has shown me that cutting back something like drinking is actually a lot harder than giving it up. It's like trimming back the number of cigarettes you smoke or biscuits you eat. Quite often it's easier to give up totally, removing the option so you're not tempted but I wasn't ready to give up drink totally. I liked drinking: I was one of those people who enjoyed it and more than that, I guess I associated it with fun times so giving it up would mean saying goodbye to my party life. I wasn't ready for that. But I was determined to do something.

Thursday 1 April 1999.

So I've got three or four days now until this whole transition period is once and for all over. Easter is the deadline, and it's well on its way. A couple of days and I'll be living by the new rules, the new me. There have been the odd couple of relapses (mini ones) in the draw up; however, I've let myself off, as there will be none after Easter.

Reasons for Not Drinking:
Always having bloodshot eyes
Always having to have one more and one more
Repeating myself (think I do this anyway)
Eating ridiculously loads (plus eating in the middle of the night)

Slurring my words / not being able to speak properly

Not remembering

Money I spend!

Drinking all M&D's drinks

Breaking M&D's hearts

Going to bed so early

Missing the entire conversation

Making everyone else feel uncomfortable

Not being able to stay out late

Not being able to enjoy different people / company

Life is about making the most of yourself in every way! Always offering your best to everyone and loving the entirety.
(Unknown)

Sunday 11 April 1999.

OK, so the whole renewal thing hasn't exactly kicked off to a flying start. I kind of messed up Thursday, Friday, and Saturday, but I'm still determined to give it my best. To be honest, facing it, I didn't really even try at all.

Must be strong — stick with my goals now and get to be who I want to be! Sometimes you just have to be brave and change direction to get where you want to go! Or else you'll just keep going on the wrong road that's taking you nowhere. It's hard sometimes, definitely not easy — but unless you make that decision and turn right around, you'll never know how beautiful and how much better that place is that you really wanted to go to... and you'll just drift on and on without ever fully appreciating it. No one's going to lead you there by the hand. You have to make the right decisions and find it yourself! Good night and God bless.

If one oversteps the bounds of moderation, the greatest pleasures cease to please.
(Epictetus)

I haven't failed. I've just found 10,000 ways that wont work.
(Thomas Edison)

The situation with Alex was, well, as unreliable as he was. I did broach the subject with him but nothing really changed which left me in rather a weak position and, in retrospect, was not really the cleverest thing to do. If I had held the strings to this 'relationship' then maybe it would have worked. But I was the one in the weaker position, the one who wanted him, the one who had shown she was prepared to wait, so really my feeble attempt at asserting myself was not too clever. Stupidly, I considered telling him not to contact me at all ever again but realised that would be both dramatic and redundant – because he never really contacted me anyway, only when it suited him. All I was really getting from Alex was heartache so actually my account with him was negative. It occurred to me I was creating a lot of drama around something that really didn't deserve it. Why did I do it? Why do a lot of women do it? Maybe because we mistake drama for love? This was a theme I'd come back to again and again.

Tuesday 27 April 1999.

I'm going to have to get to grips with things. Went out last night — got wasted, got home, and consumed entire (nice) contents of fridge. This is not going well — but I am persevering. Has been a month of renewal and reform. Have had a couple of good days (doesn't say much, does it?) — but am still on the case. Thirty days hath September, April, June, and November. Have three days left to go. Let's all hope!

A winner is just a loser who tried one more time.
(George M. Moore. Jr)

Wednesday 5 May 1999.

Ah, not too bothered about the drinking thing so much at the moment — only really when I end up pigging out heaps. Have been having a mad time — crazy but excellent in every way. I so need to live on my own now — really can't wait to get something soon. ASAP — probably next April! M&D have been on holiday for last ten days, so have had a riot — out every night and lots of parties. Weekend of 14th Val came down. Had a blast, dancing around the house, drinking cocktails, and being pure girls... hit the town by cab — joined the Pitcher and Piano posse until closing... met a bunch of new people including some flashy traders... (Hany and Simon) who happened to be going to China White, most impossible club to get into. They invited us. What a night — danced until four a.m.! They were members, so we just went to the front of the queue and waltzed straight in 'cos we supposedly knew Max. Went straight to their table piled with Absolut, Red Bull, Champagne, and danced on the podiums all night. Rest of this week I've basically had Hany (who I incidentally suspect has a strange aggressive streak), continuously on my case. Had fun with Greg for the remainder of the week except on 'disastrous Friday'. All the rest of it was great. Had Hany on the phone a lot, and Charlie phoned for about an hour, pissed and confused about his girlfriend, who seems to basically be doing to him exactly what I'm doing to Greg (not good! not good at all!). Met up with Hany and his crew in Pizza Pomodoro in Knightsbridge after tons of work drinks, and ended up having another mad night — then Friday was out with Ant and Greg and totally screwed up… got extremely pissed. Ant doesn't know how Greg puts up with me (but frankly, I don't give a shit — 'cos he totally does it too). Greg went ballistic and said he wasn't coming tonight — but soon got over it and now he is. So I will now (hoping that finally the hot water's hot!) go and have my shower, wash my hair, blah blah blah, and then go to Emporium.

Saturday 18 September 1999.

Hasn't time just flown by…

Well, a lot has happened I guess since I last wrote, though unfortunately nothing tremendously exciting. I'm doing the merged role at work — OK I guess, not brilliant. Am pushing (unsuccessfully) for a pay rise which is consequently doing my head in — along with Nick (sits next to me) who does it in also for continuously watching what I'm doing, interfering, and telling me to stop emailing my friends. Haven't spoken to Alex at all, apart from drunken nights out when I give him and Greg the routine calls and totally piss them both off. Decided not to keep contact with Hany, as I thought it was an odd friendship, and OK, he had tons of money but was a bit 'heavy' and I didn't fancy him anyway.

Work's been OK. Took a week off, just chilled out with Greg, went to Kensington Park, had a picnic and laugh. I know I totally 100 per cent want to live in Kensington one day soon. I love it.

Sam now has a criminal record, which will stay with her for five years (along with Matt and her dad!), although hers was purely for avoiding her train fare, which, let's face it; we've all done from time to time. Fortunately I've gotten away with two ten-pound fines and also gave a false address (as yet not found out). It's going to seriously affect her chances of getting her visa for Costa Rica. She's going for two years. Hopefully all will go well.

Greg is still at the Sports store and still has no money! Have resumed contact with Fabrizio. I never write, so he's requested we email. We are now doing that. Also currently emailing Ravi. Was in contact via ever more flirty and innuendo emails with Charlie. That's all quietened down now.

Still not sure exactly whether Greg's the one! Not sure — general consensus is probably not, however as yet, touch wood, ferro (what the Italians say) and everything else, it's OK! We do genuinely have a good laugh together most of the time. Ant's moving out of the flat, therefore there is 'space' for someone else. After much debate about me being anti renting etc., his folks have come up with the sum of £40 p/w and bills. Guess it's OK. Don't want to rent but do need to move out and do love West Hampstead. So we'll see what happens there, just hope whatever it is, all goes well.

The thing that does annoy me about him is that he mentions things 'Jodi' (his ex) used to do/was like etc.! Can't stand that, did it last night. Must bring it up.

Saw Valeria the other day, had to do a store visit, so picked Peterborough and stopped off overnight with her to catch up. Had one of our crazy nights!! Always so much fun — we just get each other... Talked about everything and felt so much better!

Though miles may lay between us, we're never far apart, for friendship doesn't count the miles, it's measured by the heart
(Anonymous)

The apparently infallible, globally successful Department Store I was now working for, was suddenly not doing so well. This was a time of major downturn for them and of course being such a high profile company there was loads of bad press and so they had to do something. They refused to believe anything was wrong with their product at that point (they realised that later on) and so to show the City they were doing something, they began to make people redundant. Given my total lack of enthusiasm for my job, I was pretty sure mine would be the first phone to ring on what they so dramatically called Black Monday. I didn't care. I was already looking into TEFL courses in Italy, teaching, becoming a nanny or anything else possible abroad; something to take me away from what was proving to be a very unsatisfactory start to my supposed glamorous post graduate working life.

To my amazement, my phone didn't ring that day and I didn't get called. Once again, I had underestimated my value and achievements. Or was it perhaps the intervention of luck and timing. I also wondered whether the head of my department (men's underwear) fancied me. Whatever the reason, I was still there. Life went on, work got more boring, and my feet became itchier. Before I knew it, it was time for the second Black Monday. They obviously thought that redundancy would fix a huge gap between customer expectations and the products they saw on the shelves. It doesn't of course but it happened again and once again I didn't get the pink slip. To my deepest dismay they actually offered me a new role as Buying Assistant's Assistant or something like that. They were all stupid titles anyway, like most jobs are. I would be in a different department – men's shirts (yawn). At least mum and dad were delighted that I had survived the chop. My new job was torture and more mind-numbing than the last. I spent my days moving clothes hangers around and colour-coordinating wardrobes with bland items of clothing. Seriously it was like doing community service or something.

On the rare occasion that anyone actually asked my view on something, I failed to give a dynamic response, as frankly I couldn't have given two hoots what shade of blue or thickness of cotton a shirt is. It had zero interest to me and was of negotiable importance to the world as a whole. I simply could not muster the enthusiasm. I decided to do a crap job, so with any luck, the next time Black Monday came around, I might be lucky enough to finally be made redundant.

CHAPTER 12
New Entry

"My legs are not what they used to be, Natalie."

"Oh they're still pretty good, Nonna."

My formidable grandma was getting older, as we all do. Nothing to be too alarmed about... just the passing of age and with it, the weakening of limbs. She'd always been so active, out and about all the time so her legs weakening and at times giving way was becoming a worry. We were in her kitchen, me in my usual spot at the table drinking coffee and picking at the delicious homemade fruit cake, I'd politely declined but she'd put in front of me anyway while she stood at the stove stirring a pasta sauce. The smell of tomatoes, garlic and herbs always had a kind of pacifying effect on me: so familiar, to be in that kitchen imbued me with a feeling of security that very few things did. Every Sunday we had the same family dinner here that we'd had for years. After a massive feast of risotto or pasta followed by a full on roast with her special touch and of course a homemade desert, all of us sat watching *Bulls Eye* (jazzed up darts show) then gathered around the sofas for a weekly catch-up. Today, however, Grandma was not quite herself.

"Go into the living room and have a lie down. I'll make sure it's perfect, I promise."

"Oh really! No I don't want to lie down. I want to sit here with you. I have to make sure you do it properly."

Though she had spent her adult life in England, Italy, the old country, was where Grandma had parked so many memories; she loved to keep in good contact and visit as often as she could. Now for the first time, she was talking about going for what she termed 'maybe my last visit'. This meant something; she obviously felt a change. I told her not to be so dramatic and that of course it wouldn't be. She was serious though and I was to play a part: she felt that she needed someone to help her, to hold her hand – and she asked if I would do that, accompany her on the trip and help where and indeed if needed. I was sad that she felt like this, yet flattered she chose me, plus the idea of going to Italy for a few days and casting off the shackles of this apparently grown-up but somewhat unsatisfactory life I was supposed to be living, was a ticket out of purgatory, at least for a short time. And anyway, of course I'd have simply never said 'no'. She said I'd have to be there for her all the time and not go out with the numbers of people I'd become friends with over time, just be there for her. "Certo". That's life; our elders take care of us when we are young and as we grow up that role begins to reverse. It was my turn to help. At least I could stop thinking about Greg for a while and maybe that would resolve itself whilst I was away, a breaks as good as a change they say. Then I could come back and hopefully life could begin on an upward curve again. I could have done with the break in more ways than one. I was totally bored with the shirts at work too. I was not remotely interested in which were the top sellers or how many the average man bought himself each year. I wanted out and hoped that the next round of redundancies (the store was still finding its way out of its troubled position – or trying to) would finally include me.

We would be staying in Rosalie's magnificent villa, which was something to celebrate in itself. I'll happily admit I liked her lifestyle and adored being waited on hand and foot. It was the ultimate luxury. As soon as we landed on Italian soil I breathed an audible sigh of relief. Something I felt unfailingly every time the plane doors opened to that country. Rosalie's open arms and generous house welcomed us and we settled down to a relaxing few days, catching up on gossip, eating delicious food and generally being spoiled. I didn't have to do too much for Grandma, mainly helping her get up, on the marble stairs and things like that, however I felt I had my duty to be there all the time, especially as I was only there for a short while and we'd made a deal. This was not my trip; it was hers. So when Renata, my favourite cousin of all time and friend, asked me to come out, as hard as it was I had to refuse. But she insisted.

She just wouldn't let up. She kept on and on promising that no one would know. She knew Grandma well too and understood there was no negotiating; it simply had to be in secret. Eventually I caved, "OK." I would leave after Grandma was in bed and be back to help her up. And that was when my world turned upside down.

Saturday 2 October 1999.

Wow! I have seriously met the most AMAZING GUY! Just totally hope I get to see him tomorrow. Really hope so. It's Sebastiano — Cesco (Renata's fiancé's) cousin! He is just incredible. It's insane — can't quite believe it. I feel so blown away and utterly speechless, yet at the same time I want to scream and shout about it. And we got on soooo well! It's crazy; normally I think of myself when it's late and I'm tired. But I just couldn't get tired, just couldn't — and then we kissed. Well... talk about Boom! It was just

like... BOOM! So sexy. We couldn't stop, once started. Just loved him in
every way. I can't even explain.

I want to spend more time with him. I want to talk to him all the time.
He's amazing. Hope I'm not exaggerating either. My heart's pounding
even now. I just can't wait... IN LOVE ... I think ... Let's not get too
carried away just yet — but — Yeeeehaaaa!

I felt a bit nervous driving back to Renata's flat with her, not
sure why, possibly because I knew I was doing wrong... but
nothing a glass of wine couldn't fix.

As she unlocked the door and pushed it open, we locked eyes
immediately. He stood there in a faded pair of jeans, grey woollen
round neck jumper with blue shirt collar beneath. His hair was
mousey, skin fair and appeared soft, he had a slight baby face with
bright green eyes. I felt the strangest, most alien sensation and we
stared at each other as if in utter amazement. It was almost as if I
was looking at myself in a mirror, not that we looked remotely
alike, but it was like behind his eyes I could see me, my inner self
– a male version. An uncanny familiarity that made us feel instantly
connected. I was knocked for six, we both were. Something
almost out of body was happening. We stumbled over the
awkward encounter, aware that it had been clocked by all, and
proceeded to the restaurant. The feeling didn't go away; we never
stopped chatting or gazing at each other. In fact it was as if it was
only us there. Unable to say goodbye, Sebastiano suggested we
went on to a club for a couple of hours just he and I, before
dropping me back. We were inseparable.

After I eventually plucked up the courage to tell Grandma,
never having been very good at lying or blatantly deceiving, she

made it clear that she certainly thought I was barking up the wrong tree on this one. She asked a million questions but essentially was overtaken by the fact that she felt let down. I'd cheated her.

"Natalie, you have your head turned too easily. One day in Italy and you are in love. Stupid."

"Nonna, I'm sorry I went out but I was here for you."

"Natalie, you are chasing boys. You have a boyfriend what are you doing?"

"But this is different. I wasn't looking Nonna. It was like something... well, magical really. You know?"

I wanted to say it was like her meeting Grandad, that it was something real but I didn't think that would be too clever in the circumstances. She was angry with me for going out and was, justifiably not very impressed with my judgment. I could see her point. I had landed in a foreign country, gone out for the evening and come home declaring I had met the love of my life and that it was the real thing. On evidence it could look just like any other girl's longing for a relationship, the kind of thing that happens every day all over the world and continues until you return home and real life takes over. Or they forget you. Or both.

This was different and I knew it. I had to see him again, there were two days left.

THEN... Life is so often a case of hearing the same advice and then deciding whether to take notice of it. Most of us know the things our friends or family will tell us, the advice they'll give and we know it ourselves deep down. But perhaps the point of being human is that we want to prove the exception to it. And there are exceptions. At that moment I felt like I was immune to all those warnings about love in a foreign place and distance relationships.

Sunday 3 October 1999.

Sunday, have had a good day so far, spent most of it pampering myself in the hope of seeing Signore Sebastiano stasera. Vediamo… Hope he keeps to his word at least… and that we have a great time of course. But anyway, we'll see, whatever happens I'm going to Renata's anyway. Just as a by the by, I've had complete butterflies, feel relatively sick, and want to continuously smile and jump up and down, but otherwise everything is the norm. Rosalie and G have gone to the cemetery, and I'm supposedly having a rest. However, that is quite clearly proving impossible.

Last night was just 'incredibile'… we were so connected and the kiss was something else… didn't do anything that I shouldn't but…

He really is something special, and I genuinely like him a lot! Anyway, I'm not going to go on about it, 'cos that could well be it now, over, and it probably is, although obviously hope not. But, as he said, even if it's just for now, it's still lovely and won't be forgotten (not sure how much I agree with that!). I'm usually never very good at just moving on But hey, I'm only young once – might as well enjoy myself!

Feeling a bit guilty; so spoke to Greg last night. He was sweet, not doing very much… But sweet all the same.

The question I didn't want to ask myself was, 'Am I looking for a way out from my current relationship?' It certainly didn't seem like that. I was not looking for this at all; it just came and hit me in the face. It was other worldly, spiritual and honestly felt like it was simply meant to be. I'd never felt anything remotely familiar, not with Brandon, nor Riccardo, nor Léonard even, no one had come close. This was entirely different. Like something I'd only ever read about or seen in movies.

Saturday 9 October 1999.

Not such a bad return to work. Now wondering whether I should phone Sebastiano?!

I did call! It was the right thing to do. Had a great chat!! It was so nice to hear him speaking. He seemed pleased too. Just hope it all continues. Still not exactly sure what it all means, or where it's all going to end up. However, I guess for the moment all I can do is go with the flow and see where the breeze takes me, hoping it's the right place and that no one gets hurt along the way. I do however tend to believe Fabrizio a bit deep down in that long-distance relationships are hard, if not impossible! Nothing could ever really happen anyway unless we were in the same country.

But who knows? For the time being, I'm just going with it, and hope that all works out fine and perfect.

Sunday 14 November 1999.

So basically was a great weekend. Felt odd seeing Greg, regardless of how lovely he was to me, if anything it simply highlighted that something's not right between us. I've been feeling a bit guilty actually and rather confused at the same time. Obviously, came back from Italy, majorly thinking of Sebastiano, and well... have thus had a few arguments / heated discussions with Greg and not seen so much of him. Anyway desperately wanted to be in touch with S. Waited patiently and got two letters, one photo, and we've both phoned each other. Cool! I'm also going back there on December 1st for five days. Can't wait! I know people say 'Don't! Let him come to you', but what about all the times people do go back and they find their true love. Look at Grandma. They met in Italy. He went back to England and then came back for her. It's not so different. This feels like destiny and I'm not going to let it slip away. Anyway, even if it is a let-

down, or I don't feel the same, I still have to go as otherwise would continuously think, what if...? Similarly, don't want to do anything drastic with Greg, like finish it yet, 'cos last time I did that I regretted it. I need to think it through properly, know my options and see things through to the end. So as much as I'm not sure what's going on... whilst we're having fun, I'm trying to stick with it.

So that's why I'm feeling guilty. But saying that, Greg, loving as he is, is by no means an angel. I love him lots and maybe expect a bit too much; he never surprises me, buys me things, buys me dinner, takes me to the theatre, sends me flowers, cards, etc. nothing 'for me' if he doesn't feel like it. Anyway...

Thinking of doing a few sunbeds before going to Italy, just to get my skin a little more glowing! (Know it's bad for you – but I kind of need it.)

Also need/want bikini waxed! (Not absolutely necessary of course – but should do it anyway!)

NB Two year anniversary with Greg on 22nd! Oooops, then I'm going to Italy, just hope this doesn't all blow up in my face! Oh well, c'est la vie. But hope not!

Take the good until you find something better, and in search for something better do not let the good slip away from you or die out. If you disregard it despite its worth and pursue something better, what you had escapes you; but if you remain attached to what is good, you will always have it if nothing better follows.
(Paracelsus)

Sunday 21 November 1999.
Greg and I have been going out two years tomorrow!

Well... what do you know? Sunday morning, woke up, put my phone on and have a message! Yep, Sebastiano, cool! love to hear his voice on phone. Quite chuffed. Past couple of weeks or few even, we've spoken twice a week, and so far so good; it's been him who's calling! Excellent. Not quite what I'm used to, it's normally the other way around.

Totally can't wait to go now, just over a week, really hope it goes well — sooo looking forward to it.

Who knows what's ever going to come out of all this?... Who knows? But whatever, I still feel that I have to pursue these things to the end or not the end; whatever it may be!

I have however also decided that I do have to end up with someone with a rather substantial amount of money, or at least the ability, drive, and luck to make it big anyway.

... 'Til next time... N x

PS: Got photos of S in post, sweet, but not to die for. Oh well, I guess he's kind of 'real' that's why. Am curious how I'm going to feel about all this when I get there... who knows? Hopefully just like I did before...

Greg was not stupid. He knew we had contrasting needs and after our anniversary dinner together, a few days later, we had yet another talk. He said that I needed different things, aka 'lots of going out'. I could see his point and he'd said it before but it wasn't all that black and white. "Let's call it a day and be friends..." We'd been there already yet it had never really stayed that way. It made sense and underneath I knew it too but I was scared. I didn't want to end up with nobody. In hindsight I think he was testing me. Pushing, to see if I'd actually go, it was the sort of tactic I'd use. He knew things had changed for the worse and he detected my change in attitude, my excitement at going to Italy (versus my lack of excitement at being together). When I said OK, I think he was shell-shocked. Unable to get his words out, he attempted to confirm the decision asking me over again if I was sure. I was.

Wednesday 1 December 1999 (writing diary in the sky – I love it!).

Big day is finally here – day I've been waiting for, for so long. I'm on the plane back to Italy. Here I am, all alone, just me, my diary and my drink and loving it. OK, felt a bit shattered so closed my eyes for two minutes (although probably result of the M&S Pina Coladas I bought with). I love that stuff!

I've been kind of wishing I could be famous lately, like really famous. I mean I've always thought that really but have never been nearly emotionally intact or self-secure enough to pursue it before. Now, however, I feel like I am. The Nick Ross Show *just reinforced it. I went with M; she spoke lots on it! I was really there just for moral support and to be on TV of course! Apparently the executive producer kept asking to have me say something as I had a brilliant TV look. Weh Hey! I clearly said after the show over a glass of wine that I am always more than willing to do appearances! There has to be something in this.*

Back then: to be regarded as well-known, one had to be great. Today: to be regarded as great, one has to be well-known.
(Mokokoma Mokhonoana)

I'd love to MAKE IT... although only if I could find a guy who was so totally unaffected by the whole thing that I could still have a loving relationship. I'd still have to sort out a few minor things like not being so paranoid eating wise, stop binging so much in the night and probably in fact definitely not drink so much. Although I do also know for a fact that when you're busy which of course you would be, all famous people are, you wouldn't do all this stuff. It's all only a result of boredom... you simply wouldn't have time to think so much. Anyway, apart from all those minor little things, which will hopefully become more and more minor, most other teenage/growing up issues, I believe I've pretty much overcome. I feel like I've come a long way and I understand 'me' a lot better but I still have a bit further to go — I guess you never stop learning. EVERYBODY is like this! EVERYBODY!

Anyway, nearly there now! Renata's picking me up, S couldn't make it. Just as well as I look pretty crap.

At least I'm away! Will see Greg when I get back — although the beautician said it'd probably end between us — hopefully on good terms!

It was a magical few days with Sebastiano. Better than I'd expected, we really were like kindred spirits. We just dreamily picked up where we'd left off and I returned to London carrying with me his promises that he would be over in February. I couldn't have been happier, it was like my life had transformed 360 degrees and my Italian future was looking bright. Grandma had always said '*quello che non succede in una vita — puo succedere in un attimo*' (what doesn't happen in a lifetime can happen in a second), though I'm not sure she'd have liked to apply it here. I was walking on air. Greg and I were now really just friends but I still felt terrified about letting go for some reason. I suppose it was the first time a guy has really wanted me and now I was letting go of him — with no real guarantee of a replacement. We'd spoken again about the decision and though we'd relapsed and occasionally crossed the friend line with sex, it seemed to be settled now. But with regard to Sebastiano while I should have been delighted with things turning out like this, I began to feel uneasy as I always do if I like a guy, properly. And I couldn't let go of the thought that each time a guy turns up on my territory, I don't see them the same way any more. Was I ready for a serious relationship, moreover a distance relationship? I wasn't sure. But it would be Christmas soon and then we'd be in the new Millennium. My workplace was absolute torture and I was bored yet again. If ever there was a time to take the plunge, it was now.

CHAPTER 13
A New Millennium

Courage isn't having the strength to go on – it is going on when you don't have the strength
(Napoleon Bonaparte)

Monday 27 December 1999.

Have just finished writing to Sam, where I guess I've summed up what I've been trying to say… what I feel, kind of being, that I feel sort of alone in a sense, without any real leaning posts, and I just need to find and nurture that inner strength that I know I have inside me. That it's just one of those transition period kind of things, where you don't really know where you're going, or how you're going to get there, but you know that in the end you will… not sure how exactly but you just will.

This whole new millennium thing had been really talked up. Like it was going to be the greatest thing ever and somehow life changing for everyone. If you think about it, then it doesn't make any sense. Just because the clock ticks over to a round number – 2000 – it doesn't mean that anything in your own little life will change. It's just a date, just a number. Life changes when it's ready to. That's destiny and after meeting Sebastiano, I was convinced that was how it was meant to happen. Anyway we had fun like we always have fun at New Year's but it didn't live up to expectations, does it ever…? Though I don't think anyone knew what we were expecting to be honest. I had of course been preoccupied with Sebastiano's impending visit in February. I wondered how I'd feel with him over here in my space: my track record wasn't great. I was usually bad when they turned up, the bubble seemed to burst, like they fell right off their pedestal. But I felt this would be different. I had real feelings for Sebastiano, it wasn't just some silly crush. I was sure this was the real deal or at least it had the makings to be.

Wednesday 2 February 2000.

E allora... the weekend finally came that Renata, Cesco and Sebastiano came over. Haven't written in a while as have been trying to make most of gym subscription I won doing limbo dancing at Esporta however it hasn't really worked. Do enjoy it... though would rather not have to worry about all that and just stay skinny like Kate Moss irrespective of what I did. R, C and S have been and gone. Can honestly say that every second was just completely fantastic. It's like I'm on another planet when he's around! Did the whole sightseeing thing. Seb and I kissed our way around London and he gave me a tour of the National Gallery. Probably never kissed anyone as much in all the time I've been out with them as we did in four days here. Now I feel more than a bit confused!

Sebastiano wasn't the only reason I was confused. I was still trying my best to like my job but it wasn't working and it showed. Literally everyone around me knew it was doing my head in. I wasn't good at hiding that stuff at all. The thing that kept me going was knowing I was going to see Sebastiano again in March but at the same time, it just made me even more impatient with work. It was like I had a foot in two places and that's pretty hard to keep up as anyone who has done it knows. Absence might make the heart grow fonder but it also messes with your head and you waste a lot of time daydreaming too. It had occurred to me that our relationship was built on us not being in the same place so I had no idea what it might be like being with each other twenty-four hours a day. It's like anyone you meet travelling or on holiday. There's a huge sense of excitement and you ride this wave of exhilaration but you have no idea what would happen if you were together every day. Would he annoy me? Would I still be special to him? I knew I'd be pretty stupid and naïve to think that it was perfect. I wanted to keep up regular visits because that way I might be able to determine exactly how much there really was between us.

Greg was still around – as a friend – and though we had good laughs and talked lots, I knew I wasn't in love with him. I loved him in some way but it was not the same deep, romantic love I felt for Sebastiano. I mentioned Sebastiano to him but didn't really elaborate. I didn't have a whole story to tell and knowing how it might hurt him, there didn't seem much point in going into it any further.

Friday 17 March 2000.

Was supposed to hear from Seb last night but didn't. I was looking forward to it all day and when he didn't call I felt totally empty and gutted. I've got over it now, it's almost like I just kind of trust him anyway. Hope I'm right. Normally whilst I'd be super paranoid and analytical right now, I actually seem sort of OK. I have this strange but strong sort of faith in him. All his friends and Renata, tell me he's amazing, loyal, good etc. (which should really mean nothing) as I've been told so many times you can never trust anyone but yourself. But at the moment this is how I feel and it's nicer to have loved and to have lost than never to have loved. In this instance I'd rather trust first, if that's what feels right. Innocent until proven guilty!

Love: If it's there you can't fight it and if it's not you can't force it. —
Sam.

There are some things in life you can't change and love is one of them.
— Valeria

Sebastiano and I wrote, emailed, sent gifts, talked and kept in touch religiously for the next year practically... I went there a few times and we spent incredible weekends together, getting to know each other in the country where I had always felt most at home. We dined out in beautiful little restaurants, ate fish, drank wine, danced, drove through the hills in his tiny yellow sports car, walked through the Palladian town in the freezing cold embracing each other and made love like I was dreaming, I was totally in love. We both were. The relationship was deepening and we had to do something about it. I made the bold decision to move out there.

Always finding it hard to make decisions of any kind, right down to what I should wear around the house, I felt an immense weight had lifted once I'd come to the conclusion of moving. I'd have a few things to sort out then I'd be off and that would be it — a new start. About a month after the decision was made, I was heading out to 'Loop Bar' off Oxford Street, a local for after work drinks, with my ever-faithful friend Donna for a well-deserved few drinks. We scuffle through the crowds to the bar and begin scanning the cocktail menu – desperate to get the order in for happy hour.

"Natalie." I felt a gentle hand on my shoulder and turned around. " So how are you?"

"Hi." I was shocked. "I'm good thanks. What brings you here?"

"Work drinks... can I get you one?"

"Err... yeah sure, thanks."

Brandon. Out of all the people in the world, Brandon Lad. He was so sweet, two kisses, big hug and a really genuine smile. He bought me a drink and softly tugged at my hand to pull me through the crowds.

Right, so I'm about to emigrate to pursue a new love, the apparent love of my life and my oldest childhood sweetheart who I pined for and utterly worshipped for most of my youth has asked me out for a drink! What was going on? I didn't get it; it was like someone up there was playing games with me. I simply had to do it. Never leave a stone unturned and all that, especially before making such a massive move. This could be an important sign. I had to go. I've said it before, if there's one thing I could never live with its 'What ifs?' I had to get it right.

And so we went. A brief evening out for a couple of Long Islands and a journey home together... He walked me halfway to my door (no way could I have had my parents see, they'd be all over it, anything for me to stay) and we kissed. Oooops. I know, I shouldn't have but it was just a kiss and I had to know.

Phew. It was awful. He drew me in tightly, pressed himself against me and I felt all I needed to feel to know that he was clearly quite into it – but I wasn't. I knew that I'd made the right decision. I was going.

CHAPTER 14
Following My Heart

While Mum and Dad were very supportive of me, I also knew they were doing their best to quell the doubts and the sadness they had about me leaving the UK. We all loved Italy, but it was for holidays not for life. And we were a family and families stuck together. They'd already made their concerns about Sebastiano clear and I'd assured them I understood. But in theory it wasn't all about that. Not just love. Somehow I knew I wouldn't be going if it were just for that, so I'd got myself a job, a good one. I don't know how but I did. Having found it online, I bigged myself up and applied and after they flew me over twice for interviews which I almost award-winningly blagged my way through, I got offered the position. I knew it would make the whole concept more digestible for my parents. I had embarked on this adventure in a state of high excitement but now the reality was setting in and that meant that actually it wasn't just about me going to live with my Italian boyfriend, there was a lot more to it than that. Other people were involved. And I think my parents wanted me to look beyond my Eat Pray Love vision of it all and be prepared for the challenges of daily life in Italy, with an Italian family and not approach the whole thing in carefree holiday mode. It's easier said than done isn't it when you're the one riding the wave.

"It won't be private," said my mother. "The family will be watching everything you do."

"I know."

"He's a country boy, Natalie. He wants a simple life, you realise that?" said Dad.

"I know that, Dad."

"Your life's going to change you know. No nipping out to bars with your friends every night."

"Yes, Mum."

"It will be very full on, Natalie."

"Dad, I appreciate that but you know – I'm going to have to adapt at some point right? That's what partnership is all about... so I might as well try."

"Yes, Natalie, but we just want you to see the big picture."

I promised them I did.

"And remember you can always come home!"

They were right though: this would be a whole different way of living – the lack of privacy, the complete disruption of 'my way' of life, the way I liked to eat, my exercising and pretty much everything I did. We were supposed to be getting a flat but the speed of that process and indeed of everything seemed almost in reverse, let alone first gear, so I'd be moving in with his *famiglia*. I knew how my parents felt about Sebastiano, their reservations about him, his family being present all the time and the restrictions this would place on me. But I figured that at some point I'd have to compromise me, Natalie, to fit in and to grow up and wasn't now as good a time as any to do that? If not, when would I do it?

Monday 9 October 2000.

Have been through a whole big issue with Seb, with his parents involved too, 'cos I got a bit pissed (few too many vinos) on a few occasions but I can't believe how out of proportion it's all been blown. I mean seriously I've been under a huge amount of pressure, have been so, so tired, work doing my head in here, there and everywhere, not to mention having to drive on the wrong side of the flipping road, and I got a bit pissed (a bit!)... on the weekend! Cannot believe it... Maybe he's right though and it won't happen again. Spoke to Val and Donna who couldn't believe it either. But hey, just hope it's forgotten now, 'cos it'd be ridiculous otherwise anyway.

Our greatest glory is not NEVER falling.
But rising every time we fall!
(Confucius)

Tuesday 10 October 2000.
I guess it's taking me a while to settle in here... Being with others all the time is taking its toll. First I have to join Seb's family routine in the morning, for breakfast, eat (biscuits, biscuits, biscuits), chat... and that's nothing compared to the Italians at work. So many bitchy girls and I have to sit with them for lunch (fortunately they just eat steamed veg — bonus). Then it's back home to sit with family again at night, chat, chat, food, food, food! I mean give me some space! Always, always people around me. It's like living under a microscope — I seriously feel like one of those cells or something that people keep ogling at through a lens. I just want to be free to do my own thing SOMETIMES, not be under 24/7 observation. It's painful and exhausting.

Working in Italy — even as a buyer (cough, splutter) for one of its largest fashion labels — was a huge contrast to London, in every single way. From Baker Street, W1 to the village of Lonigo, which was the labels' 'second' base, their first one 'The International Head office' being in Citadella was a shock and far more glamorous. Lonigo was really in the middle of nowhere and that meant a huge sea of change not only in terms of where I'd be every day but also the restrictions it put on my social life. There was nowhere to go and hang out at lunchtime, like Oxford Street – you couldn't pop out to the shops or go to a little place by yourself for lunch – and let's just say the Italian workplace, like all things Italian, is a law known only to itself. At this point in my young life, I should at least have known that just because a job has a cool, funky sounding description and happens to be a brand that makes highly desirable denim, doesn't mean it's going to be a cool job. Buying might sound like something you do while sitting in the front row at fashion shows but it's really about figuring out numbers – numbers of garments, dates when you need them and more numbers about how much it's going to cost. In a word, spreadsheets! I was lost in spreadsheets and it wasn't fun realising that this in fact was the job I had been hired to do. Most of the time I didn't have any idea what I was supposed to do, so I sat there figuring out ways to look busy and industrious. I found myself writing inserts for my diary in a large notebook while pretending I had my head down doing something incredibly important. It was a case of coming into work and thinking, 'OK so how much time can I waste today?' At the end of the day I'd cut out the stuff I'd written so I could take it home and stick the excerpts into my diary. If that wasn't an indication that I wasn't enjoying the role then I don't know what is. As the days passed I found the job becoming a nuisance and I felt disheartened. There were lots of outings – as well as travel for the job – and you simply had to go, there wasn't really a choice. One night there was a dinner, in a restaurant, supposedly a welcome for all the new people arriving. An inauguration dinner. They had these initiations, apparently they do this with everyone but they were different for girls and guys. We all sat down at a long table except for the finance guy who was the first 'initiation' and then he was told to crawl under the table while everyone else kicked him. I mean, I know initiations are stupid but this was way out of line and I couldn't imagine a company in the UK even getting away with such a thing. But it was to get worse. Besides me there was another new girl and it was her turn. They turned the lights off after tying her to a chair with a belt. Then two guys got up and went towards her. I couldn't believe what I was seeing. They were touching her all over and everyone thought it was a big joke, cracking up and jeering them on. Poor thing was embarrassed but all I could think of was 'Oh my God, I'm next.' I went to the toilet, stayed there and then I left. A hasty getaway. There was no way I would allow myself to be touched by strangers. I hated the company, I hated the stupid devotion the people who worked there had towards it. It was ridiculous. Honestly, some of them thought they were like part of the founding family, that simply by working there they were related or something. How does that happen? I could never allow myself to be brainwashed like that. I knew I had to get out of this place but I couldn't just walk out. God knows how that would look to Seb's family, let alone Mum and Dad. They'd have me back over in London like a shot.

Thursday 19 October 2000.

On train back from Rome, passing through Tuscany and Chianti hills (after a shitty week at the flagship store). Contrast. It's all so nice, so much to be appreciated, but unfortunately, I'm just not in the mood. I know I need to get a grip and pull myself together, but I just get so bothered by such superficial and silly things. Must move on... there are so many unfortunate people around. I should not be so superficial.

Anyway, here I am and I've been having some liquore al caffe, which is really quite nice, though full of sugar and actually quite bloating my stomach out! Nice though! And I know I shouldn't be indulging in such things on my own (though not a crime and we have to enjoy ourselves). And with all the feelings I've been going through, I decided that liquore al caffe wouldn't be such a bad idea.

Things on Mind:

- JOB Not sure if I like it at all — seriously!

- TIME OF MONTH Late. Need this to happen. Hope just stress from all the changes.

- FLAT. We have one for June (friend of Seb's) but we need one 'til then.

- WEIGHT. Want to go easy, these guys eat so much.

All the worlds a stage ... And all the men and women merely players.
(William Shakespeare)

Tuesday 31 October 2000.

Am at home (well, Seb's home) as got bitten on the eye Sunday night and it's all swelled up. Went to hospital. Seb's mum persuaded me I should be home so called Filippo, manager, who made it clear he WAS NOT happy. I mean crikey, if you're not up to it. He's so weird, like a cross between John Travolta and Mr Bean, with added short man syndrome! Think he thinks he may have picked wrong person for job... well I tell you something, it's not 'may have' its definitely have! Oh well if it lasts until Xmas and I pass probation at least then I'll have a choice. I know it's a great job and everyone would love it, but I have to like it too. And I don't! Still have teaching avenue to investigate – everyone keeps convincing me to do that. (Obviously unaware English's been my worst subject since I can remember.) Oh well, can't be that hard.

NB: how cool is it that you can find Red Bull in Italian supermarkets. Perfect! Shows how we're not really that far away.

The alcohol thing was an issue with Sebastiano and I seemed to constantly get it wrong about when and what I was able to drink and how much of it. We'd go out and have a good time and I'd think, 'OK we're at a party, you can drink at a party.' But somehow I always got on the wrong side of him in that respect, not to mention his family. That only led to more anxiety as I started to wonder if everyone was talking about me and saying I was no good. The fact that he, they, made it out to be an issue, did just that, it created one. As far as I was concerned it was no big deal. In England you'd go out, have a few drinks, get tiddly and then it would all be forgotten. But these guys were different. It was as if he thought I was deliberately doing it to spite him and no matter how hard I tried, I couldn't make him see that this really wasn't a problem – unless he made it one.

During this period I wrote a lot. My diary was my friend and was pretty much my sole concern and it provided an outlet for the way I felt hemmed in by the demands of a new boyfriend, living with his family, dealing with his culture and of course the job I now hated. I was trying to blot it all out. There was the drinking which released some pressure though at the same time created it, but my diary gave me a place to go, a real place where I could express myself without anyone seeing me or getting judgmental. It was safe. And it worked because I got one resolution pretty soon actually: I quit the buying job (where frankly all I was buying was time). I'd met an English girl who was doing really well teaching English and she'd suggested I should join her. At that stage there were not many people doing it, especially not mother tongue and the field was pretty much wide open. I wasn't looking forward to telling my parents about the job though, I kind of felt like I'd let everyone down. I'd banged on about moving away for this fabulous new job and five minutes later I quit. As much as I knew they just wanted me to be happy, I also knew they were proud and so it was sure to cause a lively discussion. I'd have to have something up my sleeve, which fortunately I did. I was going to be a teacher.

Wednesday 15 November 2000.

Being a Spice Girl or something would be a good solution at the moment.

So referring to my trusty little magical book 'A Guide To The Advanced Soul' yet again... this is what it says:

The ideal man bears the accidents of life with dignity and grace, making the best of circumstances.
(Aristotle)

You don't develop courage by being happy in your relationships everyday. You develop it by surviving difficult times and challenging adversity.
(Epicurus)

Wednesday 20 December 2000.

Back home — London! It's so nice to be back but luckily at the moment, I look forward to the prospect of moving out of family home and into the flat with Seb when I go back and hopefully the teaching too... hoping of course that I like it. Actually... love it!

Seb seems a bit edgy about moving out although he won't admit it... afraid to cut apron strings!

Spoke to him last night, he's been offered a new job, hope he takes it — sounds good, could be fresh start with me teaching English etc. Hope he didn't think I was a bit tiddly on phone, 'cos I certainly was. Think he knows me well enough — in any case is nearly Christmas so special occasion. Hate for him to be dwelling on it whilst I'm not there to justify myself. Same goes for the rubbish bag I left his dad. Hope nothing happened to that except go straight in the 'dry only' rubbish, without a minimal second thought or questionable sound going in! Sincerely hope all is fine and dandy — really you'd have to be pretty mad to search through someone else's rubbish. Unless you're Colombo of course...

I just called. S not there. His mum sounded a bit odd. Am I being paranoid? Hope so. Wouldn't be the first time!

Doesn't look like he's ringing me back.

Thursday 21 December 2000.
Mobile phone not working over here. Good — means I spend less.

Maybe that's also why Seb hasn't phoned, doesn't want to call landline? Hope everything's OK! Really hope so, as am looking forward to creating our little life together now. (Apart from it not being a normal situation i.e. I'm doing everything.) He did say some beautiful things to me before I left though, we had a bit of a Deep and Meaningful when I brought up the whole issue of him not being bothered about me leaving for Christmas plus a few other things... 'like he just wasn't really caring enough'... Told him:

- *I've gone there, not vice versa*
- *I've accepted living in house for four months when it was meant to be two weeks*
- *I've accepted to wait for the apartment 'til January*
- *I've accepted he wouldn't come for Christmas*
- *Has shown no concern about me coming back here for Christmas*
- *And to top it all off when I asked him if he found everything he wants in a girl he said, "for now!"*

I mean what? Am I on trial here? Hate feeling like I'm walking a tightrope... it really bothers me, that I know at a drop of a hat it could all change, and the strings are all in his hand.

PS: definitely lost weight in Italy. 8lbs! Not intentionally and would have thought opposite so is fab! Hope I can keep it up.

PPS: Still no sound from Seb, just checked email. Maybe it's slow?

Christmas appealed to that part of me that didn't want to grow up. It was always comforting to be in the cocoon of family and friends and this year more than ever. I didn't have to worry about who I was or whether I'd had far too much sherry (which I probably had). It was just Grandma and us plus an old family friend Henry who turned up as he was alone and then on Boxing Day my dad's side appeared as usual, a posse of glamorous cousins and lovely aunts and uncles coming together in a loud, boisterous gathering with of course loads to eat and drink. My Big Fat Greek Christmas would just about sum it up. And while I was determined not to worry about how much I drank, the funny thing is that it did affect me that day and I wondered if being around this relatively restrained Italian family was making me utterly paranoid. Sam had popped in so I asked her what she thought, anxious I suppose for some reinforcement that I was really OK.

"I don't see the point in trying to be anything else, Sam, as this is who I am and it's who everybody knows. This IS Natalie," I told her.

"Rubbish. There is nothing that you can't change. People can change, Nats, and it's a positive thing to do."

"I suppose you're right."

"NO, I am right." She smiled.

Perhaps she was and I could put this phase down to youthful exuberance or something. In some ways I wanted to change yet I didn't want to do it because of someone else. If I decided not to be party girl Natalie then I would do it for my own reasons not for Sebastiano or his family. I decided I'd give myself until New Year and then I'd make a fresh start. Before that there was Grandma's birthday. She was in a wheelchair by now and it was heartbreaking to see this indomitable spirit fading away in a wheelchair. Mentally she was as strong and sharp as ever but her body was fragile. I often questioned why advanced medicine or surgery was practised on people where other parts of them couldn't be fixed to the same degree. After a triple bypass, her heart was functioning probably better than mine, but her body couldn't support it. It made me wonder if this was the best situation for her, or indeed anyone in that position as she was so alert and smart and to be like that must make her feel so diminished and powerless. We took her to a restaurant and we all had a good time. New Year arrived and I thought Sebastiano would ring and wish me a good one. He didn't. I wondered if he'd wait until the next day, perhaps he thought I was partying but nothing happened. The night itself was, as always, a blast.

New Year's Day 2001.

So, have begun my resolutions though undecided on smoking one. Will definitely stick to the others, just not sure on smoking, will think about it and probably give that up too. Might as well! Will have to one day...

Had a fairly good New Year, though was so mad that Sebastiano didn't ring. I thought that was disgusting! He didn't come here for NY, hardly ever phones, takes everything for granted, and is only ever thinking of himself. He didn't even phone on NYE or NYD, and I thought that was just a complete lack of respect. It's like he doesn't give a shit about me. It's this take it or leave it kind of thing that really gets to me and completely pisses me off.

But I guess I have to be stronger myself. The more I believe in myself, the more others will believe in me. It's all about respect. I deserve so much more but until I truly believe that myself, no one else will.

Was completely hurt all day yesterday, constantly on the verge of tears... waiting for the phone to ring. Spoke to V who was fab as always... Then just felt I had to write him an email knowing he would get it at work in the morning. He rang when he got it and apologised — kind of — I listened and stupidly said 'OK — big kiss'. Extremely pathetic thing to say as it clearly is not OK. Just wish he wasn't so lazy about the whole thing. Will speak tonight.

**Live a good honourable life – then when you get
older you'll be able to enjoy it a second time.**
(Unknown)

Back in Italy it was full steam ahead with my new teaching career. Abigail took me under her wing and I did the first part of the teaching attachment at the school. I would be starting in a week which was a pretty scary thought and I felt I could have done with an extra week before being let loose in a business to teach English.

Monday 8 January 2001.
Can't believe how quick this teaching this is moving... only have a week attachment to learn everything... I guess there's only one thing that applies here:

**The best way to learn to swim is to
be thrown in at the deep end.**
(Unknown)

What does my Guide to the Advanced Soul say?

**Stop sitting there,
with your hands folded.
Looking on, doing nothing;
get into action
and live this full**

and glorious life.
Now – you have to do it.
(Eileen Caddy – The Dawn of Change)

*Hmmm. On Monday must remember I am there because there is
something they want from me. I am not on trial. OK.*

*PS: Made a huge mistake on roads last night – must be extremely alert
and very, very careful.*

Friday 12 January 2001.
I AM A TEACHER.
*Am at school waiting to go over the whole teaching method etc. with
Abigail and hopefully prepare my lessons. Nice morning so far... Put a
couple of pick-me-ups in coffees as long day ahead but then just won't
drink so much tonight. Guess I shouldn't have with resolutions, but just
the beginning so it's not too bad. Anyway from now on won't do it. Not
good.*

*Hope this all works out, would be great if it does, working for myself
etc., self employed! I must believe in myself and be confident! After all I
am English – what do they know?*

My teaching feedback was good. Far better than I'd expected.
I seemed to pick it up well and it seemed that while I might not be
sure of myself, just as in previous jobs and tasks, others were sure
of me. I wasn't so good at sticking to my drinking resolution: the
evening lessons of which there were far too many required a little
something and so I'd often add some cheeky Dutch courage to get
me through. Sebastiano's parents thought it absolutely appalling
that I worked in the evening, just as they thought it was wrong that

I had travelled for work with the fashion brand or attended after work functions. There was a definite culture clash here and I knew they would have preferred if I was at home preparing for and feeding their son, not to mention obsessively sweeping up afterwards. Ever watched Italians with a broom? It's their favourite pastime: they just love to sweep. They see one crumb and out comes the broom. It drove me absolutely bonkers. But as we were now moving into an apartment, I could expect less scrutiny and life would surely start to seem a bit more, well, normal.

Friday 28 January 2001.

Love the new apartment, it's amazing. Went out for Chinese New Year, all drank copious amounts of wine and guess what! Seb got drunk which was great! About time. Role reversal (shoe was on other foot) for a change. Halleluiah!

Monday 5 February 2001.

Thing is, on the one hand, things seem to be moving on relatively nicely and on the other I've been a complete idiot. The story of watching what I drink when we go out! Not here at home, thank God, that's all been fine when people are here for dinner etc. (always very couply, which I find tough and very official... ahhh). It's just that when we've been out, esp. this Saturday I did get marginally pissed, to the point of losing balance slightly — and I don't even have my boots to blame 'cos I'm still wearing bloody flats, have been for ages as foot's still not better from missing the stairs. Seb's getting fed up with it. I know exactly what he thinks of it, and I keep saying I'll never do it again, so it's getting a bit ridiculous — plus his friends are so flipping tame, it just notices! Saturday was the last resort, Seb's told me a hundred times and went mad this time too.

I was in a real tense mood before going out, lots of things on my mind, about here, everything etc. 'Thought it might have been 'time of the month' coming, but as yet — no show. Anyway, I actually felt like having a few drinks to push away and stifle the constant thoughts and dull feeling that I had, so I suppose I didn't think about what I was drinking on purpose. Anyway a few drinks should NOT have been a big deal but I guess it was and I honestly do hate myself for it. I really do 'cos it ruins everything not just in the moment but for days afterwards. Like now!

Monday 12 February 2001.

Seb and I had a good weekend. We got little business cards done so I can spread around. Had a real laugh doing it with Seb in the station (the card that is!), we were on a time limit and kept making mistakes, so was hysterical! We do have such nice times and it breaks my heart that it gets screwed up so easily by me making the same stupid mistakes!

So… I have tried to confront this and I think it's mainly 'cos I'm blocking so much stuff out. The fear of eating too much so I drink to fill me up and be happy (which ironically in the end I never am). I also worry that I might get bored or come across as boring or not be as spectacular as I should be or am expected to be. I don't know. There are just so many reasons, the most powerful being that of drinking to block out the thoughts of all these other things. Plus Seb has the habit of talking me up to people before I meet them which makes me even more nervous. He tells them I'm like a model or something. It's a vicious circle: I worry, so I drink, then I worry more because I've been drinking and so I drink more to blot that out. Or something like that. Let's face it, it all boils down to the fact that I'm just not happy with myself unless I'm completely super trim, thin, slim, skinny. All of the above.

I'm tearing myself apart inside. But I think the reason this whole problem is not getting cleared up, is that after the event, I'm definitely convinced it must stop, in between events, I'm definitely convinced it must stop, BUT just before events, of going out etc., I'm not all that convinced that I want to not drink and be all good and normal. And unless you're 100 per cent sure, you'll never make changes. It's like you're never going to win a race unless you're seriously determined to. Huge part of the problem is you have to know what it is you want. It's been so long since I've socialised without drinking, I don't know what 'it' is... so how can I bring myself to want it?

The mind that perceives the limitation is the limitation.
(Buddha)

Our life is what our thoughts make it
(Marcus Aurelius)

Saturday 3 March 2001 (in relation to sad picture I drew).
I'm trapped in my stupid, vicious head and tied up in frustrated knots. Always crying... always. Can't stop. Barred from good, niceness and beauty. Am beaten and giving into my weak and bad side and so badly suffering — need to find strength! I keep drawing these horrible little pictures (good ones) of little girls with huge tears — what is wrong with me?!

Have to stop taking the pill. Is definitely not helping.

See every difficulty as a challenge, a stepping-stone, and never be defeated by anything or anyone.
(Eileen Caddy – The Dawn of Change)

**Life takes on real meaning when you set values for
yourself, regard yourself as worthwhile and elevate
your thoughts to things that are of God – good.
There is a Higher Power, turn to it and use it,
it is yours for the asking.**
(Brian Adams – How to Succeed)

One of the things that was really bothering me was the notion of home. Where was home now? Was this really home, not Stanmore or London or England? How does that happen just by moving? If this was home why didn't it feel like home? Obviously I was missing the family, parents, my brother, Grandma and that was what home was all about. I tried to think how I'd feel if I went to that 'home' now. I would miss love surely, and this life I had now. Happily this was a time when people came to stay which was fortuitous as cracks were really starting to appear in our relationship, deep ones. I'd been pretty hard on myself in retrospect, but then aren't a lot of females? I was finally able to see that it wasn't all me: he was part of this too and he had faults. I could not be everything he wanted and in any case it would be unsustainable. But the problem is that he flatly refused to take any responsibility for our predicament and he didn't seem to enjoy our freedom in the apartment. When I came home from work he was always having dinner with his parents and so we reached an impasse and it was hard to see it getting better.

CHAPTER 15
The Light Goes down

Email from Sam
Monday 1 June 2001.

Dearest Duckie,

Sorry I didn't respond. I was on a desert island with the Kent creature... but I am back and here to tell you that I love you.

You are confused about Sebastiano and where you are living? And his lack of flexibility? Is that right? Is there anything else I should know? Is the relationship all right apart from this? Has it changed?

If you miss home, return for a while, you are not bound. True love will find its course despite the nastiest obstacles. So when you lack belief, please just believe in balance and right and wrong.

Something out there will ensure you get what you need whether you even know what is right now. It's not always what you want. I am thinking about you always and send you loving thoughts.

I have been confused recently and feeling isolated and alone in my feelings and this strange relationship. I plucked for the open communication option and it's working out. I don't understand it in every moment, but it's lovely. During my darker moments of last week, I called to you and you answered me clearly in your

voice. If you feel alone or isolated or even confused, call to me...
and sit back and listen.

So, enjoy the summer, Duckie. The world is there for your
taking. Follow your heart and dreams and don't compromise
them.

I love you, I love you, I love you. Did I mention that I love you?
Chicken xxx

When Sebastiano finally spoke about us it was to tell me that
'something wasn't right'. Though it was stating the obvious, my
immediate reaction was wounded pride, and I blurted out, "Well
I'll go home right away then." I then asked him to elaborate,
however as usual when you ask men to express themselves you
wish you hadn't because the answer just creates more questions.
In this case what I got from him was, "I'm not satisfied but I don't
think it's to do with you, Natalie."

"Seb, that doesn't make sense. It has to be me because you
wouldn't be acting like this if it wasn't. What else are you
unsatisfied with? And you spend so much time away from me, with
your parents, it must have a fair bit to do with me."

It didn't get any clearer. He didn't agree that it was me but
kept saying it was the 'relationship', oblivious to the fact that the
relationship was with me so it must be me at least in part. But that
was it. I couldn't get any more out of him and I desperately wanted
answers so we could get on with things. It didn't help when he
suggested that perhaps he'd always feel unsatisfied in some way. A
great cop-out answer. My friends blamed it on Sebastiano but I
was sure it was my fault. The surprise trip I'd planned, going home

to celebrate Mum's birthday should have been a happy time but I was utterly tormented. I felt tremendous guilt for every drop I drank. Knowing that my drinking was the thing that had sparked off this gap between us, I simply couldn't enjoy myself.

Sunday 24 June 2001.

I hope these diaries aren't getting too boring; however, I fear they are. The topic of discussion and thought has become increasingly repetitive so hope am not going on too much but clearly this thing is going to continue and will be the big issue until it's sorted out.

Just before I carry on with what I was going to say, I'll just interrupt for a minute to say that Mum is currently, right now, in the garage washing all Grandma's sweat-ridden sheets, totally soaking and cleaning some of her other things that are covered in poo! Poor Grandma is going through so much. She manages to keep a smile on her face most of the time, and when she is cheerful, it's great and means that at least for a minute or so, she's forgotten or is not thinking about what she's going through. This is all so important though, to look at life in the right perspective. She should be a lesson to all of us. All the worries and torment, frustration, confusion, and sadness caused over such materialistic and superficial things i.e. what we look like and how we are, perfection wise etc., whilst all this is going on — when the fact is that life really is short, we should appreciate it so much more than we do, without wasting away so much of it in pointless worry, striving for so much that wastes such a lot of precious time, then before we know it, we reach the point where we're older, less able and in some cases unfortunately uncomfortable too, and so much of the one and only life we have here, would have been traumatically wasted and lost in ultimately pointless worry and undue concern.

That weekend passed all too quickly, despite me willing it to slow down. I wanted my return to be to the light-hearted Italy, the one I was so eager to move to, the warm, embracing, playful Italy of long nights spent talking, drinking, eating and choosing where to have the next 'spritz'. The Italy I had grown to love so much. There's rarely anything better than summer in Italy but the way I was feeling, you would have thought I was returning to a Siberian winter, I just felt so heavy-hearted. And it was justified. Sebastiano was there but that was all he was. Just there. But while we were not strangers, we were not functioning as a couple and I certainly wasn't functioning as me, not the real me. I desperately needed his love, care, affection and more than anything, attention whereas he didn't need any of it from me. He already had everything; his family, friends, culture, home and the familiarity and security that went with all of that. Our differences were becoming increasingly visible and though I did my best to talk myself out of feeling so crap, I felt well, like you would feel if you thought your relationship and indeed, your life was going down the pan. I decided to try and get really excited about work and discovered a place called The Little English Nursery where I interviewed, did some trial days and emerged with the prospect of a proper *in regola* job. OK. So I'd have a little less freedom but a lot more security – perhaps this would in turn aid our relationship and help add to the stability and identity I was craving. There had been times in my life, many times, when I felt on shaky ground but this was by far one of the worst.

It wasn't all bad. The summer was, like all summers in Italy, pretty much cloudless, filled with languid days where, even if you were working, you were somehow not feeling the resentment that you felt when you worked in the sticky, drizzly London summers. Life was gloriously celebrated on the streets, in alfresco cafes, parks and by people sitting outside their houses, watching their barefooted children play as they put the world to rights long into the night. Seb's family had a beach house on the Venetian Riviera, not far from Jesolo, a location that was not just idyllic but undeniably romantic as well. In a place like this you shouldn't have to make an effort to enjoy yourself. I mean here I was with the person I supposedly loved in a gorgeous apartment by the sea. Theoretically it can't get too much better than that. But I was struggling to be me and couldn't quite remove the thought that it was always me enjoying his things in life, never him enjoying mine. And then it struck me: What if there was no ours, no us?

Friday 3 August 2001 (7.27 a.m.).

It's hard to be perfect! Tiring… not 'perfect' 'perfect' obviously, but my own achievable perfect, i.e. to make and try to maintain myself in the most perfect state I can be. It is possible, as we all well now know, as Geri Halliwell has miraculously and encouragingly shown the world. It can clearly be done, as not only her but many others have shown too. It is however a full-time job, hence why it's so tiring, time-consuming and stressful, constantly striving towards this material achievement. I guess if you're going to have this as your goal in life, you might as well do it without complaining or just don't do it at all, i.e. if I'm going to think like this and give so much importance to perfecting myself, then I must do it without constantly moaning or dwelling on the issue.

The other thing that I'm not so sure about and causes me a terrible amount of stress is about responsibilities and God. I'm just not sure whether God expects us to take full responsibility for ourselves and our actions / behaviour or whether He expects us to just pray and leave it all to Him. Well, this is what's confusing me horrific amounts. I find myself constantly praying obsessively, practically all day and night in the fear that if I don't keep asking, praying for what I want, I won't get it and everything will go horribly wrong. This is an incredible stress. I'm not even sure if it's the way things should be. In fact, I very much doubt it, but for fear of things going wrong, I haven't yet found the courage to try otherwise, to just let go. Should I be doing this? (Probably not as it leads to and combines lots of other ridiculous obsessive behaviour.) Or am I'm expected to believe in myself more, have more faith, trust in myself, and take full responsibility for my actions and behaviour?

I wouldn't like to try and overly control a situation, which is largely out of my hands, but I actually do think that this is the way things were intended — for us to take full responsibility for ourselves and our achievements. So I actually believe I should be taking full responsibility for myself, my actions and generally find the belief in myself (sent by God) to do it, to enable me to manage and pursue my life with my own hands in my own way... with of course the watchful, protective eye of God.

The happiest life is one without thought!
(Sophocles)
... If only!

Saturday 4 August 2001 (ten days to my birthday).
... Again on the balcony, whilst Sebastiano sleeps, watching the beach life slowly wake up and the sea welcome a new day. Well, getting to the point, Sebastiano has been very different since we've been here — very pensive and extremely distant, not affectionate. It's always me giving the kisses, cuddling, doing the touching, caring, and showing interest in

*general. Anyway, it's been very obvious that something's not right, that 'I'
am not actually much a part of his being here. He's really, barely
responsive, enthusiastic, or lively, like he just wants to be on his own. Well,
I know he's reading a spiritual, thought-provoking book about the
American Indians, the Redskins and their way of life, but that's usually a
kind of thought provoking that can be shared. Thoughts and pensiveness
that you can and want to share with your partner, your nearest and dearest
(if that's what I am, which I am now beginning to seriously doubt –
unfortunately).*

*... Got a bit tipsy yesterday, last night! We actually went out for
dinner again (wow) it was Friday, so I managed to wangle it, but for the
lack of company, like being out spending the evening with a person who is
actually absent to the situation.... to compensate, thus mildly entertain
myself, went ahead and got a bit tipsy. I'm sure that this wouldn't have
been appreciated. In fact more than likely it was despised, but all in all,
in the grand scheme of things, it wasn't all that bad and considering the
circumstances, inevitable in the hope of having a not so dull evening.*

*Anyway, going out in the beginning last night, I had to ask what on
earth was going on, in the nicest possible way, as it seems pretty stupid
being away together and doing things together if one person doesn't want
to be. Anyway, he was very reluctant to explain what was going on inside
his head as he said it wasn't all that clear and therefore would rather wait
until it was clarified, before explaining and possibly being misinterpreted.
Well, I said it's fine not to say, if you can detach yourself from the thoughts
for the time being, but as this didn't seem possible, he might as well tell
me, as he just wasn't present in the evening otherwise.*

*So, to sum it all up in a few words, he seems to be happy with our
relationship (who knows after last night though – but I mean seriously one
night shouldn't change anything), as I was saying, he says he's happy with*

*our relationship, what we have between us, but confused as he feels that
something is missing. Well, it goes on... that's it basically in a nutshell.
He feels that something is missing (obviously I've also been a bit detached
slightly here, 'cos when one person is, the other is naturally). Basically if
he really feels something is missing, it seems pretty pointless in me
struggling, doing all that I can to try and find out about work, Italy, life
here, etc., and stressing myself over the hundreds of choices, thoughts, and
decisions, when he may not even be sure of 'us', or sure he wants to be with
me! Sigh. At this point, I really frankly think it's probably best to just go
home and stop all these stresses. We'll see...*

Sunday 5 August 2001.
*There's something really beautiful about the silence and freshness of
the early morning at the seaside. It's strangely colder than the usual
mornings, but no earlier than my usual early wake (7.20 a.m.). Quite a
relief actually as the heat has been unbearable a lot of the time. (Never
thought I'd hear myself say that.)*
*The sea's not quite as calm as usual, so maybe today there'll be some
welcome breeze...*
*What a day yesterday...! Well, we got to the bottom of the
problem/situation of Sebastiano's distance and problematic thoughts. He
basically wasn't sure, or should I say isn't sure, that he loved me/loves me
any more. It was all talking about how he felt in the past, but that things
had changed, during the period of living together, it had all dulled and he
wasn't sure that he was in love with me any more. He repeatedly added
that he hadn't wanted to have the discussion, as he wasn't exactly clear
how he felt. It seems that I'd actually made him realise all this on our
countless conversations in the past, where I've brought up the fact that he
doesn't say 'I love you' often at all, rarely rings when I'm not around, how*

when I'm away, he just gets on with his life normally and how he wouldn't come and live in England. Well, it seems that I have woken him up to all this, which also said to me that he didn't love me enough.

So, you can imagine, I was heartbroken, torn, and extremely confused. We talked and talked and talked it over. I explained everything I felt, thought, and vice versa. I broke down every now and again from the shock 'cos I thought the problems were others between us. I thought they were, like where to live, here or in England — not whether we were to stay together or not! Oh well, maybe I was dreaming.

(7.45 am — breeze has gone — another scorching day ahead.)

So, as I said, maybe I was dreaming and have been all this time. I think it's the drinking personally, 'cos even if it's not to the point of being drunk, it's still a separation between two people. He says it isn't that; he says it's nothing specific. He says it's the routine that we've been consumed up in that he doesn't find fulfilling or satisfying, maybe that he doesn't have time to himself, that he's too young, not ready for it and as a result is questioning whether he really loves me. He's worried that if he's feeling this only after a year and his feelings are already subsiding, it's negative and fears it will probably repeat itself. So that's what's going on in his confused head. I said clearly things do change slightly, that's life, but in the end, it's up to him.

So, sadly, but curiously too, I was all set to return to London for good, the loss of Sebastiano, being the only real and very major one!

We'll see now…

We went for a little drink on the beach terrace bar, and he's decided he really wants to give it another go! Hmmm, I just don't know what to think or feel right now! Anyway, I'm not too sure at all of what to do. I kind of think just staying at home would be the right answer. But then I probably really will lose him. I guess that probably means he was never really mine in the first place!

How strange things can be at times. Just changing so quickly and unexpectedly. I thought we'd be together forever, the two of us. I really did.

If you love somebody, let them go, for if they return, they were always yours. If they don't they never were.
(Kahil Gibran)

The day I was due to return to Italy, 28 August, he called me and said it was all over.

"What do you want?" I asked him. "Do you want me to change?"

"I don't know what I want, Natalie, but I can't do this any more with you. I can't give you the love of your mum, dad, brother, cat."

How very sarcastic. We do not have a cat. Cocky. And that's pretty much how it went for the next month. Non-discussions about us, during which I was none the wiser to what he wanted, and right then, when I wanted answers, there were none. There might never be any. It's too easy to say a relationship broke down because of this or that without considering that maybe it was going to anyway and that's how life is meant to be. But it doesn't stop you thinking, 'Oh maybe I could have done this better, perhaps I shouldn't have said that.' You can drive yourself crazy going over old ground and as I kept reminding myself, the past was dead and buried and thinking about it wasn't going to rewrite it. Being brave

211

and grown up and everything is a nice idea though but when your heart is torn into little pieces, it just doesn't work. So I was struggling, big time. I no longer had the choice of having him and it was probably all my fault. What else could it be? Maybe there was no romance any more? Where is the romance, where people love each other for the way they are? I thought about this a lot. We can be so many different types of people and people think that to fall in love we have to be anyone but ourselves. I think the real challenge is to be yourself in a world that is trying to make you like everyone else. But it's getting harder now for people with social media showing them what everyone else is, or pretending to be, nobody is immune from thinking there must be a better version of themselves and if there isn't they have to create one.

Wednesday 5 September 2001.

So I know all the good things S has done, even if very few! Will now write all the bad things to try and see him in a more realistic light:

- *Never came here in first year, except in summer when convenient and a gift from parents*
- *Never looked for flats, Renata and Cesco did it*
- *Never came for NY, said to people, 'was too much of a drag for just two days'*
- *Never brought me little token thoughts*
- *Hardly ever took me out for dinner unless I asked*
- *Not generous — actually downright tight*
- *Never helped me find any work (others did)*
- *Always went home to his mum and dad after work, never tried to create life with me*
- *Rarely said I love you*

- *Rarely paid me compliments*
- *Fussed about coming home with me at Easter and made a very rude comment when here about boredom (frankly he'd have been doing nothing better there at all... except perhaps watching cycling)*
- *Disappeared to sign for a flat for two hours without telling me where he was*
- *Party in field, again gone for hours*

  ... Maybe I was too demanding in these things and that's prob. why he felt suffocated, lost his freedom, but I was alone and he didn't recognise my needs or think of me
- *Always did what he wanted*
- *Took the piss out of a pair of my undies*
- *Said my bum looked like a man's in black linen trousers and in Levis*
- *Said I couldn't go out in white linen dress as it looked like a nightie / underwear*
- *Looked at me like I was a complete pratt, totally pissed off in the beach with the mosquito*
- *Did exact same thing in flat with the moth / butterfly behind bed*
- *Never showed willingness to come to England or even phone when I was here*
- *Never any interest to know my family or life here*
- *Not cuddly or affectionate much in bed, after few months didn't sleep holding me or anything*
- *Totally unaffectionate with me again whilst out shopping for apartment*

  ... Could be 'cos there was also hostility on my part but that's 'cos was so annoyed he wasn't sharing any of my life in England

213

-   *Generally not affectionate, always me initiating kisses and hugs towards end*

    ... Could have been 'cos of few tipsy nights he lost enthusiasm and/or that I was there only for him really, no challenge, no fun, no freedom so he got bored?

Anyway he should have

a)   *Recognised that I was alone and needed a little more support*
b)   *Tried to understand my needs*
c)   *Tried to understand ME before judging me*

During break up and other general faults
-   *Never phoned or offered to help with moving stuff*
-   *Never asked what I thought*
-   *Dictated everything — too selfish*
-   *Not open-minded or worldly at all*
-   *Never sacrificed himself at all*
-   *Wanted what he wanted, and if it's not quite right — forget it!*

My problems (though his could go on and on!)
-   *Drinking too much sometimes*
-   *Eating a bit particularly*
-   *Demanding of his time*

Perhaps I had to face the fact that we didn't connect on a pragmatic level and that sometimes, even a deep spiritual and emotional connection isn't enough. And maybe I was kidding myself we even had that for, when all was said and done, we were actually like chalk and cheese. Everyone spouts all this stuff about opposites attracting but they still have to have something in common and we just didn't have enough of the stuff that keeps people on the same wavelength. Maybe we'd just rushed in blindly?

"You know, Nats, Italy is not like London," said my cousin Renata. "You see us all having fun but living here is not like that. We don't go out every night and go for the maximum madness like you do. We take it quietly."

I knew this. Of course I did. But I'd been rebelling against it constantly, this image of the sober, complicit girlfriend. The cheeky side of me wanted to turn things upside down, provoke and take the edge off. But why? Maybe I did it because I wasn't comfortable here and could that mean it wasn't right in the first place? I'm not sure I did it because it was always fun. And so I spent the best part of a month packing everything up and wondering how my dream life in Italy had become such a complete disaster.

CHAPTER 16
What Next?

Back in England I contemplated the ruins of my relationship and my life. Of course it wasn't that bad, though it seemed like the end of the world. I didn't work, I didn't go out, I didn't really do anything except rake over the remnants of my life. I needed answers to move on and so I spent my days and nights consulting family and close friends, Grandma, Sam, Valeria, Christopher and anyone that would listen basically. I became the relationship bore and hated myself for it. 'Listen to yourself, Natalie,' I'd think. 'You are such a drag, one of those victim women that you dislike so much. Get a grip girl. Get a life.' That was one side of my head. The louder voice was the broken-hearted one the girl who felt sorry for herself and was wallowing in it desperately. The odd email found its way between Seb and me but there was no sign of a thawing in the situation. His feet were stuck firmly in the sand and his head under it. He showed no sign of remorse or of budging. He wasn't nasty, he wasn't anything and perhaps that's what made it worse. There was no passion in the break-up. It hurt and was incredibly frustrating. Clearly the guy thought nothing would change or he just thought I wasn't worth the trouble. Both versions were equally troubling because they meant I was useless and worthless. His close friend, Diego, was in touch with me and updated me regularly, Seb was normal, calm, happy, getting on with things. I didn't want to hear that did I? Would you? I wanted to hear that he was moping, paralysed by the break-up as much as I was. Evidently this was not the case.

Monday 15 October 2001.
Who knows if he wasn't keeping himself so ridiculously busy, whether he might actually have time to miss me?

Wednesday 17 October 2001.
Have re-read diary of when we were together. It's clearly my drinking that has caused him to fall out of love with me.

Just been to Grandma's — usual two o'clock coffee and chat. She looked lovely there with her hair all done, lipstick on, nice shirt, etc. She always makes me feel a bit better, just sitting there and chatting. Am supposed to be cleaning the house today as the cleaner's done her neck in! Have done absolutely everything possible (which is nothing) to avoid yet lifting a finger. Suppose I ought to do it now. Mum's expecting it to be done and I'm not doing anything else anyway. Have interview for course tomorrow, hope all goes well, then at least that's something to do for a month. Not financially beneficial at all, but at least it will keep me busy and give me a qualification too (as long as I get on it that is).

Still hoping for a phone call, but reading back and thinking back, I rarely got them at the best of times, so it's highly unlikely that I will now!

Letter from Renata.
(*Translated*)
I know it's very difficult for you right now, but I hope that the man of your life is not him. You deserve someone who knows how to love you so much more. Really love. His is not love; you deserve a person who is more humble, who knows how to ask for

help when he needs it, non-arrogant to the point that he just closes himself off within himself and never speaks as he's convinced to be right. When you find the right person, maybe then you'll understand that you would have been unhappy like this. When you are with someone, you have to feel that they are the best person in the world for you, with his strengths and weaknesses. I married Cesco because I loved his weaknesses too: his being a bit of a child, his annoyingness, his attempt to be a superhero when he'll never become one. Another girl may hate these things because she wants a real 'Man'. I wouldn't want him any different to how he is, even though sometimes we disagree or argue.

If S had to change to work for you, it means that it's not right; it's true that you made some mistakes, but so did he. Were you happy with his faults? How he treated you, loved you, were you happy with that? Didn't you feel that you needed something different?

Don't shut your mind off with all the good memories forgetting the bad ones because that's not reality. For you to be happy, you need more than someone who just comes close. You need someone who is a bit different, better for you. More passionate, crazier, who makes you feel really loved, who brings you a flower every now and again, or a chocolate, who thinks of you other than just himself.

How should a person be to make you happy? I heard you cry so many times whilst you were here, and if you made some mistakes, it was also because you didn't have someone by your side that knew how to understand or help you. He didn't even have the strength to help you understand your mistakes until the end when you were trying to do it yourself.

Is it wrong what I'm thinking?
Renata.

I was having the 'teeth' dream a lot around this time. If you don't know it, it's the one where all your teeth fall out dramatically and it's supposed to signify change. Every time this dream turned up – and that includes when it does so now – my life changed, in one way or another. The last previous occasion I'd had it, I was moving back home to England. So having it pop up again raised a faint hope in me that maybe I'd be moving back to Italy. In practice that seemed unlikely and the next day's news from Renata that they'd all had dinner together and he didn't mention me at all, sliced my hope off at the root. It was dead and buried.

Monday 22 October 2001.
10.00 p.m.
'Girl Interrupted.'
The most fantastic film. So moving! It touched my heart and made me cry so much through it. And when I wasn't on the outside, I was on the inside as it represented so much of myself. I saw myself so clearly in it, all the confusion, frustration and madness that I feel so often inside.

All the pain! I have been doing this and going through it for years. Even when on the outside, and in the open, all may seem so normal and something else, a lot of the time if not most, on the inside I'm going through something quite different, and when I'm not, it's usually, if not always because I've blotted it out with something artificial, i.e. drinking. I thought so often during the film of things that I would like to say to Sebastiano, but I don't feel that now is the right time as am still trying to figure out so much for myself and am way too caught up in the moment. I

219

will write it down here though so it's at least off my chest, if I manage to make any sense of it.

I wanted to say that I don't blame him entirely for this whole situation — though I would have clearly liked another chance. Although I don't know if I'm convinced that continuing with me doing my very best to do things right on the spot the whole time would have actually worked for me, especially not in the long run even if it did a little in the short... I think I needed time out, this time out to try and put things right; it was time out alone that I needed. I am a complex person and not really just what I seem on the outside. I know he tried to understand me, at least in the beginning, but maybe he/you just didn't try hard enough or couldn't as I couldn't really understand myself. Very few, if any people really do understand me, and this is because I haven't really understood myself. I kind of hide away from lots of things and try to create my own little world, actually with a large sense of unreality and oblivion, to escape from what I'm not sure of or what I don't understand/like/or feel comfortable with. I thought I would be able to work it out with you, that you would be able to understand and to help me, but, on the other hand, how could you, if I couldn't really understand myself or therefore be able to explain it to you? I thought you were stronger, or maybe I was expecting miracles. Whatever, it didn't happen. I feel that I need someone stronger for me, someone that can help, guide and stand by me; but then maybe I need to try and figure out, help, guide, and stand by myself first. This is why I think I need this time. I need to sort my head out. Although nothing's 100 per cent clear, I obviously know more about what I'm saying than you do, which is also probably why the whole thing ended. I tried to explain to you a couple of times, but never in very much detail. I don't know if it's that you couldn't understand, didn't or just didn't want to. I think as time went on, you more and more just didn't want to.

And in fact writing all this, the more I write, the more I feel that I shall probably never give this to you at all — on the one hand it's a shame as you will never really get why things changed, but on the other you would also most definitely cancel out any vague, possible future hope (if there was any) 'cos you'd think I was just a complete nutcase, which obviously means that you were/are not the one for me. I am however just trying to be honest to myself. I am not perfect as we all know, as clearly nobody is, but neither am I much of what I often seem on the surface. It's much more/I'm much more complex than that. I'm sorry that you couldn't see or understand it or stand by me, but maybe the timing just wasn't right, or it just wasn't right at all, who knows?

PS: Had that tooth dream again. But it was less severe this time.

PPS: Some spiritual help.

God does not offer temporary relief;
He offers a permanent solution.
(Isa. 54: 10 Hag. 2: 4–5)

Fear can be easily abolished by not looking always to
the bigger picture, but just little pieces at a time.
By taking one step at a time, one day at a time,
everything becomes so much easier.
God gives us enough light to see the next step,
and that's all we need.
(Ps. 27: 1 Ps. 23: 2)

Don't Worry
You cannot control the past, but you can ruin a perfectly good present by worrying about the future.
(Phil. 4: 6–7)

Take One Day At a Time.

Even with such good friends to lean on, I felt like I was still the relationship bore. I didn't want to be her: I wanted to be Natalie, the funny and cool girl who didn't let things get to her. But she was gone and who knows, she might have been gone forever. Each relationship we have changes us in some way and some have the power to change us forever, so maybe this was my big moment. But honestly, where was I going from here? Sam's belief in destiny was always helpful and even though she was in Australia, travelling, at the time, she found time to call me and give me her brand of tough, but unconditional love.

"Duckie, I am so hurting for you right now."

"I know but it's all my own fault, Sam."

"No it's not, Nats, that's crap, you need to look at the bigger picture."

"Ah yes fate again, what's meant to be…"

"Of course fate. What else is there?"

"Maybe I've ruined my destiny by getting pissed so much? Maybe I've drunk my destiny?"

"I don't think so. Destiny is much stronger than any liquid, Duckie."

Other friends weighed in with their contributions, agreeing almost unanimously that if he really loved me and believed in us, then the drink would not have made a difference. That made me feel better for about a second, until I realised that it meant he obviously just didn't love me! I felt like I was going crazy. Day after day I was dragging all this pain, confusion and frustration around with me, opening it up for whoever would give me some new piece of advice, wishing for them to tell me what I wanted to hear: That it would be OK, that Seb and I would get back together and this was just a temporary blip. Somehow I managed to give myself a swift kick and yield to the suggestion of a CELTA course, one that would give me the official credentials to teach English to foreign students. It was a six-week intensive affair and Grandma had kindly offered to pay. I applied and was accepted but quickly found I was totally unprepared for the amount of work involved. It was utterly intense. The other people on it, albeit a nice mix, were really gung-ho and I felt like a pale imitation of a student by comparison, which I suppose I was. I wasn't in the right state of mind to take on such a thing; I could have been knocked down by a feather. I was a total wreck but I tried and pulled out as much determination as I could find. It wasn't just the amount of work though; I also really struggled with the entire concept of the teaching methodology. Plus it really annoyed me that I (well Grandma) was paying so much for the course, it should be a guaranteed pass, which it wasn't. I wasn't ready for that. I struggled and in the middle of the pain and the tears, I managed to settle down a bit and found some really great acquaintances in the class. It reminded me of the camaraderie we'd all had together in Nice. (Like when you make a choice, meet others who have made the exact same, and you just kind of get on.) How long ago that seemed. Anyway, I did pass but I kind of messed up as well. Given the unexpectedly high level of my pass they said that all I had to do was one small assignment in Italian and they'd award me the equivalent certification to teach Italian to foreign students. But I was done, finished, absolutely drained and I just left it.

If we all did the things we are capable of, we would astound ourselves
(Thomas Edison)

Monday 26 November 2001.

Got email from Seb. "It's me, Ciao... come va?"

????? So long... nothing's changed. I mean he's not seen me since he made his concrete decision, so there's nothing that could have really changed, as far as I can see anyway. I will however, reply politely and remain diplomatic. (After all I am British!)

Wednesday 28 November 2001.

OK so two days later and I've written back to him.

Hello — qui va tutto bene, Ho finito il corso per insegnare. E' stato dificilissimo ma molto interessante. Ho conosciuto tanta bella gente (sul mio piano mentale). E' stata una bella esperienza. Il sole splende qui... quindi. Tutto positivo. Te come va?

(Translation: Hello, all good here, I've finished the teaching course. It was super hard but very interesting. I met a bunch of great people (on my wavelength). It was all a great experience. The sun's shining here, so... everything's positive. How are you?)

I checked my email constantly for a reply from him. When it eventually came it was a flimsy, nothing sort of reply. He chatted loads, as if you know, we were best buddies or something. Why do men do that? If he made the big effort to make contact after a long gap, why do the pen friend thing? I mean say something… 'something'. Once again, I took my begging bowl out for opinions and the general consensus was there was nothing, absolutely not a bean for me to get excited about. And so I replied in a similar fashion. He did it again. And then it stopped, confirming everything I'd thought about online communication (which was pretty new at the time) and now feel even more strongly about: it just makes things worse and rarely takes you forwards – until it's taken offline. After much insistence and persistence from past clients and colleagues I'd arranged to go and do the Gold Fair in early January, to translate and interpret for a couple of companies I'd worked for previously and I was looking forward to it. Something constructive, paid and of course in Italy – ironically being closer to the problem felt like it could help. Mum, Dad and Grandma were vocally against it, predictably, and thought it a bad move to even set foot in Italy. I knew they were worried about me being hurt but I thought they were being unnecessary since if you looked at it logically I was making a forward step and not shrinking back into myself which could only be a good thing. I was missing my life over there terribly, just as much as I was missing Seb, that much I knew. The idea of going back, to be a full-time English teacher was one I was tossing around in my head. That led me to thinking about how I'd had it all, not so very long ago. A boyfriend, a job in Italy, the country I love, a beautiful place to live, weather, food everything. And I'd fucked up. I'd well and truly fucked up.

Monday 10 December 2001.

Medium I saw with Donna said that he saw me here, not abroad, but guess I can't take everything he said as gospel – shall have to see.

Lots of talk amongst friends / family of getting my diaries published one day, since the topic was brought up. Don't know if it would work, or would be a good idea. Would certainly be brave though. Totally exposing – well, will look into it though, just for curiosity, if nothing else. Would be like running out through the world and everyone I know completely naked.

Will be curious to see if he writes on Monday. Tarot cards on internet indicate this! Also said to forget hoping for an old love on Tuesday. So either he'll write Monday, but Tuesday I should assure myself that there's nothing in it.

I wonder if there is anyone else out there for me. I guess I'll never really know, until I completely put S out of my head! Which is proving to be a struggle, to say the least.

Ask for spiritual guidance then follow up on hunches, leads, or inner promptings...

Guess the Tarot card thing was right actually: there was a sign from Seb this morning, but not a message. He just forwarded me an email from Elena (from work) with no msg – arsehole. Anyway her message was dated a week ago, so I wrote back, 'It took you a week to send me that?' Just to prompt a response. Anyway he wrote back explaining, and we conversed a bit. Said he felt like he was in limbo, 'in pausa' in life. Didn't seem too happy. I wrote back saying he should take the time to reflect upon himself and read as the pace of life will soon pick up again and he'll have no more

time. He wrote back agreeing, saying that we had the same conscience.
Tarot also said, however, firmly not to read anything into the contact.

He signed off 'Ciao Nat' as in 'bye — don't write back'. Must start
believing more in what will be will be.

No matter what it may look like, there is still an avenue
for fulfilment. The Buddha became enlightened only
after he had done all that he could do and given up.
(Siddhărtha Gautama)

Tuesday 11 December 2001.

Yia yia died. (So that's two grandfathers gone and now a
grandmother.)

I love Yia Yia, she is, was, always has been and always will be a pure
soul! May she rest in peace forever. Amen.

Why do they all go at Christmas?

My usual delight in the lead-up to Christmas was absent. I just
wasn't interested at all. There's simply no worse time of year to
be heart-broken than the festivities, when by default you're meant
to be happy. After receiving those cryptic and useless emails from
Seb I'd developed an obsession with getting back together with
him, which as you can imagine was more than a little unhealthy. I
kept telling myself it was not going to happen, though part of me
kept hoping. Then something struck me, something that made me
cry fresh tears. I thought back to when Greg and I were rocky in
our relationship, how I contemplated ending it silently for so long
and how sometimes we'd argue about partying and that prompted
me to let go. The minute I did, he just wanted to get back together

straight away and wouldn't accept that I was going or finishing it for real. But he still wanted me. This time the shoe was on the other foot: Seb was doing to me exactly what I'd done to Greg. What goes around comes around.

Friday 14 December 2001.

Hmmm — have definitely put on a few pounds too many. Have been seriously overindulging lately, and it's not even Christmas yet. Not good. Must get back to how I was when I was 'super upset' about Sebastiano, not that I'm not still 'super upset' now, but when it first happened, I lost weight, a lot, and how I was, looked and felt then was great, much better figure wise. Shall just have to be focused and get on with it. Time before Italy getting shorter (excellent — can't wait) need to get in A1 form asap!

Still hope Seb comes to see me. He's never shown enough interest in the past I guess, but let's hope that things change a bit. Can only hope, then wait and see.

Funny things happen in life.

I really do believe all that I learnt from 'The Celestine Prophecy'. Fantastic book! And of all the rich and touching things that I learnt, the one thing that sticks in my mind is:

'Nothing happens by coincidence.'

It's crazy. I really believe that it doesn't. Nothing happens by coincidence... situations etc. and we never meet people just by chance. This is what is so strange. I learnt something today that I am in control, that I must be in control of what I want/relationships etc., that I don't have to accept things if I don't want to etc.

I went to a sort of interview (language in business/Emily Roberts). I met a lovely woman (Emily), who explained to me about teaching, their process, etc., probably to take off in the New Year! She was the one who said about being in control of what you want, i.e. that you don't have to accept things from people if you don't want to. Well, how strange! She had decided when she was twenty-two that she wanted to do something different. She went to Italy and ended up staying there for fourteen years; she had various relationships, and then at one point, she just suddenly decided/felt/realised that she had to come back to England. So after fourteen years of being in Italy, she came back here, and within a year met and married her husband, soon after, had twins and has now been happily married for nine years. How weird! She says she's still different, that when she goes to collect the girls from school, in the playground with the other mothers, she still feels different. Now the worst thing is that I strongly feel and believe that I would feel different (that different thing), here, but not in Italy. Strange as it may be, I don't think I'd feel different over there, well, a bit yes of course, obviously, but a positive different. I think that's what I feel, that there it would be a positive type of difference and here a negative different!

I felt I'd bored a lot of people with my relationship drama and was fast running out of sympathetic ears. In fact, I'd even managed to sabotage what should have been a perfectly easy night out by crying floods of hysterical tears in Pizza Express in West Hampstead. Not only that but the cry-athon stretched to include Donna and Veronica, who had come into the loos to find me and both ended up sobbing too; the three of us were sat on the floor, balling our eyes out. By now I'd cried over most of North London and I was decidedly fed up with myself and my tears and what felt like my neediness. But that didn't stop me from clinging on to hope like a dying man. I'd told myself that I had a life before I met him, so why couldn't I have one now. It didn't make sense that the period of time I'd spent with him should dictate everything but then this stuff never really does make sense. You can't rationalise when your emotions are running wild and actually trying to do it, just seems to make things a whole lot worse. I decided to make new plans and this time I would keep them. In this I was aided by a new journal. A 'Bridget Jones Diary' (who I happened to love and could easily relate to), one that you could actually write in that someone had given me for Christmas. It was great, just a gimmick really, your basic page-a-day diary that began with a note from Bridget, her resolutions so to speak... which I simply Tipp-Ex'd out and wrote over with my own:

On Boyfriends:
-    Just want Sebastiano back
On life:
-    Want to get it sorted and be happy and content.
On couples:
-    Nice / fine as long as I am in one too!
On weight:
-    Always keep it down. Takes twice as long to lose as it does to put on!
On choices:
-    Always difficult but always listen to heart and follow gut instincts.
On Matchmaking:
-    Can work at times, almost did with Sebastiano, if we get back together, then I'm all for it.

New Year Diet Plan.

OK, so not really a diet as such, but regulation of eating regime. Need to seriously get on the case. Initial plan of action will simply be to no longer overflow cereal bowl in morning so that it's bigger than Mount Everest and not to eat huge handfuls out of the bag first too (regulate size of bowl and content).

Secondly, to not eat at all in between meals; thirdly, totally regulate alcohol intake and completely eliminate it where possible, i.e. mostly. Fourthly, try to keep more on the move than I have been lately. Fifthly, try to eat as little rubbish as possible.

NB: Cannot wait for gold fair — a week and counting...!

Miracles happen to those who believe in them
(unknown)

Sometimes when you approach things the right way, they have a way of paying you back. I'd gone to the gold fair in good spirit. I was looking forward to translating and interpreting and I was also thrilled at the thought of being surrounded by the emotional warmth and undoubted physical comforts of Aunt Rosalie's home. I had no thought of getting in touch with Seb, as much as I'd have obviously loved to see him but of course word got round and it was he who made the first move. (Always believe in miracles.) We went out and I kept a careful eye on my drinking. I wore my tight black trousers, boots and a fitted black shirt slightly unbuttoned at the top, my winter tan was just right and my hair had been straightened to perfection. The attraction between us was still palpable, as strong as ever. So we saw each other again and kept doing so night after night. And then I dropped the ball, or rather I had a bit too much to drink. I was feeling stressed and overdid it, and of course he reacted as I knew he would, with disappointment and disapproval. In retrospect, I think it was part of my unrealistic drive for perfection, wanting to project a new improved Natalie. I was quite prepared for it to end there but he'd been thinking he said and he wasn't ready to let it go. I was back on track and seriously had to get my act together. Hoping and praying he didn't change his mind, I began planning my return.

CHAPTER 17
Rientro in Italia

Tuesday 29 January 2002.

Well, hard day, didn't do anything but conversations, discussions, thoughts, and confusions — just generally tiring. Grandma really really irritated me, actually is constantly irritating me loads about this whole issue, that I decided to let her in on. Nightmare. If she says anything more about it, one more time, I'll go mad. Had a good conversation and talk with Dad about the whole plan / direction / ideas, which was good and more than compensated for the debilitating issue before with Grandma.

... Why is it that those closest to us manage to rile us up so much... particularly when we know they are completely right?

Email from Sam Wednesday 30 January 2002.

Duckie,

I'm sorry this will have to be short. I have only a couple of hours left in Oz and too much to do.

I was so excited to receive such a beautiful email, so clear and self-empowered. I am proud of you, Duckie. You've done really well. Stay focused, don't drink, and work on your dreams still. If you have no expectations of your relationship with Sebastiano, then not much can go wrong. Make sure that you have a strong enough individual life plan to survive regardless of any relationship knock-backs. Still, isn't it just right that none of us can direct the path of true love? Regardless of any efforts to hide from it, chase it or manipulate it, what is destined will be.

Kentdog will not be joining me in Fiji. He's sill in Zimbabwe. He's down. His life plan isn't working out for him and he's swollen with pride. He's uncommunicative. It's all good though. My life is fair; it is full of wonder, enchantment, and trail magic. I answer to nobody but myself and abide by my own rules. I am not alone, as I feel the presence of my friendships close. I am settled in the knowledge that what will be, will be. If Kent and I are to work, then beyond the laws of space and time and beyond lust, desire, or will, it will be. And if it isn't to be, then so be it. I am living every day with an open heart. If someone rocks up and changes my life, then I will love it and be open to it. Life is about unplanned collisions that transform us. I don't want to hide away for a second or retreat to bed to dream of what once was.

I love you, Duckie, I'm Fiji bound. Good luck with all.

Chicken xx

Wednesday 30 January (one week completed, no drinking).

When I let go of what I am, I become what I might be. *(Lao Tzu)*

Decisions made now. Am going back for a period of time to see what happens. Must admit that everyone in Italy (except for Rosalie and except for all the others actually) just mean: Renata, Cesco, Seb, and Zia Rita (Renata's mum) are driving me quite mad regarding this problem resolving. I've tried to say enough is enough now, but they keep on and on… it's driving me mad and hope they stop and that it all just goes away. It's the whole issue, talk of seeing someone, a psychologist or something. It's doing my head in. Maybe they're right — maybe not, but I just need some time.

Sunday 3 February 2002.

Listening to Enrique Iglesias in room — lovely! I bought it for 'Hero', but it's all great! Last night was Martin Pinto's b'day again ... I didn't go as couldn't be bothered to tube it all the way to Old Street with my verruca trouble! Anyway turns out C&V drove in the end — but hey, I had the evening that I wanted anyway. Chilled at home and watched the film I wanted to see. BBC2 (obviously can't remember the name) was really good, not particularly nice, but good. About four people 'thirty-somethings' in Camden and their lives, loves, obsessions, manias, paranoias, differences, diversities, insecurities, etc. Was really good, a real eye-opener, basically clarifying and confirming that everyone is pretty messed up inside, in their heads actually and we shouldn't be fooled or disheartened by the strong, together facades that so many people seem to be able to put up. Really was good to see, when you think that you're the only one with all this madness going on in your head, that you must belong to the weirdos group — where really you're no different from anyone else, or at least no different from the majority. Seems that everyone has their paranoias and insecurities, and the important thing is to just not get too caught up or bound up in them!

Be like a very small and joyous child, living gloriously in the ever-present now! Without a single worry or concern about even the next moment of time.
(Eileen Caddy)

It was now only ten days until I returned to Italy. I didn't want to think of it as a return as that made it sound like same old, same old and it simply couldn't be that. Meanwhile I was doing nothing, just floating, semi-aimlessly in that twilight between departure and arrival. I felt like I hadn't done anything useful for a while and knew with my dismal work record I had to get that side of life resolved when I got there. I didn't just want to have this little life in Italy with Seb; I wanted to prove I could be successful and I suppose the idea of making mega loads of money went along with that so I'd fixated on that notion. By the end of the first week in February I'd hit two weeks of not drinking, a milestone really and I was pleased with myself considering that, at the time, I was dealing with yet more emotional upheaval. Or maybe that was just my regular life. Maybe my regular life was meant to be this chaos, constantly up and down, starting and never finishing? Surely not? There was a certain element of change to it, of newness but it was, ultimately as yet really quite unsatisfying.

I've never been someone who can leave things unfinished and so in my mind, good or bad, I had to go back. Naturally, I fluctuated between excitement and apprehension, sometimes both at once. During my preparations, I'd heard very little from Seb himself. I wondered why that was and told myself that he was just waiting until I got there. But that thought also nagged at me, the fact that he didn't see the need to make an effort was an issue I'd had with him all along. I started to doubt his sincerity particularly as, during the lead up to my arrival, he was totally silent. No word from him at all.

It made me anxious, though I guess he knew I was going, so it was sort of game over – no need to make any effort. The anxiety was predominantly due to not knowing how Seb would behave and how genuine this whole desire to give it another go really was. I was dubious about his commitment. As I always thought, and was now living first-hand as direct confirmation, what goes around comes around. Perhaps this was payback for what I did to Greg? Still there's nothing like a fresh start to a relationship although you could argue that once it's been tainted with doubt, regret and at least one break-up, it can never be box fresh again. On the other hand, you could also argue that you enter this phase better equipped with knowledge about the relationship, so you're not making hazardous guesses about each other.

So while I was returning with plans to improve myself and had already completed my third week of not drinking, in anticipation, I was also coming back well aware that he had to change as well. I had to set the same high expectations on Seb as I set on myself. He had to be more attentive, definitely and not pretend to do it; he should be more worldly, open to travel, want to move, learn, investigate, and improve his mind. I couldn't cope with him thinking Brendola was the centre of the world, in fact it was his whole world and the pinnacle of adventure for him was cycling around it. He also needed to be interested in my origins and that meant London. Up till now I had never felt he was interested in who I was and in having some of that in this relationship: his angle seemed to be about squeezing me into the mould he had in his head. Armed with these thoughts in my mind I felt I had made progress.

The return was not easy, not at all. I was staying at Aunt Rosalie's and juggling interviews for various jobs, determined to wait until the best one came along but not sure if I'd know it, if it did. (Let's face it, my track record of choices so far had been pretty appalling.) Stress led to more stress, I became run down and I got a virus.

Friday 22 February 2002.

Still not well. Thought of doing sunbed to make self feel better, but think it maybe best not to go out of house. Am still doing nothing work wise, hoping for the Gambellara job just for the security of it if nothing else. Obviously hope it's nice and enjoyable too if I get it that is. In the meantime, am using the time to relax, catch up with myself, progress along my spiritual investigation, awakening, uplifting of self, and to try and get better too before signs of cold and fever develop further. Time therefore being used wisely.

- *Debating whether to have ciggie, know it's no good for throat, but will probably have it anyway and attempt to go to a pharmacist later (doubt I'll get round to it realistically).*

After applying for a bunch of jobs, I got the job in Gambellara that had been offered by a girl I knew. It was in her father's company. At the time it seemed like the best option and, unlike teaching, it was stable. I only got the job because unfortunately the girl who had it previously had been having an affair with my acquaintance's father, which as you can imagine did not please her. In order not to have to see her every day – the job included sitting at reception – she moved the girl to the back office and replaced her with me. She knew I wouldn't have an affair with her father but that's not to say he didn't try because he did, constantly. I was glad to have a job particularly as Seb wasn't exactly beating a path to my door. Or even calling me. I was living with the mother of a friend now, who gave the room for minimal rent. I had my independence and was 'looking after myself'. It was a tiny room, classically Italian, dark wooden floorboards, wooden wardrobe and desk and yellow dressed bed and curtains. It looked out onto to the condominiums' car park but it was fine. It did the job. There was a small TV, which couldn't maintain a static picture, and I bought myself a CD player on which I played the kind of music girls play to themselves when love's ambiguity is eating them up. For me it was Enrique, carrying with it some of those home securities and Jessica Simpson, who I'd recently discovered could bellow out some pretty emotional tunes too.

Seb and I were, well, I'm not sure where we were or what we were. Our Hollywood-style fantasy romantic reunion didn't eventuate; instead we met up sporadically and he seemed to be ambling through it all. But here I was: I'd made the effort to come here and my hands were tied. I had to forge ahead with this and nobody could make it work for me. I knew I had to create my own life first. I was getting increasingly impatient with not drinking, not to mention bored. It had, however, got to the point that the drink thing loomed over me so large that I was absolutely paralysed at the thought of touching a drop. Sure it was dull but worse than that, I felt threatened by it. The feeling of empowerment I'd attained from not drinking was actually minimal and all I was left with was the notion that 'If you drink, you lose it all'. And that should have told me that something was still not quite right. I

239

should have taken consolation in the fact that he was, at least, talking to my cousin Renata about us. She assured me that I was the only one he was thinking about.

But that doesn't help does it? I mean words are great and smarter girls than me have fallen for them but we all know that actions are where it's at with a guy. It seemed that Seb couldn't quite get over me as Natalie 'the party girl'. He was having problems with acceptance, the acceptance that he needed to stop tarring me with that particular brush, as it wasn't helping us move on. In a strange way it wasn't encouraging me to change. And, so, I waited.

Friday 22 continued...

Really not sure what's going on! Just don't understand why he doesn't call at all!

I wish I knew what was going on. I wish I knew if he was going to ring!

Saturday 23 February 2002.

Am in a little bed at Renata's and Cesco's in their spare room, lying here again by the little red, heart-shaped lamp, writing, where I recently wrote Seb a letter of a few thoughts and feelings (which incidentally has not seemed to have had any effect whatsoever). It's Saturday night and he didn't even ask me what I was doing! Where I was going? I rang him, I repeat — I rang him — today just to try and be casual; he was going out with his friends tonight but didn't ask about me. Last night we went out for Diego's b'day, which was all nice, had a good time although I'd say he was cool on the affection. Few good signs but just a few. Still trying to make out what his real intentions are and frankly quite doing my head in. Clearly and obviously very negative, I know he says he needs time, but this

to me seems to be getting us nowhere fast or nowhere at all for that matter.
Shall have to try to clear this up soon — will see if he calls in the week.
Perhaps I should let him know my loose time frame for this trial so he
doesn't think he has all the time in the world — that was Dad's advice, and
I guess he does tend to be right.

    Monday 25 February 2002.
    Really pleased that Seb rang this morning to hear about the job, was a
bit put out frankly over the weekend that he hadn't bothered to ring at all.
At least he rang this morning and said he'd ring again with more time —
this was good. Was really quite chuffed. He rang again tonight, so really
pleased at that, although I honestly felt the phone call to be a bit cold. We
spoke for eighteen minutes (according to mobile); was a relatively nice chat
with a couple of breakthroughs of a little giggle and real communication
(of laughs), but the rest was really all pretty surface! Not the most
effervescent of phone calls (almost a bit forced). I fear now that as the call
wasn't that fab, it won't encourage him to call more often. I wasn't super
superbly chatty, fun and silly, though I wanted to be. It was difficult as
although so much has been said, so much hasn't and there's still no
conclusion and I have no idea what he's thinking.

And so it seemed Seb and I had swapped one impasse for
another. His erratic behaviour went on for a painfully long time
and frankly it was messing with my head. We saw each other every
now and again, but an actual proper reconciliation was nowhere in
sight. I often wondered if this was a good idea and perhaps I should
have just called it quits. At this point, I had loads of people giving
me good advice in the form of, 'If he calls, he calls, if he comes
back, he comes back, but you need to stop thinking about it and

get on with your life.' Now this is probably the greatest single piece of advice in the world and it makes incredible sense but at the same time, as everyone knows, it's seriously hard to do. I would have loved nothing more than to be able to compartmentalise this and move on but the point was that I was only really back in Italy because of him, well because of us.

But there was no 'us'. So I was faced with the choice of 'giving it time': another of those great nuggets of advice that everyone gives you, or putting it back in the box and forgetting about it. I mean theoretically I should just leave it in the hands of God, surely? But I was scared to, scared that if I turned away from Seb he would slip out of my reach and then the opportunity would be lost forever. When I did see him, it wasn't bad but it wasn't good. Aside from his distance, I was not enjoying not drinking at all and I think I might have resented him for it. I kept telling myself that Gisele Bundchen didn't drink or Gwyneth Paltrow or lots of others but the fact remained: I liked to have a drink and I wasn't going to give it up forever.

Tuesday 5 March 2002.

OK, so everyone's throwing food in my face! Not literally — but you know what I mean. First, I thought the whole idea of the 'mensa' (daily lunch in the cafeteria) would be a complete nightmare; then when that didn't seem to be quite so bad after all, I came home knowing that she's (Giuliana — mum of house) not here and I eat loads (some apples and kiwis, a whole tin of beans, and a whole tin of tuna), then Guido the son, who also lives here, comes home loads later, cooks, and brings me in a huge plate of pasta to try. Well, said I'd eaten, but couldn't refuse, as it felt rude. So had to eat that as well. He did however also bring me a glass of wine, which I did refuse. I explained why I was avoiding drink (which I don't know whether was a good idea or not), just hope he doesn't relay to his mum. Wouldn't want that, just don't know how someone will interpret it and wouldn't want her to think badly or disapprovingly of me at all. But anyway — I didn't drink it! I returned it to him, said again, that I was avoiding it for a while and that he could have that little bit extra.

Sunday 17 March 2002.

Spent night out with Sebastiano — was nice, we went to Bassano, had a pizza and some laughs... progression has been made. Still feel there's something in the air though. I wonder if it's the not drinking... I notice it in the quiet moments, and it feels like they last forever. I wonder if he feels the same. Renata and Donna tell me it's not that and that there have to be some quiet moments, which he's probably not thinking about or analysing at all. Maybe they were there before too, just I was so much mellower with some drinks in me that I didn't notice.

Tarot reading

First of all said story with Seb was a finished story. Over. I kept asking similar questions, but she said it came out that there was a chance that things could get better but for now it's over. He doesn't feel love for me. He feels affection, but is not in love with me. Just fond of me. After continual related questions, it came out that there is a possibility for the future, but he wants to see me happy, relaxed, self-sufficient first, not moaning on about us, the relationship, etc. (Knew it!) He is too bogged down with the issues of the past and is blocked. She saw lots of conflict, discussion, suffocation, arguing, and tension; there is no way the relationship will move into a progressive commitment right now. He needs to see a new fresh start, not the past. She said in the past two months his feelings had died a death for me! (God forbid — but then I guess it did look that way.) She said he's still very immature and doesn't want any hassles at all. Just wants an easy life, no heavy conversations or hassles, but what was in my favour was that he was very attracted to me. I need to back off, and hopefully by the summer things could be different — but for now nothing. In about eight months I should be feeling calmer, more serene, but things will not be getting more serious 'til a lot longer than those eight months. Any future together would be a long way off but not altogether excluded. He wants to see the attitude of joy and being easy-going in me, not feel the weight of it, though for the moment he is not ready for anything serious at all. In five months something materialises on the job front for me and I'll soon be going on a journey for work.

Easter is supposed be a time for reflection and boy was I reflecting. I was reflecting so much I didn't do anything else. I spent those few days back in London with Mum and Dad (without Seb, naturally) dissecting, analysing and replaying what had happened and what could have happened. Being at home, away from the Italian bubble, enabled me to step back as well, and to ask myself if Seb was right. You had to wonder what was holding us together and to this day I still can't answer it, other than perhaps my need for a romantic fantasy to become reality. Returning to Italy I saw no evidence of his interest in me, indeed he was pretty much invisible in those early days I was back. I figured this was his way of dragging things out to a dead end, rather than confronting them. Typical. The relationship wasn't right and I knew it. I knew it then and I know it now but back then I wanted it so much to be right and I was too weak perhaps or too stubborn or too needy to admit it wasn't.

Still I wasn't totally without independent thought. I'd been living in a straightjacket since we – laughingly – got back together and I needed to break out of it. I knew not drinking was annoying me and frankly right now it wasn't serving much of a purpose. What was I trying to prove to Seb and would it even be enough for him? I decided it wasn't worth me not living my life and for God's sake it had been three months. Three whole months of not drinking and trying to prove I could be Natalie the Not Party Girl. My father told me to wait a bit more but I figured that if it wasn't over with Seb then, it would be soon so I may as well do the things that made me happy. Just a little one here and there. I had learned a lesson though and realised that the alcohol should not be the focus of the evening, just a part of it. I noticed that when I wasn't full of drink I was so much calmer, and able to look people in the eye and speak to them and feel in control. So it was a good thing and I was determined to keep it that way while enjoying the odd glass or two. That decision in itself relaxed me and Italy suddenly looked like the fun place it could be. I still dreamed of Seb's return. I fantasised about our reunion and what it might be like. It got me to sleep, helped me sleep and gave me a strange sort of comfort. Funnily enough, the more I did it, the less I needed to and soon I felt myself feeling strong and whole again.

As it goes with men, the more distant you are, the more interested they are and now, Seb seemed to be showing much more awareness of me, even as a friend (we still hadn't gone back to being lovers). One night we were both invited to the same dinner party. I knew I had to keep the alcohol under control. I was so tired while I was getting dressed that I decided to have a couple of very small vodka Red Bulls to relax me. Then, I thought I'd only have one glass at the party and everything would be cool. Wrong. I got wasted. Everything went wrong and I just wondered if I could do anything right. I couldn't even stick to simple rules I'd made myself. I often thought I should not have kept going home as it enabled me to avoid any concrete decisions but my brother was getting married soon and I had a dress fitting. So off I went again and it was nice, especially seeing Sam who is always so inspirational in everything she does and says.

Stardom.

Must admit, I'm really curious / concerned about this whole fame issue. At the beginning of the year it clearly said that I was going to become famous. It also said that it would most probably be connected to foreign land! The other day at home I asked 'Tatiana's Chronicle' the question (purely for fun), and that too said that fame awaited me. Well... let's hope so, I mean, I really do hope so now, have kind of got my hopes up! Just can't really foresee how exactly this could happen. Do not have any links in TV or the glam world, but am clearly still hoping!

... To be updated!

Tuesday 7 May 2002.

Spoke to Donna last night (and practically used up all calling card). Anyway was definitely worth it. She's so amazingly positive over this whole Seb thing. I just can't believe it and I have to say apart from the beautician at Visage in Stanmore, she is practically the only one! It's always great to speak to her, though don't want to delude myself either. She just seems totally convinced that if I just get on with my own life, totally, and become stronger and independent, without him and do my own thing, he will come back to me. She does also insist, however, that it cannot be a facade. I really must believe in what I'm doing, in creating a new life for myself. It must come from within me. Well, we shall see! I guess that was the initial plan of coming back here after all — I just got caught up in the security blanket of Seb, which actually in reality, certainly wasn't very secure!

Thursday 9 May 2002.

Had a nice chat with Grandma last night, which was good, without friction on usual topic, which was long overdue. Mum, however, managed to rub me up the wrong way — saying that of course I'd find somebody that'll love me unconditionally. I mean I can't stand that sort of thing, so certain in something that cannot be certain — it's painful to my ears like the shouting about being happy thing — I can't bear the tempting of fate! Well, heaven forbid I didn't and please God that I do, but I so could've done without hearing that.

However, no one will ever be able to love me that much, until I love myself that much.

PS: I'm supposed to be becoming famous at some point soon. I really can't see exactly how this is going to happen; however, it would be much appreciated at this particular moment in time.

CHAPTER 18
The Predicted yet Unexpected

My rental situation was getting a bit tricky. Nothing to do with the woman I rented from, she was fine. But her son had always had an odd way about him. At times, knowing I was not drinking, he'd appear at the door of my room with alcohol as if to say, 'Go on, take it.' On other occasions he'd bring pasta to my room on a tray with a flower, smile and leave. There had always been something unsettling about him and I could never figure out what it was. He looked rough, unshaven, and kind of dirty with scruffy clothes hanging off him; he spoke very few words and disappeared all day. I later found out that he was in fact an ex-convict. I didn't need to know any more and decided to keep my door locked while I looked for a new place to live. In typical Natalie fashion I got ahead of myself and announced to my parents I wanted to buy. They quickly took an axe to that proposition and pointed to the various tax implications that could arise. Let that be a warning to anyone who thinks it's easy to live your own version of *Eat Pray Love*. Somehow I don't think discussing tax implications would have helped the plotline.

I saw a perfect little *appartemento* in the centre and arranged a viewing. Pulling up in little my white Peugeot 106, slightly hot and flustered I spied the estate agent, an Italian straight out of central casting; tall, slim, tanned, rugged longish brown wavy hair and bright blue eyes. All of this was enhanced by a pair of perfectly faded Levis, a navy Ralph Lauren polo shirt, and a killer smile. He eyed me up and down as I got out of my car, slightly overwhelmed and growing warmer by the minute. I was wearing my sexy, tight Diesel jeans with tassels, thin, pale blue floral shirt and high-heeled brown sandals and was satisfied with the way I looked. However I was far more satisfied with the way he looked.

"Buonasera."

"Ciao... Sono Valentino."

"Natalie... piacere, you're the agent." We were both clearly taken aback.

"Yes – where are you from?"

"London, I'm English."

"Dai... che bello! I love London. Come... Let's go in."

It was distracting trying to view the flat with this ridiculously handsome and charming man at my elbow but I managed to stay composed. It was in a great location and a great flat: small, one bedroom, little white bathroom, bright kitchen, living, dining area and a small balcony, perfect. I decided to take it. I kind of got him in the bargain as well; he had my number and before long was calling inviting me out: we began seeing each other socially and I loved hanging around his crowd. They were fun, cool, and loved to party. Suddenly those days with nice but relatively sombre couples in the Sebastiano group were forgotten. I may have not been that far from Brendola but I was in another world, a world that suited me far better. And just like that life switched gear, new friends appeared, my phone was constantly ringing and I felt like I was living again. And to top it all off, Valentino offered me a job. He was opening a new estate agency and wanted me to work there as PA/office manager. It was in the centre of Vicenza, plus the pay was far better than my current salary. And then in a final twist to my transformation from moping, lovelorn Natalie, he and I started having a thing – not a relationship, not a fling but well, we were sort of seeing each other. I panicked slightly as to how this would affect the job proposal, but apparently there was no need. In yet more proof that life in Italy is a million miles away from anything in the UK, he said that the job was still mine and every thing was fine. It was no big deal he said, shrugging his shoulders. We liked each other. It was 'natural'.

Thursday 13 June 2002.

I do love it here, it's just I sometimes don't want to accept it. I don't know if it's M&D, C&V, and G or what, but there's something that just doesn't seem to let me just relax and enjoy life and the moment... this then generally sends me into crisis state. Don't know why? If it's the family, knowing that I'm really a part of that but I'm not there? Or if it's just that I wonder quite how sincere everything is over here? Or if it's just all too good to be true? Difficult equation to figure out! Not sure of the answer. But I guess, given that I don't feel like going home right now, I should just relax and get on with being here knowing it's currently where I'd rather be. Or maybe I should think in a more adult manner about things and make more solid decisions? For the future... Move in a direction that's actually taking me somewhere? Not sure if the sporadic unease is due to the family not being here, not sure if it's that? Or the fact that I'm drinking alcohol again, when I go out (only when out) if maybe it's that that makes me feel not so good about myself?

Saturday 12 October 2002.

OK — so still haven't got round to writing my summary of the summer, just way too much, however will identify it clearly when I do. (If I do.) Just thought that as for the first time in ages, I actually have a moment of time to myself that I'd write a few lines.

It's horrible outside, rainy and wet. Am having a 'sfigato' couple of days. Today I nearly got run over whilst crossing the road from supermarket to the Tabacchi, wrote a message to Valentino that I regret and yesterday drove into the back of a BMW! Luckily, he let me off; I was actually looking at myself in the rear mirror at the time!

Valentino's being as mysterious as ever (to be honest I'm quite done with maniacs!). Renata says I should just stay well clear of him (she doesn't like the crowd... well of course she doesn't), but who knows? I mean who knows! Haven't got a clue what goes through his head, only know that either working together will bring us inseparably together or establish that there is no future for us as a couple. Anyway, whichever of the two, I'll just have to accept it and will hopefully find out quite soon. Bought a rug today for flat. Who knows what's going on inside Valentino's head?? — I doubt he thinks about me though, at least not as much as I do him. Just have to see — time will tell.

While Valentino was well, being Valentino, I met a guy called Tommy, a very well-to-do man who took me everywhere and pursued me avidly. His crowd were hard-core party people too. Everyone was drinking to excess and taking drugs so it made me feel like I was the good girl in all this, as one thing I didn't do was I never took drugs. And they were getting far more drunk than me. I felt vindicated in some ways. I wasn't that bad and Sebastiano had made me out to be some kind of reckless social butterfly. Now

I was surrounded by a whole bunch of them and I felt rather tame. It wasn't all men, men, men. A girl needs her girls too and I'd met Lucia. Lucia was like me, similar build, blonder, very chatty and knew tons of people. She'd even lived in Cambridge for a while studying; we hit it off immediately and she became my partner in crime. She was a good person and someone who proved to be there for me and as it turned out, would always be.

Thursday 21 November 2002.

Well, it's been a long time since I've written. It's almost the end of the year and I'm only halfway through the diary, look at that! (Am on July) a first for sure — I usually don't have enough pages. I guess it can only be a good sign though as it means I've been busier and probably more relaxed. Not of course that I haven't still had 3,000 questions going round in my head, but I've just not sat and written them out. Lots has happened and strange situations unravelled. I'm now working with Valentino too. So, sort of been changing slightly, slowly but surely. Really am just following things through as they arise, hoping that they take me to the right destination and if not, that a big red light will kick in with a massive diversion sign forcing me to change route, without me having much to do with it. Have to pray and have faith that this will happen. I don't feel able to make such a drastic decision by myself just yet. I need the right road blatantly illuminated for me, and this is something only God can do I believe.

Am kind of improvising at work at the moment but hope it all goes well in the end (as have also turned down a good teaching job with a school… As school Manager!), was very unsure what to do, but I ended up sticking with this. I guess I felt I had to see this through, plus wanted to be in a solid Italian environment, more so than constantly with a bunch of English

*teachers. I would never have imagined working with Valentino every day
— how funny (sometimes) and sometimes not! He's a bit nuts. Often wonder
if school would have been a better idea, but not sure, and at the end of the
day Valentino issue went on for so long. I figured I might as well give it a
good shot. Didn't quite get what I'd be doing in the school anyway.*

*Valentino: Whatever is going to happen there?? I'm trying to look at
it as a sort of working holiday for a couple of years to see how things go.
He has so much going on in his private life and work for that matter that
I doubt I'm even in his thoughts but 'whatever!' Am not even sure what I
want, so pretty pointless fretting over it!*

Tuesday 26 November 2002.

*Life's definitely proving to be a bit strange or rather very strange. Can't
seem to get my head around anything at all. This morning have decided
it'd be nice to have a wacky London clothes shop in Vicenza. Thought it
would be a nice career move. Guess I need to give the job with Valentino
more of a go first before judging anything too fast. With him, nothing
really growing/changing but think he's probably weighing up the
situation a lot before deciding anything. The more you do that, the less
productive anything is anyway 'cos it's become a headache before you've
even started or at least I think so. Myself, I'm just going to be keen and
take things slowly and calmly both on job and personal front. Also would
never have expected the situation with Seb and not too sure how to handle
it!*

Men, huh? Can't live with them, can't shoot them. They say
women are prone to changing their minds but honestly what is it
with guys and this business of running off and then coming back at
the last minute? Why do you have to almost disappear out of their

lives before they decide they really want you and then they come back and expect you to be exactly where you were when they left? It all began with the roses outside my front door. Not just roses but lavish poetry – beautifully written, declarations of undying love, apologies for past behaviour and sad requests for forgiveness.

I was thinking back to Donna's wise words when I was last in London. She said that guys don't act until they actually feel real loss and what that means is that nothing you do really matters. That includes playing it cool, getting on with your life, being mysterious – you name it, it simply will not work until it hits them that something is gone. It was weird. The thing I'd wanted so much had transpired but I wasn't sure if I wanted it any more. It wasn't just that I was having fun and seeing other guys: I had moved on in lots of ways. So I was thrown into this process of reconciliation that I wasn't sure I really wanted. He was calling all the time now, acting like nothing had happened and his behaviour was annoying me. Actually it was making me angry, livid at times. After all the heartbreak he'd caused, the lack of communication and the complete disregard for my efforts he was here throwing himself on my couch – and acting like he owned the bloody place!

Why did I not feel what I'd felt previously? Sitting across from him one night in a restaurant I just didn't want to be there. As much as I tried to like him, to love him, to pull out all those feelings from before, to feel them again, I just couldn't. I had to give it a shot; after all, this was what I'd wanted for so long but no matter how hard I tried, I just couldn't actually do it. Not at all. Things felt broken and there was no way this was going to come back together. I looked at Sebastiano and all I could see was a sad, little boy who had just been allowed out into the world and wanted desperately to experience something but had no idea – or lacked the courage – how to go about it.

Thursday 2 January 2003 (London).
I've really decided that the real answer to a hell of a lot of my problems is to become famous. In all fairness it is a lifelong dream and I've now got to practically thirty, without ever doing anything about it. Some may say it's too late now, but others may say it's never too late. Not really too sure what I can do about it, but it would definitely be an achievement to become superbly famous before the year is up! What A RESULT! I really want to be famous! It's going to be the answer to everything – just unfortunately not all that easy to do! Must look into it.

I had a new neighbour, Éloise. She was French. We were both in the same boat, both Italophiles, both following a dream and searching for the unknown pot of gold at the end of the rainbow. It wasn't the most natural of relationships – I don't think we would have been friends normally and definitely not in London but living in foreign countries makes for strange bedfellows. We shared some great times, spent hours discussing our dilemmas regarding whether to stay or go. We shopped, got our hair done and she even read my cards, which kind of weirded me out as she was quite good at it. Because we were rarities in Vicenza – namely foreign girls – we were very well looked after. Flowers, wine, dinners, we were never short of any of them. Or dates. Being reasonably attractive was all we needed to be. And then Éloise went all Single White Female on me. You know, the film about the flatmate who takes her flatmate's life. She didn't exactly do that but she began to copy the way I looked with intricate detail. She copied my clothes, she dyed her hair, cut it the same way and did her make-up like me. Imitation is not flattery; it's really freaky. We ended up falling out, quite dramatically. Though, I suppose I shouldn't have been surprised: she was French and deep down I'd never really got on with them.

Monday 3 February 2003.

Well, January has certainly been the weirdest month. So much has happened. Grandma died, which has been the biggest upheaval thing and a real shock and change to everyone and all of us, but I think especially for Mum and me. Really pray that we both find the strength to move on brightly and positively.

When we were younger Charlie and I would talk about the people we love dying and he would be all mature, telling me that I had to come to terms with it, the fact that everyone would eventually die. He'd be driving me home after one of our many evenings out in London from the theatre or some swanky bar where everyone was far more mature than us. We would arrive back home but there would be no one there. Panic bells would ring loud in my head and my heart would start pounding. We both knew everyone would be around the corner at my grandparents, as something would have happened to Grandad. This was always the case and as we turned the corner M&D's car would be there with all the lights on in the house and an ambulance outside, stretchers at the ready. Grandad would then be carted off to hospital with everyone left in tears consoling Grandma or emphatically silent. Charlie thought I should be prepared. I think it was a blessing that I wasn't home when the news came that Grandma died, as I don't think I could have handled it. I got the watered down version but it was still excruciatingly painful to hear and I was heartbroken and desperately sad. Ironically I was neither home for Grandad's or Grandma's deaths, two of the hardest things I've had to go through, and I'm sure there was a reason for this. I clung to the fact that I, we, had got through Grandad's death, I still felt him close although not physically and we could cope, yet of course Grandma's was a much more dramatic departure. But that was just who she was and how she would have wanted it. The church she'd attended for so many years was overflowing with mourners both from the UK and Italy and Andrea Boccelli's 'Time to say good bye' echoed through the bleak, cold walls as the coffin was gracefully carried through. The sun shone brightly at the funeral but then the snow fell like I had never seen before and everyone was stranded. We had people staying wherever we could fit them. It was almost as if she was leaving her mark, the snow and the mountains being in the depths of her heart. It was humbling to see how one woman's life could touch so many people. She had been a huge force in my life, as well as a haven and refuge from everyone and everything including my own confusion. I thought about the most recent arguments we'd had, where she'd been unimpressed with my life choices and wished we hadn't argued. I had known she was right about things, completely right but I hadn't wanted to believe her or accept it. After the initial shock, days and weeks after I wondered if this was a sign too. It might seem selfish to say that but I'd met Sebastiano when I'd gone to Italy with Grandma for her last visit. It had happened immediately and I'd grasped it as some sort of sign that

I was meant to have a romance here too, a real one. I think I wanted so much to have a love story like Grandma and Grandad's in my own life, that I told myself it was meant to happen. But clearly Sebastiano and I were not here for the long haul. We were not here for any length of time and I had to face the knowledge that my Italian romance was over. I actually no longer had any purpose being in Italy except to feed that part of me that insisted Italy was more fun than being back at home in London. The attention I received from men for being different fed my ego and boosted my self-esteem. There was sunlight, parties and a suspension of reality that I couldn't have back in the UK. Meanwhile I could pretend to myself that I was planning some major assault on life, like becoming famous, and I had a purpose. But I didn't. I had absolutely no purpose in being in Italy and when I look back, I was really going round in circles.

CHAPTER 19
A Close Encounter

Tuesday 3 March 2003.

Well, work... Am metaphorically speaking, breaking my balls for peanuts and I'm getting a bit fed up of it. Must try to keep positive. For the first time tonight am letting my hair dry naturally – first time in ages I mean – straightening it all the time has dried it out and it's not achieving the desired effect with the desired people anyway!

Maybe with those not desired but I am not interested in that. Whole confusion and dull situation with Valentino: absolutely nothing positive growing there. Can only see him getting excited about various other mysterious phone calls, where his response to the call is that of the relationship kind and he then moves into the meeting room. So there's clearly no hope there. Seems ours will just be a working relationship – though seriously need to earn more money and frankly I could be!

Shitty film on tonight. 'What Woman Want', Mel Gibson – everyone thinks it's good. I think it's shit.

I'd taken a little trip to Siena to meet my friend Donna from London and her boyfriend Adam. It was fun but when I returned to Vicenza on Sunday night my car had been towed away from the railway station, where I'd parked. It turned out I had not seen the *vietato parcheggiare* sign that was pretty much hidden from view at about knee height! I had managed to get a fine for parking, a tow away fine, a fine for keeping it in the tow away place and to top it all off, the police noticed my insurance had expired, so for good measure there was a fine for that too. Could it have been any worse? After a very, very nice pleading phone call to my cousin Renata to come and rescue me from being stranded at midnight, I made a very, very nice pleading phone call to my brother begging for funds, to save me from financial collapse and thankfully he obliged. That's one of the annoying things about Italy: how they seem to manage to extract money out of you for every tiny single thing. But it's also so much fun and the dilemma I was facing was that I was well aware I wasn't really building anything in Italy, neither in material/financial terms nor in long-lasting love. So the question I was asking myself and Mum and Dad were asking me constantly too was, what was I actually doing in Italy? My job was unsatisfactory, I was working for a psychopath and there was no potential for serious love on the horizon. I reasoned that I was having fun; my life was – except for the job – an endless round of drinks, dinners, days at the beach, clubs and parties. That wasn't bad when I looked at it. (Dad once said I was living like Tara Parma, which to me was no bad thing at all, though we all knew I didn't have her foundation to fall back on.) I was living for the moment, something that I rarely saw in London. When I thought about returning to London, all I could focus on was the thought that I would not have any of this. Well yes, in a sense I would, I still had my friends to go out with etc. but essentially I'd be a number... that's what you are in London, but there I was 'somebody'. It wouldn't be the same, anyway. Plus it would be like going backwards not moving forwards, I was convinced of that. I couldn't see how returning to London was a positive step of any description. Here I felt so much more passion for life, just getting up in the morning was easier while there I felt I'd be living life looking through a window, removed from that passion which defined Italy so much for me.

At this point I was going between London and Vicenza quite a bit. I went back for Easter break and then returned to Italy for a wedding, which Sebastiano attended. I don't know how it happened, perhaps it was the emotion generated by the wedding, but I ended up sleeping with Sebastiano afterwards. We just *cogli l'attimo* as they say, grabbed the moment. No harm done. It didn't make me feel attached, as I'd long since passed that point. Funny how that happens. There are always strange couplings at weddings. Or arguments. After that, I'd gone back to London for a week and then I returned to Italy with a strong sense of needing to find something to hold on to. Or rather, if I'm being honest, someone. Alessio was my glimmer of hope. I liked Alessio's company, he was someone I was attracted to, extremely good looking and a good friend of Tommy. However he'd always had a girlfriend, with whom he was living so he was off limits. Suddenly he didn't have one and it all proved very convenient for me. Alessio was seen as a bad boy, a bit of trouble who hung around lap-dancing clubs (which seemed to be in abundance in Vicenza for some strange reason) and the warnings made him even more attractive. He came into the office where I worked, regularly, as he was a friend of Valentino's. He started coming in more regularly as Valentino was selling his house and so we began a flirting thing, which led to more flirting and became increasingly exciting. After some weeks of this I bumped into him at a party and we ended up kissing.

I soon found out his ex was a lap-dancer but he'd had a child with someone else and was being stalked by a previous girlfriend. I should have known there and then to let go but that's me, I always like to step into the fire. I was unsure whether to go any further even though he kept texting. That brings me to another point about Italy and small towns like Vicenza: there was no middle ground with the men. Either they were slow, weary, provincial with no ambition and needed winding up like a wind-up toy or they were off their heads on drugs, troublemakers and looked super, super cool. There was no other way with them.

Thursday 5 June 2003.

Mum and Dad and Christopher & Veronica here for the wedding (Luciano & Gabriella). Alessio just texted to say he's at Villa tonight. I said I'm not going down alone. Hope he didn't get the wrong idea, he said he'd ring 'dopo cena' – hope he does, he's such an adrenalin rush! We'll see.

Well that night, that Friday night that Alessio said he was going to Villa Bonin, I broke every rule in the book. He was very persistent!

Had a lovely dinner with family then everyone went back to their hotel. I went back to the flat, touched up make-up and jumped in a cab to Villa. Drank and danced 'til closing, stayed at Alessio's, overslept and was late for my hair appointment in the morning, where I was supposed to meet Mum.

"Hello Mum."

"Natalie, what happened? You look terrible."

"Umm sorry I'm late. I didn't mean it."

"I was so looking forward to a nice morning together and look at you, you can barely speak."

She was right. I was no good for conversation. I was no good for anything.

"Sorry Mum. I really am."

But sorry didn't cut it. My mum had come for a lovely weekend to spend quality time with her daughter and her daughter had gone chasing after a bad boy Italian, spent the night with him and now looked, well, pretty trashy. How I hated that about me, my thoughtless impulsiveness. I'd spoiled that moment just like I'd ruined things for her when, once on that lovely cruise with Valeria in the Caribbean, I came swaying along the corridor, starry eyed, still in my dress from the previous night. It was clear I'd been up to no good. It's not the kind of thing parents need to see. Sometimes I was so stupid.

Saturday 14 June 2003.

It's the hottest it's been here for fifty years, 38 degrees during the day and 32/34 in the evening. Driving the car if you put your hand outside, the air's hot. Stifling. There's no air.

Am supposed to be going to Tommy's house today. A different Tommy (Tommaso Brillo), who has a huge house in the hills with a pool, he's invited us up to chill around it and in it. Valentino will probably be there as he's Tommy's friend too. Is so hot can't even open blinds for fear of letting heat in! V bought me two bags by the way – he's in a nice phase... No idea what goes on in that guy's head.

Tonight there's a pool party, which am really looking forward to – 'Palm Beach Party'. Can't wait. Alessio won't be there, though he knows about it. He's at the beach every weekend. He's generally a nightmare –

exactly what everyone told me. I emailed him what I thought: that he was wasting his life with all these women. It was like he had everything but nothing. I mean he's totally loaded, lives in a palace and nurtures nothing.

No one knows what he is able to do until he tries.
(Publilius Syrus)

Sunday 15 June 2003.

(How strange that I wrote the above phrase yesterday! Right on Saturday.)

Saturday night after a fantastic day at the pool with everyone, mucking about etc. then quick turnaround at home and back out to the pool party in the evening. After a totally excellent day and night; (however having drunk way too much) I had a car accident.

Car's a write-off. Lost it. Thank God, sincerely, that I am still here. Big, big car accident, was tired and fell asleep in the car. Horrific mess, but again as I said before thank God (seriously) that I am still here. Blood everywhere, gashed my head and nose open but so far nothing worse, and I sincerely, sincerely pray that there will never be anything else wrong related or non-related to that. Well, I have ten massive stitches in my head, six-inch scar but hopefully it will go away quickly. Mum and Dad have been over, came over immediately and C&V come tonight, can't wait to see them, just hope no one brings up drinking conversation with them. God forbid! They all did (Renata's parents etc.) with M&D, and it really made me mad! I'm supposed to be resting not getting wound up! I will not have it nor accept it.

Everyone's been so good apart from Seb, Renata and Cesco, who are all obviously worried, etc. but just stressed me out (Renata & Cesco did actually also help a lot though).

Other than that so many people have been nice though, Luca, Alessio, Tommy, Lucia, Chiara, Antonella, Andrea, Enrico, Pieropaolo, the other Luca, Alessia, Valentino, Valentino's mum... so many people.

Everyone came over to visit and brought stuff, was really heart-warming!

Better to lose a minute of your life than lose your life in a minute.
(OPERATION TRAFFIX)

Tuesday 1 July 2003.

One thing that really does bother me is that by now I would have been working nicely on my tan. I would have logically been relatively black on face and body whereas I am in fact relatively white! Realise that this should be least of my worries, am fully aware of that. However nevertheless is bothersome. Have not been in sun for ages, would normally be super tanned by now. Not fair.

Massive panic yesterday as doc refused to take stitches out, as there was too much bruising and swelling below — blood clot. Had to go back to hospital and was there for three hours trying to drain it with syringes. Not very nice at all, just pray to God this is the last of the troubles now. Want it to heal and disappear and forget it ever happened.

Am questioning a lot of things at the moment, must admit. Have got Crispi looking at jobs in London just for the sake of it and am not looking forward to going back to work here with Valentino the Psychopath. Not looking forward to it at all, but if he gives me grief I'll just change my attitude and leave — though obviously would be so much nicer if things just went well.

After the stitches were out I spent a couple of weeks in London where I decided to forgo any thoughts of future decisions and just enjoy London, really enjoy it. There were a couple of mad nights with Valeria after which I returned to Italy to join Lucia at her beach house in Caorle, the ancient Venetian beach town with just enough to keep you busy but not too much crazy nightlife. We had a group of very hot guys renting the apartment below hers, adding a certain frisson to the trip. One day I dropped into the apartment, just a quick loo diversion from the beach. Lucia always laid the loo paper on the seat before sitting, as her parents were a bit older so of course I did the same. Desperate not to miss a moment of the sun's rays, soon as done, I raced back out, wearing my tiny bikini, when I heard a roar of laughter from the boys' terrace.

"Ah ha ha ha."

"Guarda – look at this…"

"Ehi… Bellissima – is this the new fashion?"

The searing heat had ensured the loo paper had stuck firmly to my legs. My Sophia Loren moment was ruined. I couldn't imagine her ever making a faux pas like that. That summer was beautiful, balmy and crazy, as it tends to be in Italy. Random dinners out in the open air, with fresh local food and copious amounts of delicious wine. We'd drive around in convertibles, singing at the top of our voices as we made our way to beach clubs. It wasn't total hedonism, we still went to work but nobody did very much and it wasn't expected. I'd started teaching English, on Tuesdays, at the Devon school, which I really enjoyed. Weekends were more of the same, just more intense fun. Occasionally an enquiry would arrive from home. "What are you doing? Anything? Are you sure you don't want to come back?" I ignored some, replied to others.

I felt like I had a whole family here, not just my Italian real extended family but also all my friends. There was such an openness and honesty in our relationships that you would never get back in England.

And there was Antonio (Anto). He was one of Valentino's best friends, not the most beautiful boy like Alessio and definitely not as 'bad' as him, but he had something I liked very much. He began taking me out after I'd taught at the Devon school, each Tuesday. He texted me lovely words every night and every morning. He often drove me home from work, took me anywhere I needed to go, paid for everything, gave me cuddles and was lovely. Everyone began to tell me how much he was into me: he'd never really been seen out with other girls and now he was simply always with me. You know how some people are just comfortable, you just fit skin to skin? Antonio was like that. In Italy they say *una cosa di pele*.

Saturday 15 November 2003.

Evening at most amazing fish restaurant, Cinzia e Valerio followed by clubbing at Manamana with Anto.

OK — fantastic evening, Mama Mia! We ate so well, incredible. It was all amazing. Anto was a complete and utter angel. He ordered all the right things. I was on such a high from the food and the whole atmosphere. Shame I wasn't with the man of my dreams, would have been such a perfect situation. Life would have been perfect! C'est la vie. He's great and we had a good time anyway.

He ordered:

Octopus and king prawns

Lobster spaghetti

Half a lobster with king prawns and langoustines

Dessert
Perfect wine all the way through
Dessert wine
Coffee, Biscotti
3 digestivi!
Amazing... and then on to Manamana.
Sometimes I feel like I'm living like a movie star. Dad said it once and
he was right!

It was not the first time a friend became a lover. It's amazing how that can happen. One minute you've put them in the friend compartment, quite sure they're in the right place and that you don't want to jump into their bed. Then, by some strange twist of fate, you see them differently. Suddenly Antonio's blondeness was attractive, his green eyes mesmeric, his lean body and his tall, strong presence positively captivating. And there was his mystery which was really rather irresistible. Sometimes he went all quiet, which I didn't really understand. He'd simply say he was 'depressed' and very little detail would follow. He certainly played his cards close to his chest. There were times when we would have amazing fun, when he'd be totally in control and then others where I would not hear from him, yet another Italian lunatic to add to my collection. During the winter I went home for Christmas holidays and kept in touch with Antonio. He seemed different somehow, erratic and subdued.

Back in Italy I met up with him and he was a man transformed, not in a good way. I immediately thought his withdrawal from social life and general reticence must be me and he'd lost interest. I guess it's just a thing we do as women: we think that it always has something to do with us. This time it didn't. He'd spiralled into a deep depression and the doctor told him he needed to virtually clean up his act and to cut out all vices and rebalance his life. This included sex as well as drinking and smoking. I was mystified. I couldn't understand where all this had come from. We were involved so I had to care but it was very hard to know what to do. I would find myself sharing his moods with him, which did me no good. And then I found out that he actually did have a problem, he took a lot of cocaine, a lot and this accounted for his rapid and massive mood swings. I didn't want to judge him. I don't think it's our place to judge anyone: we're all fallible. The only judge is really God, I guess. I just felt for Antonio and I felt helpless.

Friday 30 January 2004.

OK — so seems like a big change period is coming up, and not really sure quite how I feel about it. Since I've been back, lots of people have been a bit down (I think basically due to the usual routine they've been doing for years, but not entirely sure).

At Christmas, I was half thinking of attempting going back to London for a go but couldn't commit to a date. Thought perhaps around Easter. Anyway, was going back for V's b'day on Jan 23rd, so had plenty chance to talk about it. Dad rang saying he'd found a flat and they'd put an offer in. Seemed perfect for me and that if there was anything holding me back from returning to London, like not having my own place etc., this could be a good solution. They did however insist on it not being any pressure!

It is however close to impossible to find flats in decent areas that are actually affordable. If I'd have had to do it all off my own back, find job, flat, etc., it would have been a massive headache and made going back even harder.

I went round the flat when I was back, but my heart wasn't in it 'cos at the moment my heart is here. I hoped I'd feel different, but I didn't. It was very difficult. However, on other hand, the alternative is: nothing. It's stay still, stay doing exactly what I'm doing now and not achieving anything. So in all sanity, even if going against the heart in the beginning, it is not an opportunity that I can turn down. It's a beautiful little flat, in a beautiful little close in Stanmore, near shops, station, close to all the family and M&D are willing to help finance it by guaranteeing it for me. Not sure when they'd be able to do that again as age would be against them. I basically at least have to accept as a try.

And that's what I told them. I'll try my very best at the whole thing, but if my heart isn't in it and I honestly will give it my best, wholehearted shot, but if I'm not happy or at peace after a while, I'll have to pack it all in, rent it out and come back here. Dad said that's fine and we could even sell it.

Don't know why he said that — wasn't thinking of that, would always want to keep the investment, no matter what. I love property. I think he was just emphasising no pressure.

Well, all this takes me back to some dreams I'd had not so long ago. One especially where I was asking a psychic where I should live. She was telling me the pros and cons of both. I remember she said basically that in Italy it would be fun. I'd have fun and probably write a book. Yet in UK I'd be more stable, no more back and forth on planes. Well actually would like to write a book have always thought that, with all my diaries. Wouldn't need to be in Italy to do that. Could do it there too, anywhere for that matter, would only do it, if and when I reach some kind of conclusion in my life. And I'd call it 'HOPEFULLY' (hoping that it would still be appropriate and apt as a title).

I spent the last few weeks in Italy in a whirl of hedonism. Play, play and more play. I moved out of my flat and into Éloise's as she'd gone back to Marseille for the summer. Antonio was still around, more as a friend really and I cared about him. And I met Mr Gillette, introduced by Isabella who had become a good friend and fixture in my 'Italian family'. His name was Dario but I'd dubbed him Mr Gillette because he embodied the looks of a Gillette model, plus he worked for them. We liked each other, clearly, and so went out a few times. What a contrast he was to the others: calmer, mature, older and there was something else. But I had no idea what it was. The inexplicable thing was that the old Natalie would have hung on to Mr Gillette as some sort of sign to stay in Italy, she would have hung on with her fingernails probably. But I wasn't doing that. I felt really calm with him and I wondered why. We had a lot of good times. He took me to Tuscany for two days and it was idyllic. It was like being in a movie: we drove there in his navy convertible BMW, stayed in the most picturesque places, visited towns and vineyards, ate in the best restaurants and generally lived the dream. I look back now and I can clearly see that Mr Gillette helped me make that step across the bridge of change.

CHAPTER 20
Back For Good

Mr Gillette was a turning point in my understanding of what I needed as a woman. He was a huge digression from every other man in my recent past and he not only showed me what a man could be, he showed me how respectful, calm and well, normal (rather than hysterical) things should be between a man and a woman. When I returned to London he continued to contact me, calling me almost every day. Those calls were significant in my life: they reminded me I'd finally taken a quantum leap and so, when he didn't call on occasions, I missed him. Deep down, however, I knew it was the right thing to do, as getting addicted to his contact would do me no good. I had taken out the positive things of our meeting and I decided I was fortunate to have that. A few of the Italian crew came over for my thirtieth birthday – Lucia had been visiting for a while – and he joined us too. I loved having him there but couldn't fathom why he was so strange and distant and trying to discuss it with him didn't get me anywhere. Perhaps it was the 'he's on my territory' syndrome. It seemed that each time someone foreign transplanted themselves to my home ground, however temporarily, things didn't feel quite so right.

I saw him after that in Italy. I'd gone to see Lucia and he rang and took me to Lake Garda for the day. Again it was lovely. He seemed to want to talk and tell me about his life and I learned he had a brother who was unwell, very unwell. But, strangely, I didn't learn a lot about him. Other than that his brother's illness inhibited him from letting go and enjoying himself, almost like he felt he didn't deserve it. The whole situation sent me into a panic, what was I getting myself into: I actually had a panic attack while I was visiting Italy, which led to me drinking and texting him while not in the best frame of mind. Drink and text are not great bedfellows and my output was predictably dramatic and pathetic though at the time, of course, I probably thought it made sense. What my poetic words did to his head I don't know, as he didn't manifest much sign of it and continued ringing me. After a solid week of doing so he informed me on the last phone call that he couldn't ring every night. I told him I'd ring but he didn't acknowledge the remark: the fact was that I never rang. It was my policy. And a good one I think. Anyway it all went very strange after that. I knew he was busy but I also knew he was, and is, Italian, so one should never expect anything smooth or logical!

Tuesday 14 September 2004.

So here I am back in London, not really knowing what the future holds for me. I know it was the right or at least sensible, no, I think right and sensible thing to do, to come back with the whole 'flat' option, and the flat is looking really lovely and quite simply gorgeous! I've done it out all in white, with huge cream corner sofa, glass table, put a breakfast bar along the wall in the kitchen and decorated it with multi-coloured ethnic cushions on the sofa and on the bed. It looks a million dollars and I love it... but I must say that I'm not exactly bursting with enthusiasm about this whole situation, everything... London, Mr Gillette, all of it. I haven't got a clue what's going on with Mr Gillette and London's just well... London, I guess. It's great but I guess it's just the fact that I didn't exactly choose to come back here from my heart, and heart's natural decision. It's just not easy at all.

I've finished the temping job in the Italian law firm which was great 'cos it was easy to get to and was just temping, so wasn't really real. I am now however working for Darren Redbourne (friend of Crispi's) who's the MD of a financial company. Him and Hayden, the other MD, needed a PA, so that's where I fit in. I mustn't overdo the use of internal mail or office email, which unfortunately, after a week I have already managed to do. I must tone that down – absolutely 'cos I do have loads of stuff to do and definitely don't want them to think that I am not doing it or taking the P at all. Definitely don't want that. Have to be really grateful to have the job. It's not easy to get a permanent job – this is one (practically): there's a three-month trial as a standard company procedure but hopefully... So I should calm off the emails until then I suppose. But it's a job, which means money, which means you can have choices, therefore all very Important!

Saturday 18 September 2004.

'Tis Saturday now, first two weeks of work over. Bought what looks like a lovely book yesterday. Don't know if it's going to be positive or negative at the end but was compelled to buy it. 'Italian Fever' it's called.

Still desperately miss Italy but is still in my interests to give it a proper good go here too. No matter what the outcome, it's still really important and can only help me to become a richer (internally and externally, characteristically and materialistically) stronger and more complete person.

Hmm, I really don't know what will happen in my life. I still have no clue what is going on with Mr Gillette, it's doing my head in. Think I'm going to have to forget him. I don't think he's doing enough or will do *enough. I'll see if that changes, but at the moment it seems like that. Would like to think I was wrong but...*

    I don't want to dance with someone who doesn't want to dance with me!

I admit it would have been nice to be able to make a clean break from Italy and see London as a positive move forward but I was struggling to do that. It wasn't just Mr Gillette I was pining for: I was missing Italy in itself and if you asked me I would have probably replied in superficial terms and talked about sunshine and parties and food (though food is not so superficial, is it?) but it was that quality of joy I was really missing. To read that you'd think I'd been plucked from Vicenza and put in a cold, dark prison. OK London could be cold and dark but it was definitely no prison and when I was on form, I enjoyed myself. I just preferred being there and I suppose it may have had something to do with the fact that it wasn't as 'real' a life as being in London. In Italy there was still room to pretend and dream whilst in London, surrounded by adorable but logical, sensible family who want to put things in boxes for you, there wasn't really the room for that.

    In retrospect I was making the classic mistake you do; I was trying too hard to get it right instead of exercising a bit of patience. I was hugely impatient for London to fall into place that I wanted it too desperately and when it didn't I'd forget I'd only been back five minutes and ring the alarm bells inside myself. As for Mr Gillette, well that fizzled out. It had to really but first there were discussions, debates and lots of analysis which is a really bad sign: frankly if you spend so much time discussing a relationship you're not really having it. There were the predictable tears (mine) the heartache (mine) and then it wore itself out. I did the only thing I could do. I went to a tarot reader, Magical Miss Stefanie of Golders Green.

"You should not return to Italy, not now as it will be difficult and a struggle for you," she told me.

Well yes, but I wasn't planning to. I was impatient for her to give me something.

"There is someone but you have doubts about him, someone you already know. He will want to come back into your life but you will have already met someone here, in February."

And that… is how it was all back on with Antonio again. I had barely swept aside the residue of my relationship with Mr Gillette when I clutched back on to Antonio. I was desperate to retain my links with Italy and my Italian girlfriends had said as much. It was like swinging back and forth across the river on a rope. I couldn't let go as I might fall in and then where would I be?

Tuesday 30 October 2004.

I really do seem to get obsessed by people. I think since I can remember, I have pretty much always done that. Mr Gillette and now Anto (again). I am clearly doing it with him now. Funny how that situation went. Good, bad, good, bad, really good, really bad, black to white then disappeared during his depression then came back. OK, fair enough he didn't come back saying he was madly in love with me, wanted to marry me and have his children but he did come back and was full of smiles, hugs and kisses. I MISS HIM.

He was so lovely this time in Italy. As lovely as he was though he was not proclaiming his undying love.

As usual my parents threw their opinions in the ring though who could blame them as my love life wasn't exactly a great secret.

"You have to make sure someone's interested in you, really interested, Natalie, rather than just you chasing them." That was my mum.

"Mum, I'm not chasing Anto for crying out loud. We've decided to see each other and he makes an effort, not like the other Italians."

"Which doesn't say that much," pointed out my father.

"Dad!"

"Anyway you left Italy and showed you were not interested in him. So how do you know he will take you seriously?"

"Dad, I left because you kindly offered to settle me into London with a flat and remember when I came to see it, Antonio was having a low time so the poor guy probably thought I'd deserted him."

"It's all a bit shaky to me," said Mum.

"You don't even know him so how can you tell? Anyway I have to give it a chance and at least see it though to a natural end."

"But you need to settle, you can't keep flitting about or you'll find suddenly life has passed you by."

I sailed reasonably steadily towards the end of the year with Antonio coming over a few times and me going there. I loved his calm but also his propensity to be whimsical and childlike. His continued capacity for mystery I found annoying. Meanwhile I was given the names of a couple of Italian guys who'd moved to London. It was nearing Christmas and it was just the extra spice I needed.

Wednesday 5 January 2005. (A few days into the New Year, looking back at the last few days of last year...)

Lots has happened, has been ages since I've written, guess the whole Christmas period just took over! I'd been emailing this guy, Paolo Bevilacqua, a friend of Isabella's. Never got around to meeting up so I told him to come to our office do! Didn't go down too well with the office but never mind, shouldn't be so narrow-minded! I ended up staying at his, as was late and he lived in Notting Hill. Nice guy, nice flat, very wealthy, bit of a computer genius but definitely not my type.

Next event after that was the girls coming over for NY! I was so looking forward to it. In the meantime, Lucia had put me in touch with another guy from Vicenza who now lived in London. Edoardo, he rang me and we spoke for forty minutes, seems like a nice guy. Apparently the whole of Vicenza had been in love with him. I didn't get any hopes up though, not after I did with Paolo, then it was a let down, but was a nice chat and we said we'd be in touch.

Still a bit confused about Anto, the girls were over so I talked to them a lot about it... I wondered if maybe the distance now broke him off, but he knew how much I loved Italy so really don't think he'd have had any difficulty in telling me he wanted something more from me – he knew I'd jump. The girls agreed!

Had a great time with them all here NYE was fab. We all got ready at mine in our evening dresses, had champagne cocktails then set off to meet Mart, Nicole and others and Royal Garden Kensington for black tie do... was fantastic. Masses of champagne, great long meal, excellent music and Greek music... Laura got sick, threw up and broke her dress. Lucia traumatised her feet and had to keep putting them up. I got glass in my foot and Cri just danced non-stop with the Greeks!!

I ended up meeting with Edoardo, a very good-looking guy with olive skin, chiselled features, dark hair and general air of Italian hotness about him. We struck up a friendship just after New Year and I felt happy that I had someone in London who maintained my Italian lifeline. I realised I was clinging to the Italian past – which was still a present for me – but I found myself unable to let it go. Edoardo pointed out that it was natural to idealise something in the past when you felt uncomfortable in the present.

"You are putting it up as some sort of model for life so much, Natalie. I understand how you feel being here again but I think you only remember the good, and superficial things about Italy."

"I'm not sure that's totally true, Edoardo. I'm aware of the negative things."

At least I think I was.

"I can only say what I see and hear. And you, you talk mostly about the parties, the fun, the whole social scene and its normal when you're young to do that but you can't really build a whole life on that. And if you want to, there are parties in London. You are always out."

"But it's different in Italy, Edoardo, you know that. It's more... light, less responsibility.

"Ah," he said. "Now we are making sense. Less responsibility is the thing that attracts you so much. But you know; as everyone gets older these things change. Think about it. It's not about where you are in the world, it's just life. Soon these people will marry and have children. Or they'll not marry and go away to work. Or they'll find other things to do that are not parties. Nobody does this forever. You can't live on hedonism. Well, OK you can, but it's a very dangerous and uncertain route to follow."

I didn't think I wanted a life of pure hedonism and I told him that. I was worried he thought of me as a party girl. I began seeing him more and I liked that he was mature and made an effort, the lack of which was always my beef with previous Italians. It didn't exactly race along – us – and he seemed to be taking it slowly. Any slower and it would have been backwards but he was in control, probably because I was so anxious for this Italian connection in London, I was more needy than I should have been. Despite his insistence on going slow, there were instances where he'd be totally full on and then a red light would pop up and the inevitable screech of the uncertain relationship brakes. As a person he was super smart but almost too analytical, at times I found him rather heavy and tiring. As we got to know each other another fact was revealed, an important one. I wish guys would reveal the stuff that really matters at the front. In Edoardo's case it was his yellow fever, that passion that some men have for Asian babes. Call it what you like, the desire of many guys to possess some sort of oriental woman in their life is prevalent. And Edoardo was one of them. He had it bad.

He'd had a Chinese girlfriend and from our conversations it was evident that he wasn't over her. This sent out a clear signal. I clearly was never going to be who he wanted. Sometimes you have to accept that people have their little predilections and no matter how much they try to pretend they don't, it comes out. I had a track record of trying to transform myself for past lovers but no matter what I did, I would never be an oriental babe. Our relationship soon collapsed and he went on to hook up with and marry a replica of his ex. I wasn't surprised in the least.

Thursday 3 February 2005.

London is such a beautiful town. Last night, even though I was moaning to myself about having to wait around for a while before going to Paolo's for dinner, I actually did have a really nice time. I had a Pina Colada, walked along, all wrapped up warm, scarf and gloves, as was snowing, walked along as the dark was setting in; the lights were shining brighter, neon sparkling, snow falling and people rushing about! Benetton window looked appealing, so I end up trying on a few things and buying a couple. Nice! Fun! Then gave a few people a call... I proceeded to walk along a very busy Oxford St, then caught one of the buses Paolo had said I could take to his. Hopped on and got off at Notting Hill. Well, I don't like him in any romantic way at all but did have nice evening. He made lovely fish for dinner, which I have to say, was delicious. He really went to town, did sardine bruschetta, cocktail di gamberetti, spaghetti frutti di mare, lots of white wine and tuna steak marinated — which we couldn't eat. Was a nice evening. I stayed there as just couldn't be bothered to go home. Didn't touch him one tiny bit. Just couldn't and wouldn't. Totally impossible. Got up, had a nice shower, he has nice smellies, which is good and he prepared breakfast so that was nice. Sat in gorgeous, big flat completely decked out in Italian furniture — he'd imported every item of furniture from Italy — in the centre of Notting Hill, with a wonderful cappuccino in a huge big cup as I like, and the most wonderful Panettone to dip in it. So all in all a wonderful Wednesday morning brekkie in an Italian style Notting Hill. Then hopped on the bus to work. Much prefer that to tube. Lovely. Got off and walked down Regent Street, window shopping the rest of the way. A very pleasant evening and morning.

Contentment is not the fulfilment of what you want,
but the realization of how much you already have.
(Unknown)

Friday 11 February 2005.

Sometimes you know, I think it's not good to want for too much! It can really make you not appreciate what you've got. I believe this is really true. OK, it's good to want for some things but to want for something too much really does come in the way of appreciating what we do have.

Well, it's Valentine's Day on Monday! And from the fear of not actually getting any invites, I've ended up with three! I could almost cry. I feel like I've been through so much — obviously nothing compared to lots of people, but in my own personal world, that's how I feel, especially in the romance, boyfriend, love area! I'm actually so chuffed, touched, pleased, surprised, and basically happy! Just hope that I enjoy it now and have a meaningful time.

Wednesday 2 March 2005.

Off again — would frankly like to take tomorrow and Friday off too and just be done with it! Have to be careful though as bonuses are coming up and am keen to make a good impression (if not too late).

I must admit, I really could get used to this staying at home thing, I really could. I'm sitting here in my beautiful little flat, watching the morning programmes, doing my washing, putting my things away, tidying up, having a cup of tea, etc. whenever I want. I really do like it. I so wish that I could get together with someone I love, get married and not work any more. I really just want to do exactly that and then have a couple / some beautiful happy and healthy kids to go with it and all us live happily ever after. Wish I could just do that now.

The secret of change is to focus all of your energy not on fighting the old, but on building the new

(Socrates)

CHAPTER 21
Decisions

The thing about decisions is that they only work if you make them and then stick to them. A decision that is made half-heartedly is not a decision: it's just more indecision. This very aptly described my state of mind in 2005. I had absolutely no idea what I wanted – other than to meet the man of my dreams and/or become famous – and my refusal to decide on a path in the medium term meant I was living my life without resolution. With one foot in Italy and one in the UK the only way to live was relatively superficially, because let's face it unless you commit yourself to something that is all you're doing. Now, being a party girl, superficial could sustain me for a while but I wasn't going to be able to build a satisfying and substantial life on such a flimsy foundation. My parents knew it, boy did they know it and of course they reminded me of it... frequently. I can hardly blame them, nor can I fault them for getting irritated with me: I think if I were them I would have been thoroughly irritated with my constant toing and froing, my inability to stick to a job for a decent length of time and my habit of constantly looking over the horizon.

Having been the relationship bore, I was now the Italy bore, my indecision spreading far and wide with kind, tolerant and increasingly patient friends, giving me their views. Isabella was one of the people who could always be counted on to be wise and thoughtful. She was a friend of Valentino, the estate agent in Italy and a divorce lawyer, so what she didn't know about relationships wasn't worth knowing! She was at least ten years older than me, maybe more and her general worldliness and sophistication, along with her pragmatism, made her a great friend to me. When I flew to Vicenza I now often stayed with her; she had a gorgeous flat in the centre of town. Between her and Lucia, I felt secure and I suppose this drew me to Italy as much as anything. Not that I didn't have my friends in London but I suppose I was constantly looking for signs that one place had the edge over the other. Plus Italy had Antonio for whom I was still pining. At the beginning he'd done the running and I'd been a little so-so. Now I was bombarding him with letters and texts, offering pretty much everything I could to make it work. My pursuit of Antonio and all things Italian in general proved to be too much of a distraction at work, where much to my dismay, it was duly noted and commented upon.

Tuesday 12 July 2005.

OK, so just feeling totally fed up, bored and complacent. I just want something exciting to happen in my life. I'm certainly not getting any satisfaction or joy out of things as they are at the moment.

I know the last thing I should be doing is complaining, especially not after such a tragedy that's just happened, i.e. 07/07/05 — terrorists blowing up underground and a bus and lots of completely innocent people like you and me horrifically dying. I should be so thankful for my life and for all that I have, considering that I travel on just those trains every day, as does Christopher and loads of other people I know.

Thank God, seriously, that we are OK, and I totally pray that such a horrific thing never ever happens again.

But nevertheless, I'm still not happy. I should be so grateful for all that I have, which I also am, it's just that it's not making me happy — or at least not happy enough to feel relaxed. I'm so bored with everything. I miss Italy, I miss love, I miss Anto! I miss feeling like ME! What can I do? Anto is a complete player, sweet, nice but also a liar and has a bad substance habit along with other problems. We talk, we don't talk, we see each other and we don't. Insomma... niente.

Had a slight hiccup when over there — after having decided to totally avoid him, ended up caving in and kissing! Anyway wasn't looking at things realistically. Now am back on with the ignoring thing. Clearly not any sort of relationship, just a nice boy who's got caught up in the wrong world and frankly can give nothing. Don't know why he bothers hanging on every now and again as he clearly wants nothing from me, neither does he want to give me anything.

Am going to Italy for a week at the end of next week. If he's around I will just ignore him (if he tries to get in touch that is). I will only be thinking of myself this holiday. And it is going to be a complete holiday. So I'm missing that real love, the romance that turns into real love — I guess that's the big problem number one at the moment.

Anyway, that's that, established and annoying but at the end of the day on the Anto front what do I honestly want doing with someone like that. I terribly miss love, proper love and real affection.

Never cry for the person who hurts you.
Just smile and say: "Thank you for giving me a chance
to find someone better."
(Unknown)

The other thing is that I'm clearly very much missing Italy too, just the closeness and togetherness of it all. In reality having spoken to quite a few people, it's not all it's cracked up to be (that's locals telling me this) what with a total lack of sincerity, lots of back-stabbing and a general who gives a shitness... There really is an awful lot of all that, so I guess all the going out is great but on a superficial level.

- Oh dear it's clouding over and all I wanted was an hour to relax in the park!

- Just had some gorgeous chicken left over from the barbie. Gorgeous. Must appreciate the small things in life.

That year I turned thirty-one. Just like that I was over thirty and I couldn't quite believe it. I was more confused and messed up than I'd ever been. I'd decided I'd rent out the lovely flat Mum and Dad had helped me buy, as I wasn't there enough. A couple of days later I was made redundant and though I didn't enjoy the job I felt, as I do in these situations, that the choice had been made for me so that annoyed me. If you think about it, it's funny really, since I couldn't make any real choices about my life myself anyway! They were having drinks that night and of course wanted to say 'farewell'. I resisted but the crew at work, full of irritating pity, convinced me to come out for one and so I did. I was surprised that being there brought tears to my eyes and then the oddest thing happened. One of the girls pulled out her perfume, held it in her hand, then sprayed it and I thought, 'Oh my God, I know who that is. It's Grandma.' The second I saw the bottle, I knew instantly. The only other person in the world who'd worn that perfume – Paris by YSL – was Grandma. Until this day I had not smelled it anywhere in a long, long time. I knew then that she was there with me, watching over me and it was all going to be OK, I was sure of it.

Ask yourself if you're really happy and you cease to be.
(John Stuart Mill)

Never one to overlook a coincidence I was struck when Brandon appeared again. He seemed to have this uncanny knack of popping up out of nowhere when I was leaving or thinking of leaving, as if to remind me that, yes, there were good-guys left in the UK and indeed he was one of them. I had to wonder if there was more to it. He'd inexplicably popped up when I was smitten with Sebastiano and now, just as I was looking for another reason to go and work in Italy, here he was again. On the tube! Despite him living in the neighbourhood, I'd never bumped into him before locally, so why now? He asked me out and I said yes, all the while trying to push that kiss to the back of my mind, that awful one we had before I went to Italy to live. We went out the next night. It was odd because we were both nervous and, as a result, talking rapidly so that there was absolutely no space. He asked me out again before we parted for the night, so I guess it couldn't have been that bad, at least for him. As for the kiss, well it was a bit better but I can't say the fireworks were going off. His presence sent me into a whole panic about Life vs. Fun and what I was supposed to be looking for. I often look back now and wonder why everything had to be such a big deal, not just for me but for other girls as well. Why on earth did it all have to come with so much drama? Why couldn't it just be life without all the hysterics?

I occasionally found the answers watching *Sex and the City*, which I adored then and still do. It gave me a strange sense of peace. Yes of course those four girls had lots of money and amazing clothes and seemed to go out more than they worked but their dilemmas resonated with me. Why couldn't we be happy with the guy next door? Why did we put ourselves though agony over a guy who didn't care about us? What was really important? All these questions and more were part of not just my life but those of my girlfriends as well, though, admittedly, at times I was just too self-absorbed to see it. We were all making it hard for ourselves, just like those Carrie, Miranda, Samantha and Charlotte, did on SATC even though they seemed to have everything going for them. In fact it seemed to me that the only people who weren't hitting themselves over the head all the time were the boys I knew, the old crowd especially. I envied the way they just got on with being who they were and didn't seem to be constantly looking over the horizon for the next best thing.

Thursday 16 February 2006.

Well I would love to inject a positive note into this 2006 diary but as ever... the time just wasn't coming. So here I am, laying on the bed in London, listening to the rain outside (which, in all fairness, there hasn't been that much of lately) and am about to get ready to go to work, AKA Very Boring Time Killer — but at least I like chatting to the girls. Major plus point. It is 16 Feb, day rather expensive mobile phone bill comes out of my account and two days after a very alone Valentine's Day, where my only company was a piece of salmon (delicious at least) my parents (guess was better than being alone, alone) and numerous episodes of SATC. Hallelujah for that at least.

No contact with Anto again. I was quite rude to his last text — totally against my will but I know I can't handle what he has to offer. The New Entry (Umberto) is fast becoming the fasted New Exit ever. Next please! Also am totally panicked about small circle of hair missing on head. Ahhh — am actually seriously worried about this, though refusing to let it get me down. Must definitely get it seen to ASAP, i.e. tomorrow.

What is happening to me? Ahhh! I ask and totally pray that things get better. At least we're all going out in the city tonight for Georgie's birthday which hopefully should be a laugh... though I clearly need some much more powerful changes than that in my life right now. I really do — pray they come.

Wednesday 22 February 2006 (seven thirty a.m.).
REALLY REALLY MUST STOP STRESSING. Must stop stressing about the small things in life, as it has absolutely no effect on the big picture.

It just doesn't — I stressed about the pilot I was matched up with in case I liked him and it interfered with a possible to return to Italy... then with Brandon appearing same time as teaching position in Italy, then I didn't get the job. Then I decide I'll probably go to Italy once this temp job is done and along comes Umberto — another spanner to spoil my plan, more worry — then he turns out to be a dick and disappeared anyway. Seriously — they all sorted themselves out — my worry did nothing — had no effect on circumstance whatsoever.

I have been stressing way too much for absolutely nothing. A big patch of my hair has come out, which has been diagnosed as Alopecia. God, God, God Forbid! I really don't want to think about this at all, but it happened and they say it's triggered by stress. Must stop stressing and let the future take me where it has to take me and let it take care of itself. No matter how much I think of it and try to manipulate it, I could never possibly imagine what it has in store for me, nor steer it. I must stop being afraid of not noticing or missing opportunities as if they are there for me to be noticed or picked up and acted upon, I will notice them, no matter what – and if I don't then I am not meant to. I have to accept this and simply enjoy the day. I pray now that my hair gets better and that it never, ever, ever happens again.

So what did I do to get over my restlessness? I booked more trips away, that's what. With my temp job finishing soon, I decided I needed a break and who better than to break with but dear, sweet, wise Sam. We booked a trip to Cyprus and then, just for good measure, I booked a trip to New York where I'd be joined by a few friends, SATC style, though I'd be staying with Flynn who I'd met while studying in Besançon. He was one of those crazy Americans, who actually turned out to be a very good friend and we'd exchanged visits already. I had no strategy or plan for life but if anyone had been looking for one they'd probably say I was scared to stand still in London. Flynn had always liked me and was gracious (mostly) when I didn't reciprocate his romantic feelings. It was cool of him to let me stay with him in his flat in New York; we'd always got on well and he was someone I felt I could really talk to. There weren't many guys I could discuss this current level of stress with but he was really good about it. Before I went out there we'd had a chat about where I was at:

"Don't understand why you're stressed out. Is it job related? Or is your personal life not working out?"

"Not job, hon. I think that's it largely subconscious. Probably more personal life. Seeing as I'm not too bothered about career.

It's the personal side. I think those four years in Italy changed me a lot."

"Don't worry too much. You've got Cyprus coming up and then over here to New York. Things fall into place when you let them."

Do they? I hoped he was right. He always said the things I wanted to hear. I told him that.

"That's because I'm wise, Nat. You're a good one too. You used to be so carefree but it's an odd age we're at now."

It was a very odd age. And it seemed to be getting odder.

Wednesday 8 March 2006.

Am thinking of going to Italy for a month in May. Don't really know why. I guess I'm hoping for some kind of illumination, either to stay there or to come back and actually want to be here. I just wish that I had some sort of passion!... some sort of satisfaction either in a person, a partner or a job, just something of mine. I know that it's something I have to find myself and maybe create, but I just can't seem to. There's nothing worse for me than being emotionless. I guess this is partly why I want to go to Italy for a little bit. I wish that something would come along for me, either a job or a partner... something. Just jobs never seem to work out and men never seem to either.

Whether I don't like them enough (Charlie, Brandon, Flynn...) or they don't seem to want me (Mr Gillette, Anto, Edoardo, Umberto,) I really wonder if it's me. I can only think that perhaps they think I drink too much. Gosh I don't know. I really haven't been much at all lately. I mean in comparison with years ago, am so different. Just don't know what it is. I'm thirty-one, going on thirty-two and can't seem to move forward in these most important areas. I need to feel a passion for something. I have tried, put myself out there, am receptive, giving everything my best shot, I'm praying constantly for something, just anything to wake me up and make me feel alive! I feel like I'm not really LIVING living! And I find it frustrating and suffocating. I just want to feel alive. Have been praying for a long time for this now, must never stop believing. I know...! Just...

Valeria dreamt of me eating bread, which she said symbolises 'patience'. I must have patience.

Life is not easy for any of us.
But what of that?
We must have perseverance and...
Confidence in ourselves.
(Marie Curie)

Had a little chat with Mum tonight, which was very nice: didn't really resolve anything but we shared. I was upset and talked a bit, we had a small chat. Was nice. I don't like bottling up, but I often find myself doing it for fear of feeling more frustrated by what people may say in response (those close to me I mean). Anyway was good and worth it! A problem shared is a problem halved!

When you go through a hard period, When everything
seems to oppose you ...when you feel you cannot even
bear one more minute, NEVER GIVE UP! Because it is
the time and place that the course will divert!
(Rumi)

CHAPTER 22
Desperately Clinging on

Ah Yannis. If only he had been the answer. Yannis, the type of boy your parents would lock you up to keep you away from. Beautiful and aware of it. That sublime combination of an angelic face with masculine, chiselled bone structure. Tanned with long black hair, he had undeniable presence. And suddenly, just like that, my void disappeared. I decided I'd found my soulmate in Cyprus. I was enchanted by the mystery of yet another culture: I've always loved hearing men speaking another language to each other – it's quite sexy.

Sam and I had wandered through some of the usual British type tourist spots in Paphos before hitting on the fun crowd. Yannis and his friend took us out on their motorbikes, all around the island. In my needy, vulnerable, confused state I decided he was the man for me, why my father was Greek so surely this was meant to be. Talk about clutching at straws but I did and I convinced myself this was meant to sway me away from Italy. Like most of these Latin based cultures where the only day that matters is today and the only time that matters is the minute you're in, he was not so good at keeping in touch when I was back in London. It took a week before I heard from him but of course he said he'd sent me lots of texts and I probably didn't get them.

As a young woman, you desperately want the holiday romance to be the one. Nothing could be more perfect and you get to tell people that you met in a beautiful place and it was all meant to be. As we know, it very rarely turns out quite as sweet, beautiful and uncomplicated as we wish it to be. The truth was that Yannis was five years younger, he lived in Cyprus and we were at very different phases in our lives. But that didn't stop me. I began to tell myself he'd met a younger, more beautiful girl and thought this was my way of being realistic. But the whole thing was really me kidding myself. Not that it stopped me continuing to do so. I'd learned the Greek alphabet, impressing my dad in the process and my sentences were coming along. I decided that in future if nothing else came out of holiday romances, the desire and drive to learn the language is not to be underestimated.

Sunday 23 April 2006.

So made a big mistake, didn't I? Didn't listen to the right voice in my head. My own fault entirely. No news from Yannis since last Monday, so I decide to send Happy Easter text (Greek Easter). I had totally decided to send it today but my gut feeling said wait and so did Grandma's voice in my head. Stupid me, sent it, he replied by text saying he was actually looking at some pictures of Cyprus I'd sent on email there and then, so obviously if I'd waited, he'd have got in touch with me first via email and who knows what nice stuff he'd have written, instead I just got a text back. Nice but nothing major. Well I don't believe it's changed anything in the long run (Sliding Doors movie scenario) but I would have felt miles better today had I left it, checked my mail, and seen his message and then sent Happy Easter. Oh well, will not chew self up about it and lesson learned: Always listen to your gut feeling, the little voice in head, always and to Grandma's responses! I do feel however that the issue here is more how I feel than the outcome.

New York provided a great diversion. Flynn had been living in a flat in Manhattan with a group of guys for a while now so knew all the good places to be. I hadn't seen him for a few years so it was a bit odd to begin with. When I did see him, I knew again, there was sadly no attraction on my part. It was a shame, I thought. Here he was, such a great guy and he was so into me but I wasn't into him. But he treated me like a princess and it was brilliant. He paid for everything too so I returned to London feeling completely spoiled. If only I was in love with him.

Tuesday 16 May 2006. After New York trip.
New York taught me a few things. Nothing I didn't already know but let's say it confirmed them.

a. *NY is a great city for fun, very easy to enjoy yourself. Moderation is boring.*
b. *If your gut feeling tells you something, it is usually right.*
c. *If a man likes you (I mean really) he will treat you in a way to make it clear.*

With work fast approaching its final weeks I was in a real quandary about what to do. Italy, Cyprus or what? I'd found some teaching options in Cyprus but they didn't merit spending too long over there, as the lessons were so few. It would end up being a huge holiday. Yannis had shown no interest whatsoever so what I was thinking I don't know but it just shows you how long you can ride the coat-tails of a holiday romance. Even one that seemed to have ended. I kept sending Yannis the odd message, telling myself that it was up to me too, to keep things going. I mean I couldn't just leave it all up to him, could I? Of course I was lying to myself but I wasn't ready to tell myself that. Despite a deep sense of unease at my general life direction, one that seemed to be consistently built on fantasies, I didn't seem ready to give that up just yet. I decided I had to give Italy one last crack.

I could tell you about the parties, the sunshine, the food, the endless parade of gorgeous boys, the trips, the aperitifs, the clubs, the passion, and the joy. But you've heard it. I'd heard it. But I still kept telling myself that is what I would miss, that this stuff was what life was all about and that it would break my heart to not have it within reach. Do you want to know the truth? The truth is that I didn't need to return to Italy that summer to know what I would find out. I didn't need to make yet another big move. Like most of us, I knew deep down that it wasn't going to work, that I was off on one of life's wild goose chases when all I had to do was slow down, calm down and just let things be instead of always pushing for the next thing. But I went. And I went without the rose-coloured glasses because I was probably tired of wearing them. There were all those superficial things that I'd coveted so much but it wasn't enough. Because the truth was that all it did was remind me I wanted something substantial. Something real. And I wasn't going to get it by living like this. The only answer was staring me in the face. I had to get back to London. I had to accept that I was growing up, that this need within me for stability and certainty was real and needed to be listened to. It was a nice summer. And then, as if to give me a nudge, the job I'd lined up teaching turned out to be a bit chaotic. My new teacher friend who was supposed to give me a room said the room was no longer free. It was the beginning of the end.

Tuesday 12 September (Book).

I'm really keen to write a book. Not an entirely new thought — I've thought it many times before — basically about my life — what I've learnt from it and what I believe, however small, I can try to help others, who maybe feel similar to me in certain things or have felt etc. Anyway there are various points I'd like to cover and for that I'm not sure where to start exactly — not right now. What I'd ideally love to do would be to get together all my diaries, from wherever they are, all of them and begin to piece together little by little the journey of discovery of life, the world, people, everything... feelings, etc.

There are numerous titles I've thought of for it, to try and transmit the contents of the message that ultimately I'm trying to give, which are:

Things Do Happen
The Light At the End of The Tunnel
Sometimes Everything Just Isn't Enough
There Must Be More Than This
The Joy of Living
Now It's Time For Me to Be Happy
Life's Not So Bad After All
The Princess Within
The Big Question Mark
The Lion That Can't Express Himself

Never regret or judge anything you did, do, or are; you are so much better than you think.
(Unknown)

I left Italy feeling like my world was caving in. I'd resorted to staying on someone's sofa, a filthy sofa at that. It was freezing, I got bitten all over by little insects from the grim furniture and I ended up in tears. And that is how it ended.

Better to be slapped with a truth than kissed with a lie.
(Russian Proverb)

CHAPTER 23
Hip Hotel Group

The real discovery of the voyage consists not in seeking new lands but in seeing with new eyes.
(M. Proust)

Recruitment agencies were getting on my nerves. I think they are one of the most dispiriting experiences you can have. Most of the time you feel like they're pretending to be interested and are really not that interested in your details at all. You spend an hour talking to some girl called Emily, Charlotte or Annabel and she writes all this stuff down and then you never hear from her again. Or, she rings you with a job she says is 'made for you' but it has nothing to do with your aspirations (and not much to do with your qualifications) and you know they just want to get it off their books so they can collect their commission. I got this temp job, well temp to perm like everything is really, at a very exclusive Hotel Group, a place populated with high-rolling VIP types. They worked hard but there were perks to the job, the money was good and there was an atmosphere of positivity so I decided I had to give this my best shot.

One thing I really wanted to do was try and keep up my languages and maintain my connections with people who worked in that area. In between languishing in the reception area of recruitment places, waiting to be heard and then ignored again, I went to the language fair, just to see what was happening. There was a guy there who was showcasing his business – Speak the Lingo – that did pretty much everything to do with languages: locating foreign students, finding schools and work for them, organising trips and social evenings. It sounded exactly like the kind of thing I would have enjoyed doing. It was a commission-based business so I decided I'd do it in the evening, working on his Italian programs. We started seeing each other out of work hours. Interestingly, I didn't feel any attraction when I'd met him at the language fair however later when I went to his often and found myself with him alone, away from all the bustle, I sensed something between us. I wasn't sure how much it was reciprocated: we'd only been out together a few times and nothing had happened, yet.

This was the first English guy I'd met that I had a romantic interest in and it might have been pure coincidence. However, in the back of my mind I was recalling the woman I'd met a while back, who'd also lived in Italy, Emily Roberts. She'd told me that after finally returning to London, she literally met her husband-to-be the next day. Was I, at last, at the hands of fate too? I'd decided to be broad-minded about English guys, unlike every other time I'd returned from Italy and Jason seemed a good place to start.

One night after a jolly evening of French language learning and conversation at the Bar Room Bar, we drank rather too much wine and ended up kissing madly. That was when I should have found out he had a girlfriend. She lived in Spain but a girlfriend is a girlfriend, whether she's onsite or not. One of the girls who worked for him told me, so I decided we'd better have a chat and confronted him.

"Jason, I know we've only just started seeing each other but I need to know if you are seeing anyone else?"

He looked a bit put out. "No, why should I be? I've just met you."

"Yes but someone told me you already had a girlfriend. I need to know the truth."

A sheepish look. "Well yes," he said crisply. "But she lives in Spain so we don't see each other all that much. It's just one of those things that keeps going you know."

I didn't know, I was really none the wiser. We went out the next night, had a chat about it and it was all pretty unclear. "I want to see you," he said. And like lots of girls do, I decided the girlfriend was a big deal.

Monday morning... 18 December, (after Office Christmas Do).

Absolutely exhausted and off to work again. Hope it's OK! I can't deny that I'm not upset that Jason never called over weekend. Yes definitely let down about that — especially as I thought he was trying to prove himself, supposedly! Well, I certainly wasn't going to phone. Won't speak to him now before he goes. I'll continue to work on the Italian night, however as I'm keen to do that. At the end of the day we've only kissed. Though it does seem that a lot of what he has to say for himself is apparently a lot of rubbish by the looks of things.

Well c'est ça. Not going to stress about it. Just going to hope that have a good day and week at work! Certainly tired — very hopefully will wake up soon. Also desperately hope there are no jokes or comments or even dodgy thoughts in office re. Friday night! Ahhh — just got to face the music! Fortunately Holly was far worse than me, ending up smacking waitress's backside and falling across the table smashing all the glasses. Let's hope they focus on that!

Wednesday 10 January 2007.

Gosh, well everything seems to have happened so quickly. I guess I do miss Italy a lot in certain ways but I still feel that right now I should be here.

Feeling unsure of:

Work: Much less to do at the moment. On one hand is good, means I'm doing my own stuff (yahoo etc.) but feel guilty in case I get caught or what they think of me.

Solution: Don't worry about it — look and be serious. Don't ever get caught, make sure all work is done. Know and believe that if the job is for me, I'll keep it and if it isn't then I won't.

Men: Can't seem to get Jason's girlfriend issue out of my head, therefore don't trust him, plus not sure he's right.

Solution: Talk to him about it. Take it slow and take it easy: no one says it has to be forever, or at all if I don't want.

Italy: Miss the fun, light-heartedness and social side of things.

Solution: Go for weekend as soon as have the chance. Know that it's never going away anyway. Think of financial benefits here and make most of it. Don't forget fickleness and uneasiness of life and friendship there. Think of my good friends here too.

Also feeling anxious because:

a)   I am not happy with nor proud of the way I am working — as I have been doing tons of personal stuff.

b)   I am not happy with nor proud of the way I am eating at work, as purely to save money I am not being seen eating sandwiches at my desk/lunch etc. and I think this creates unnecessary distance.

c)   I am also not really happy nor proud of the way I am eating at home in the week, as again always seem different to others (this

303

is OK at times but not always).

So these things will change.

I will work harder and more conscientiously in the office, absolutely, totally make it noticed... and I will do the 'Italian night' stuff at home! Otherwise, am simply doing two jobs half-heartedly, and this is simply not good enough – will definitely dedicate different time slots to each job, concentrating solely on one at a time. (It's only in the dictionary that success comes before work!) I will definitely once or twice a week have some lunch at my desk, pay for it and eat it as the others do. I will definitely do this to unite myself. (Eating together is an important ritual bonding and uniting people in many different environments: it is important, very, very important actually.) And at home I will vary what I eat some evenings too – definitely.

Jason went to Spain, came back and he was different. Different in the way men are when they've been with a woman they like. I think too often women make distinctions in their own head about a man's status to persuade themselves they have a chance with him. I told myself he was on the verge of ending it with his girlfriend but of course that was irrelevant. There was a woman there before me. And she was not totally gone. As these things often are, it was too messy, he was being selfish and I was being stupid trying to find a spot for myself amidst it all.

He who does not know how to look back at where he came from will never get to his destination
(Jose Rizal)

It was time to shift my focus. And that shift would be to my job. Enough of men, enough of the language business, it wasn't going anywhere anyway. My day job, I would whole-heartedly throw myself into that. I was working for one of the biggest hotel groups in the world it had to be worth the effort. I was surrounded by high flyers. I don't mean my immediate colleagues, I mean the guys I worked for. All of these guys had had been educated at the best schools and they even came from titled families, like one of my bosses, Matthew. Expensively dressed and perma-tanned with that confidence that comes from being wealthy, they carried themselves with confidence. And they all had a glint in their eyes: these were the quintessential bad boys, out for fun. Wives, mistresses, the lot. And the singles were never single, they were players. They could have what they wanted, when they wanted it. As such the lifestyle that went with the job could be amazing and somewhat exciting. And that included us, the PAs. We were constantly on call: for the years I was there I had a Blackberry permanently glued to my hand ready to deal with whatever request, reasonable or otherwise, would come up. These men were used to having everything done for them and they wanted it done pronto. 'Nothing is impossible' they'd say and they'd mean it, there was a will and a way and we had to find it. I recall having to ring BA once because the top guy was running late and wanted the plane held! They could be demanding and petulant and I soon realised this Hotel Group and places like it, well they were cults. This was most definitely a cult, a place where a bunch of very definite, very strange characters decided who was in or out. The founder was Mr John Cassidy. He had as many women as he did banknotes. Of course the so-called girlfriends didn't know that. They'd turn up to the hotels thinking they were the only one for him when, in reality they were just part of an ever increasing string. It amazed me that these women didn't understand that: it's a basic thing with guys who are that wealthy.

After a few nights out at work events, I realised that I was in with the jet set, the real jet set. That life in Italy, those parties, the dinners, the clubs – it wasn't anything compared to this: this was Hollywood style living. Having not given much thought to having lots of money before, I began to appreciate the things it could buy and the lifestyle it could fund. And, I must admit, it was exhilarating, the idea of living a chauffeur-driven life appealed to me.

Thursday 12 April 2007.

Don't think I've EVER been so busy in a job… I don't think – not quite! It's been so crazy these last couple of days. I've been going nuts. I was so looking forward to having Matthew back in the office after his trip and he's just behaving like a complete arsehole. One day all smiles, sweet emails with smiley faces, jokes etc. and next minute all formalities, no fun, no jokes, no smiles, just black and white and regards Matthew. (I don't know some people are so weird!)

I guess before he thought it was fun to have a bit of flirting going on, now he's prob. found someone else so it's all formal and back to business with me! Who cares! If that was honestly all it was or all it was going to be then who cares.

Also…

I must stop worrying what other people think of me, largely related to girls in the office. Whatever I do or say… I'm always paranoid about what they think, how they interpret it and then how they bitch. Well I'm just going to ignore it and put it out of my mind. I made one mistake yesterday, last night, and that was indicating to Lauren that Sofie and Holly are not that serious about work — 'that' I totally shouldn't have said, as Lauren is two-faced. Must learn from that mistake.

Another dilemma is that Harold has said I should go to the new hotel opening in Portugal and cancel Sardinia with the family. That's thrown a spanner in the works. (It's mums 60th!) Can't ignore that.

For the first time in my life I was actually doing a job instead of pretending to do it and I was enjoying it. It was crazy and hectic but fun. And sometimes it was so much fun I didn't know how to take it. One day, a particularly sunny Wednesday, two of the bosses invited the PA's to lunch. Sofie and Holly accepted Matthew and Ryan's invitation but I couldn't go as I had a lot to do for Harold. Afterwards they came back, with champagne naturally, and Matthew put his arm around me, in what was a consoling gesture I guessed. There was more champagne and then Matthew sent around an email inviting everyone to Henry J Beans to watch the football. We were all rather drunk and I'd had quite a few strong cocktails.

"How about a hug, Natalie? A hug for me?"

It was Matthew. What was he playing at? Honestly I couldn't work that guy out.

He was insistent. "Come on you know you want to give me a hug. Pleaaaase… I need it."

"OK then." Who could resist those puppy dog eyes he was pulling and the poor me with the frown and turned down lip. I gave him a full-bodied hug without hesitation.

The night progressed to Boujis where things progressively got out of control. Holly ended up in A&E. I woke up the next morning, not remembering how I'd got there, without my phone or purse and I started having recriminations asking myself all sorts of questions and answering them negatively.

"What sort of girl does that? What will he think of me? A girl who is truly girlfriend material doesn't do that. I am not the kind of girl who men would think could be a great girlfriend and wife. I hope I'm wrong but how on earth could he or anyone want to know the real Natalie when they've seen this drunk, blubbering one. She's awful."

But this soon got forgotten as there were plenty more parties in all the best London nightspots and of course their hotels, where the champagne was both superior and unlimited, obviously. One night we'd been out at the Mayfair Bar where I was having a joint birthday party and Matthew had been throwing some rather extreme and energetic dance moves with me.

"Hello I'm Giles, and who might you be?"

I was taken aback as I took in the man in front of me.

"Hello, I'm Natalie. The birthday girl. Pleased to meet you." I was sure I was blushing. What a man! He wasn't conventionally good-looking but it didn't matter. He was charming, urbane, dashing and immediately cut a swathe through all the men in my brain. He literally wiped them aside. He was older and he had that knowing way about him. If there was one thing that I remembered after what had become a blur of an evening, it was his face as if it were a Polaroid. I had to see him again. A few days later I was sending thank you emails to all those who came so I decided to get his address and send him one as well. He invited me out and it was like a fairy tale. We had incredible dinners in the most beautiful places and later on, we would stay in equally luxurious and decadent hotels. He was totally captivating and it was hard not to fall for him. He had that aristocratic bearing, a royal connection and, as I found out later, a spectacular stately home in the country, which almost put Blenheim Palace to shame.

I was baffled by his interest in me. He was constantly in contact and incredibly insistent and persuasive about spending time with me. I hadn't been with a man who showed jealousy really so this was new, and actually rather flattering. Of course I should have looked further into it, I should have asked questions, I should have let my natural instinct lead me. But I didn't. And then I found out what I probably had buried in my subconscious: he was married. It didn't worry him of course. He was part of that charmed, moneyed circle where mistresses were par for the course. I tried to break away. He offered me a flat in town, money, everything to be his mistress but I struggled with it. He wouldn't let go, sending flowers, turning up at work and following me home. I don't think I've ever felt so conflicted about someone but really, I knew no good could come of it. It ended and I spent many nights (becoming all too familiar) with wine, cigarettes, sad songs and the faithful girls on the end of the phone for company.

Organising the latest hotel opening was sheer hard work, for all the PAs. It was to be in Rome so we hopped on the plane and off we went. Yes it was glamorous, incredibly glamorous but the work behind the scenes wasn't and there was lots of that. We were sat in this beautiful Roman villa with walls covered in frescoes for dinner the night before the opening – a thank you for our efforts and a motivator for the next day. It was a warm night; we'd had music by candlelight outside for the aperitivo and the champagne flowed, well, like champagne always did at these events. My colleague Sofie and I had become good friends but with her party-loving nature and natural German penchant for drinking, she was just as dangerous as I was so I have no idea how I thought she'd monitor my alcohol intake at this event.

The meal itself was incredible. To be expected. Food was one of the hotel's strong points along with many others of course. The aim was perfection.   They prided themselves not on being Michelin star but their own far grander star. Most of the other girls and people organising then went back to the hotel but Sofie and I stayed on.

"We go out now. To a bar I know."

It was John, 'The Boss', and what he said, went. There was a whole bunch of us: clients, some rent a crowd type model girls of the type you always find around these men, and Mr John Cassidy himself who was insisting that I should squeeze up right next to him at the tiny table in what seemed more like a strip club than a bar. After a short while my two immediate bosses – Matthew and Lee went to leave. I rose to go with them but was quickly persuaded to stay.

And so we partied on ceaselessly it seemed, the champagne, wine and vodka making a direct channel from the bar to our table without interruption. It was early in the morning when John's driver dropped us off at the hotel. He and the others were staying at the new glamorous hotel. The PAs of course were not. I barely slept that night but miraculously was ready on time for the opening the next morning, albeit in a wiped out kind of way.

It was the strangest of days. The opening itself went brilliantly. John was on great form until there was a bit of a scuffle and then he disappeared. I saw his face change but thought nothing of it.

When the ceremony finished Matthew appeared in front of me.

"He wants to see you."

"Who?"

"Cassidy... John."

"Why? Why me? Is everything OK?"

"No it's not. He wants to talk to you."

"Oh my God."

I am not sure why but John seemed to see me as a confidante and so I went to see him immediately. There had been problems with a senior partner, serious problems. Strangely he wanted to talk me through it all so I sat and listened and then told him I'd better make sure I got the evening's proceedings under way, in order to not spark any concern. I quickly went back and changed. All very awkward; I didn't know how to behave as my phone kept ringing with John wanting to talk. It was turning into a surreal evening.

"I want you to sit with me."

It was Matthew.

"Here. Sit here close to me, Natalie."

Well how could I refuse? I didn't want to. At this point my energy had taken a huge dive: no sleep, massive administration burden and John's puzzling need to confide in me had taken their toll but everyone still wanted to party and so we did. As the evening's dancing wound down, it was back to the hotel bar to blow even more money.

A waiter stopped us. "Sorry – e' chiuso, is closed... But of course I open for you."

"No, no... don't worry! OK back to my room guys." It was Matthew.

At that point the group halved and the rest of us settled into Matthew's opulent accommodation to deal with the business of drinking. And that's when I forgot what happened. All I know is that I woke up in his bed, wearing my party dress. This was duly removed by Matthew's masterful hands and what I think both of us had anticipated for some time took place.

As I struggled to get my clothes back on I heard Matthew's remark, "I've waited sooo long for that." For my part it was OK. Not earth shattering. But OK. What do you expect for early morning, post-drunk sex?

Now I had a problem. I was not in my hotel. My hotel was down the road. And I was here in an evening dress in Matthew's room. Not good.

Thank God for Pablo. Pablo worked on the sales team, had started shortly after I did and befriended me from the start. He'd taken me out, all over Europe from Verbier, skiing (my ludicrously Bridget Jones attempt at it) to sunbathing in Sardinia, Lugano, for an exquisite lakeside party, his home in Spain, regularly lavishing gifts and affection. Not least a Gucci handbag delivered sky high whilst flying first class to party in Dubai. He was desperately trying to start a relationship with me but I didn't want it. We'd had the talk and all was clear. We were just good pals. And right now that's just what I needed, a good pal. Nervously making my way down the grand corridor, I held my shoes in my hand, tiptoeing, head down, shoulders hunched hoping that none of the other bosses would come out of their rooms. I spotted Pablo, began whistling, coughing and making all the sounds I could to get him to turn around. He looked at me, nodded and without asking a question about why I was there, (he almost annoyingly always did the right thing) escorted me downstairs, while keeping an eye out.

"Wait here," he said, leaving me in a recessed doorway, "I'll check the place out."

He returned. "It looks bad. There's a whole bunch of them standing in the foyer. You can't go out the front."

"Oh shit. What are they doing up so early? Pablo, what am I going to do?"

With the élan of a master spy, Pablo scoped out the kitchens. "It's the only way," he said. He dragged me through the kitchens, past a crew of really rather unsurprised chefs and kitchen-hands, and out into a back alley where he found me a cab.

I took the lift to my floor unseen and then it hit me: I'd left my key card in Matthew's room. I'd have to go all the way down to reception and ask for one.

"Nat. What are you doing?" It was Sofie. Still in her evening dress too.

"I could say the same." We giggled.

"Oh you know, just partied and forgot where I was, so just coming back now."

"Yeah, me too. So much dancing." Dancing my foot. Sofie knew what I'd been doing but we were not going to discuss each other's indiscretions now.

That day we all went off to Matthew's birthday do early evening. It was typically extravagant, typically Matthew with beautiful, willing women draped all over the table. We moved from an exclusively cool restaurant to an equally exclusive club, just near the Spanish steps. Matthew was flirting with everyone. Fortunately I had no expectations. That's just how he was. He liked to conquer. They all did.

CHAPTER 24
Tom, Dick and a Few Harrys

The excitement of working for the golden boys of the Hotel Group was starting to wear off. Yes the money and perks were good however these guys expected everything to be done for them at all times. It was a wonder I wasn't asked to wipe their arse. At times their entitled behaviour wore thin. The commute meant I was starting to feel like the pale, washed-out people I saw on my ride into work every day and had vowed I'd never become. I think now I may have also suffered from what had always plagued me: once I realised I could do something, the interest wore off and that was starting to happen here. I could do this job with my eyes shut and so naturally felt less interested. My pursuit of the elusive 'BIG THING' that would change my life continued. Way back I'd put in an application to be a host on *The Big Breakfast*. They actually wanted someone to cover Denise van Outen for one week. Huge opportunity. My application was accepted but when I was questioned over the telephone I went to pieces. Basically, I blew it. But deep down I'd never given up.

"You don't really want that life anyway," said Dad.

He was adamant that any brush with fame would lead me into a dark, dangerous spiral, one that could only end in the gutter and would almost certainly involve something unsavoury. Both my parents were believers that hard work was what got you somewhere and that any instant attainment of 'success' was not real. That didn't stop me trying again. I decided to apply for a new programme: *The Apprentice*. It looked like fun (and to be fair I think in the early days it still had some unpredictability about it). So I applied and I got through to the next stage, which meant an interview.

Looking suitably professional in my little black dress I arrived to find hundreds of people waiting. My heart sank: I'd thought I was at quite an elite stage of the process. Still it was fun waiting in the queue, chatting to everyone and finding out what each other did. Everyone seemed incredibly friendly and I felt, perhaps incorrectly, that we were all in it together. That was my big mistake.

We were lined up and then a voice from the twilight said, "Tell us what you could bring to *The Apprentice*."

This was my big moment to prove I had IT. I felt supremely confident, as I'd heard what the others planned to say: they'd told me while we were in the queue. So I was totally honest, sincere and to the point.

I can't remember correctly but it was something like, "I have thrived in a multitude of different industries both in the UK and abroad, working with and for a variety of extremely talented people, ultra high net worth individuals and successful, multi-million pound businesses. My experience enables me to manage, problem solve and achieve in a wealth of environments and my knowledge provides the confidence to succeed."

And then I heard the others and I realised I had been set up. They all gave completely different answers to what they'd told me, each obliging the producers with something outrageous, witty or controversial. Basically they were going to make better television than I would. Fame would not be mine, again!

Since our Rome walks of shame, Sofie and I had become even closer at work. It was good to have someone to go out with after work, a colleague who shared a similar disdain for the Eurotrash princes who paid our salaries. One night after a particularly demanding day at work, we decided to cut loose and headed to the pub, our local, The Lamb & Flag, where we proceeded to down large quantities of champagne. I actually think we managed a sneaky M&S Pina Colada in the office before we left, such was our desperation. They asked me to join, so I went along too. It was a steak house in Fulham – Sophie's – and it was a good evening. More wine and champagne supplemented by some protein. Sophie fell asleep at the table and it was at that point that Hugo, our host who I'd met previously, decided to put her in a cab. He called one for me and as I got in, he kissed me. Not a light 'thank you for the evening' kiss but a rather definite and determined kiss.

After a few texts the next day – as is the modern way – we started seeing each other regularly. On the face of it he was not who I'd imagined myself with. Quintessentially English, rosy cheeks and rather reserved. But I'd told myself that I needed to be open to new things and that included men I might not have considered were for me. We had fun and I was aware from the beginning there was no great emotional connection but I decided that might come in time, once he got to know me. Plus I needed to give English men a go. I told myself I was on a learning curve. Like a lot of women I think I knew this was a dead end. He never mentioned the future. In fact he studiously avoided it. He made no discussion of marriage; it simply didn't seem to be on his agenda.

For my part, I was determined not to jinx anything by being the one to mention it. As a thirty-something woman I knew that would be the kiss of death. Any question that brought up kids or marriage would probably terminate the relationship. No, I had to wait for him to do it.

He never did though. We carried on having fun but it was becoming increasingly empty. Our holiday in the south of France which should have been the pinnacle of romanticism, a fortieth birthday in St Tropez, followed by a drive to Portofino and after a few nights there, Monaco, left me with a head full of question marks. It was fun yes, but if that didn't bring out the emotion in him what would. And then he took me to Paris. Upon hearing that we were going Sofie said she was sure he'd propose. And so were the rest of the crew. I tried not to think about it but as the weekend wore on I could see that it wasn't going to happen. He gave me a gift of sexy underwear. He always gave me sexy underwear. Perhaps that was a sign that he didn't want a wife and I'd missed it.

One day out of the blue, he let out a flippant comment to the effect he had no interest in marriage or kids.

"Why didn't you say that before?" The only words I could get out.

"You never asked."

"You had opportunities to say it though. Why keep going out with me?"

"I thought you were happy with the way things were, Natalie."

I wasn't happy. I was pissed off that he couldn't love me in the manner I wanted: totally. Why couldn't he? Why couldn't anyone? What were they looking for? Brandon, who seemed to have an antenna for when I was 'single and lonely again' sent a text out of the blue inviting me to his birthday dinner which I went to. After an adolescence of fancying him like mad, I wasn't sure how I felt about him as an adult. He was a nice guy and part of the old days so I enjoyed seeing him though in truth I didn't feel he was enough for me. We'd tried. There had been a brief interlude where it seemed almost impossible to refuse the trial of dating. I felt I had to follow the signs. We were both mystified as to why we kept appearing before each other and mutually agreed it had to be worth a try, perhaps the powers that be were up to something. We did our best, well he did but I was present. We had meals, did the cinema, drinks and kissed but it became a struggle. A couple of weeks was enough for me to know that he wasn't the one for me, not the person I'd conjured up in my head all those years ago. As is so often the case. But why did he keep springing up?

Monday 2 November 2009.

Three weeks away from what would have been my first-year anniversary for a relationship that I really thought might go somewhere, the first relationship that could go somewhere in the past ten years and it ended. Such a shame. Hugo and I, the couple that everyone thought would end up together, have ended. I must admit, it did feel like something was wrong, based on his lack of expression of true emotion and his lack of ever mentioning the future at all. In hindsight it was a total giveaway. But we had such a great time. I certainly hope that my doubts didn't manifest themselves on him but frankly my doubts were a direct result of his standoffishness with regard to all that issue; then there's the fact that I did still get a bit pissed now and then but far far less than before and sincerely I'd hope that was not related in any way to his not wanting to take it to the next level. (Plus every single girl in that group does exactly the same thing and he's always with them.) He says he doesn't feel ready and doesn't know if he ever will. He's forty-four for God's sake. How old does he have to be! Quite a few people said I should get pregnant but I didn't want to do that as I didn't want him to resent me, or be a single mother and it frankly could've gone either way so that was out of the question.

I'm sad and baffled how he lets something so good go so easily. However, as he says, he is selfish, thinks with his head (or possibly his penis) and not his heart, is not emotional and open.

So I'm reading this book that Donna gave me, a self-help book and am hoping it will bring me more happiness and another lovely relationship that will actually take me somewhere as opposed to standing still, which was what was happening with Hugo. It's all about positive thinking… blah blah but there has to be some truth in this as there are so many books written on this. Be positive; know what you want, put the right vibe out there and good things will happen! I can but try. I really am fed up from sadness in relationships and loneliness too. I really thought my time had come (even to the point I put the date we got together as my security pin number on various accounts), but obviously not.

Tuesday 3 November 2009.

Anyway, I'm reading this book. Wine and ciggies help. I'll have to cut them down but I need something to help me get through this. Hopefully I can replace the wine and ciggies with a new and wonderful man, someone to share my hopes and dreams with.

I wanted to make a list of all Hugo's bad points… in order not to lose sight of the stark reality, so here we go:

- Didn't call much

- Never said anything nice emotionally

319

- *Always on his terms*
- *Always went back to his place first before going out knowing I didn't want to*
- *Never expressed extreme emotion either way*
- *Never asked about any of my friends and family*
- *Never really wanted to see me more than two or three times a week*
- *Always kept a strong personal life*
- *Never talked about a future*
- *Not flexible*
- *Moaned a lot about the world, grumpy old man style*
- *Stuck a lot in his ways, would never budge*
- *Didn't put me first*
- *Didn't talk about anything important*
- *Never let himself go with kissing*
- *Never showed real passion towards me*

I do still torture myself about having drunk too much. Had I not ever got drunk perhaps he would have considered me for a future, though this was largely related to me feeling insecure. I hope there's nothing wrong with me — why no one ever seems to fall in love with me. I shall do my absolute best to be a better person and hope that I fall in love, in a love that is reciprocated. Now I hope that I sleep!

After the mess of Hugo my mother decided to step in.

"I've paid for you to join an introduction agency," she announced one Sunday lunch.

"Mum! I don't need one of those. They're for people who can't meet people."

"Nonsense. It'll be good for you. And they're for everyone. They'll match you with the right people, ones that suit. This one is very up-market. It'll be a good chance to meet different kinds of people. Anyway it's no different to meeting people through friends, really."

She'd paid quite a lot of money for me to have these introductions so I thought, 'What the hell.' I made an appointment to meet one of their staff and discuss my 'preferences'. After a bizarre interrogation with an agent, at the fifth floor bar in Harvey Nichols, of all places, that consisted of in-depth questions like revealing where I went shopping, what sort of food I like and similar mundane things, I was 'matched' with some dates. There was Graham, a sweet, strange looking workaholic who had his own business and desperately tried to talk it up and make his deals sound huge. Unfortunately the figures I was surrounded by at work made it seem as if he worked in a chip shop. Jason and I had a couple of drinks at the Blue Bar in the Berkeley. I noted that he ate his peanuts in an ugly way while staring desolately out of the window. He calculated a perfect two way split in the bill. Fergus was Scottish with an accent so thick I could barely understand him. He also had a problem making choices. I had to choose the restaurant, the time, the wine and even his meal. His only positive was that he owned a townhouse in Hampstead but I had no desire to see it.

Wednesday 9 December 2009.

Btw — is day after office Christmas party that I organised very well, I might add. And then I proceeded to be the only one who got really drunk and said a bunch of inappropriate things. Nice things but inappropriate.

Great — am so completely mortified, utterly and completely annoyed at self. Absolutely ridiculous but no one to blame but myself. I just feel so flat at the moment. I know that I'm only good and OK on red wine now, so have no idea why I didn't think about that and drank gallons of champagne. Totally stupid and will not do it again — definitely. Will not think about it any more. It was a Christmas party, an office Christmas party — that's all. It's done and dusted and everyone will now forget (I hope).

Tuesday 29 December 2009.
(Sam's Birthday and Grandma's.)
Sam's in Costa Rica. I called her. Grandma's in heaven — I spoke to her too. Well I wished her Happy Birthday.

I really owe my wonderful parents so much. They have always put me first in everything, and never, ever faltered in their constant and unconditional love, care and support. That is no small feat and not something that many people could honestly say they have behind them — or with them always. Even when they're gone one day (something I do not wish to think about) I know that I will always have that.

I think this must add to my expectations for a man, to be all that my parents are to me. To make me feel loved, as secure as wanted and as cared for. I guess they have a pretty high target to reach but to me that is what love is, real love at least — all or nothing.

Having gone down the route of the introduction agency to no avail, it was a mere slippery slope to a blind date. His name was Jack. I am not normally into curry houses but he offered Noor Johan where a sighting of Hugh Grant was always possible, as it was that night. Sadly the person sitting opposite me did not look like Hugh Grant. He was shortish, chubby, a rugby build – not an elegant rugby build but the short, squat kind of rugby build. No sooner had he sat down than he uttered the words, "I won't be staying late."

"Fine." I mean what can you say.

He suddenly felt the need to elaborate. Perhaps it was my brief response.

"I have to go to Berkshire you see."

He spent a lot of time in Berkshire. And so, eventually, did I. I can't tell you how I ended up seeing this man I had no real immediate attraction to and not a great deal in common with but I think I was still in my 'give it a chance' phase. It was strange how it happened. Even the physical thing: I wasn't into him at all and he did all the running at first. And then suddenly it was me. How on earth it happened I have no idea. Perhaps I was needy at that time? On the other hand, I've always been open. I can only explain it by saying the guy radiated confidence. And that was truly attractive. His racing green Aston Martin, horses and lifestyle added to it all of course. There was always the feeling too that I couldn't have him, and of course that kept me hooked.

At weekends I became a polo watcher and then we'd inevitably end up partying with his friend Marcus, who had a girlfriend, an actress who was twenty years his junior. He took me on a holiday to Thailand, a seriously expensive holiday, staying in luxurious hotels. Travel is a great measure of a couple. It ruined Greg and me or perhaps helped in a sense too. And this trip was not working. There was distance between us and paradise wasn't helping because no matter where you go, you're still the same people. And we were different people trying to make it fit.

Returning from Thailand he seemed to leave me for dead. I had no idea where we stood but I knew for sure I wasn't a priority. What did I expect? The guy always showed up late, always had an excuse, and always had somewhere else to go. I was not important to him. That really should have been enough for me but if every woman took flight in those situations, there might not be any relationships. Sometimes men need time to realise you matter, though I think I already knew time would not make a difference here. Increasingly he'd just take off to Berkshire and not tell me and I'd be sitting there hanging on the telephone for his call. It was really rather pathetic of me. One night we went out for dinner opposite his house in Clapham. It was going well really, until I spontaneously poked him in the arm. He flipped, truly flipped. That was a red flag for me. If a guy you're going out with gets angry about something like that, he doesn't feel that much affection towards you. We had big discussions. Big and useless discussions that got us nowhere. He looked me in the eye and basically said, "I don't know what I want from this." And that was when it all fell apart and I was left asking myself why a man couldn't want me like I wanted him.

CHAPTER 25
Old Times Come New

God, self-help books and fortune-tellers had done their best to guide me through the years but I didn't reckon on one other piece of assistance. Facebook. I discovered it at a time when I most needed the reassurance of old friends. For that I will be personally always grateful to Mark Zuckerberg and co. for creating this amazing vehicle of opportunity. I'll admit I was a late adopter of social media: I really hadn't bothered with it much so while everyone was discovering Facebook pokes I was still in the dark ages. But I joined and was delighted one day when a message popped up from one of my old school chums, Naomi. Who could believe that after eighteen years of not speaking we were in touch again? And then thanks to the beauty or the beast of 'writing on the wall', essentially letting the world know your business, the others started turning up. There was Kim who'd been at both secondary schools with me and soon we had a group meeting organised. There had been marriages, births, deaths and careers but the best part was that everyone was just as I'd remembered them and hopefully they thought the same of me. The first meeting was just some of the girls and really we could have been back in the school common room especially when I said I'd found some of the guys on Facebook too and got back in touch.

We decided that we'd have to get the boys involved in a gathering but there was so much girl stuff to catch up on, we thought we'd better keep them out of it for now.

The day went on, and it was blatantly clear we just didn't want it to end. Endless glasses of iced white wine, all of us clustered around an old wooden table, we were the last to leave the place. And our gatherings continued, showing me that there is nothing better than open, natural friendship. And at that time in my life, it was what I most needed, giving me a sense of calm I'd not managed in a long time. And of course when I told them about my inability to find love, they assured me it would come and did their best to make me feel that I hadn't totally fallen on love's scrapheap.

But I was still struggling with it all. The thing I was realising was that I had gone out of my way to please all of these men (shall we name them... Sebastiano, Antonio, Hugo... blah, blah... and now Jack) and they really hadn't done too much to please me. I'd done it thinking they would fall, irrevocably, in love with me but of course it hadn't happened. I said this to a younger colleague who asked my advice one day. She too was struggling in her search for love and respect.

"Why doesn't it work, Natalie? I do everything I can to make things right and then they turn around and throw it back in my face."

"It doesn't work like that," I told her. "You know the number of times I've fretted, cried, schemed, prayed and did everything I could to get a man to notice me, to really notice me, it just didn't happen."

"Do you have to play hard to get, is that it?" She was asking the question we'd all asked ourselves.

I personally don't believe it's about playing hard to get. I think it's about being true to yourself and not compromising your morals. Once you lose the essence of who you really are you give others the same impression, the impression of someone who doesn't have the self-confidence to be themselves. And the fact is that it's that confidence and pride that attracts people. Trying to 'man please' is a destructive experience and leaves you feeling disillusioned and used. I knew that, I knew it very well. A relationship based on a forged projection of yourself is unlikely to go the distance. It's unsustainable. Based on the fear of revealing your true self, it simply generates more fear that ultimately either destroys you or the relationship. It's the fear that needs to be conquered.

It goes back to the theory of 'if you love something let it go...' which lends itself of course to destiny. I'd had my beliefs in destiny, fate, what's meant to be and all that crushed to say the least... Once upon a time, I'd have sworn by it – not from experience of course; desire more than anything. But as it does, life happened and tarnished those ideals. Whilst I would have liked to have that hope, I'd become more focused on practicalities. It was then that one of those unexpected things happened.

At work Mr John Cassidy was still treating me as some sort of confidante: since the issues with the senior partner he'd called me in for a number of chats and I'd done my best to sit there and listen. Often he just wanted to say things he felt and I knew I wasn't expected to say too much but just to be there. We got on well. One day, not long after my first Facebook reunion with the girls I needed to get a message to him in a meeting. He was in the goldfish bowl meeting room where you could almost see but a frosted pane of glass prevented you totally seeing who was in there.

"Who's Cassidy in with?" I asked the receptionist.

"An external."

"What's his name? – Need to know if I can interrupt."

"Oh some guy called Charlie Brooke."

Charlie. Charlie Brooke. School Charlie? How was it all these people were coming out of the woodwork?

I had to see. I crept along the meeting room wall and tried to see if it was indeed my old school friend. It was impossible to see so I got down on my knees to peer under the frosted glass section. I was doing my best to be subtle but unsuccessfully apparently. John Cassidy spotted me and not surprisingly, came out to see what I was doing.

"Natalie, are you crazy?"

"Mr Cassidy, Sorry I needed to talk to you then heard you with Charlie Brooke; that's one of my oldest friends – I wanted to check it was actually him."

"Is it?"

"I can't see."

"What does he do, your Charlie Brook?"

"He works in property."

"Wrong person. This Charlie Brooke is ex SAS. He's helping us at the new Hotel opening"

It was funny, so funny I decided to email Charlie. I knew he'd never changed his job so although we hadn't seen each other in years his contact details remained the same. He loved the story and suggested we meet up for drinks. It actually took us a few months to make that meeting: every time we'd schedule and reschedule something would go wrong. Almost uncanny as if something was coming between us. Probably no bad thing as I was still trying to figure out what on earth had happened with Jack doing my best to rectify it and get us back on track, once again banging my head against a brick wall. Anyway, I certainly wasn't putting it off and I knew Charlie Brooke, good old dependable Charlie would not bullshit about something like this; life was just getting in the way. I wasn't concerned about it: he was a friend and he always would be no matter what happened, unlike the men I'd dated who had just disappeared.

A few months later, Dani organised our much-awaited follow-up. It was Italian, somewhere behind Carnaby Street. Having been late the first time, I really wanted to be there on time. It was summer and it happened to be one of the rare hot days that London gets. The tube would have been bad enough without my high heeled brown sandals breaking the heel snapped off one of my shoes. I tried to ram it back on and enlisted the help of a couple of strong men to help me but it didn't work. I was in Pimlico; having sold my original flat, I finally managed to buy one just where I wanted, in town. It was tiny but I loved it. So I had to hobble the rest of the way to the tube only to discover that I was apparently the only Londoner who didn't know the Victoria line was out of action.

"Shit," I said to nobody in particular and put my arm up to hail a cab. Miraculously I got one almost immediately and asked him to take me to Carnaby Street via a shoe mender.

"So how's your day?" he asked.

"Well it's not great. Look! I've broken my sandal and I'm supposed to be at this reunion of girls from my school but I can't even walk in this sandal which is why I need to get the shoes repaired."

"Give it 'ere," he said. "I'll fix your shoe."

He decided to multi-task, driving while he attempted to force the heel back on the shoe, slamming it against the dashboard. Things were not looking good. The roads around Victoria were full of diversion and there were no shoe menders in sight. The only open one I knew of turned out to be closed. I decided I'd buy new shoes when I got there. There were lots of places around Regent Street. It would be easy.

But getting there was to prove even harder. I got out of the cab as the amount of diversions meant the clock was going through the roof, I decided to walk down Piccadilly. It wasn't far, once the other end and I'd be there. My aversion to reading the news meant I also had no idea Gay Pride was on. And so it was that I got stuck while the procession passed by, my destination barely minutes away but in reality far, far away. Needless to say the girls loved the story, and more screams escaped when I revealed that I'd randomly recently been back in touch with Charlie Brooke, and more to the point, that we had actually been trying to meet up. They couldn't believe it. It was wide mouths and squeals.

"You're in touch with Charlie, Nat?" gasped Kim in semi-disbelief.

"I always said you two should be together," added Naomi

"Yeah we're meeting for a drink supposedly, but it doesn't seem to be happening anyway."

When Charlie and I did eventually manage to meet up it was near my flat in Pimlico, at my new local, The Orange. He was a little late but he'd kept me updated the whole way as to why and when he arrived it was lovely. Actually it was more than lovely. As he walked in, it was like a giant light bulb had been switched on – and it simply got brighter throughout the course of the evening. I felt a current of warmth, a feeling of lightness run through me. Something strange had happened, I felt released from the chains I'd been bound in, and I felt something was very different. Charlie had always treated me well way back when, taken me out to lovely places and been patient and kind. He was no different now, except that he was a man in every sense of the word. Something was right, it was so right I was terrified. I realised that what I had been wanting to feel was what I'd felt with Charlie but couldn't get with any of those other men. It was Charlie, who at sixteen, set the bar high and nobody else had matched it. One drink led to another, then a meal and it ended up being one of the nicest, most comfortable, real evenings I'd had in a long while. We did it again. And again.

Time went on and the contact continued. We were in touch in a different way to that which I had become accustomed with anyone else, except Charlie himself of course, many years ago. His contact was always constant, his words appeared real and his actions, well, they couldn't be faulted. Just as before. It felt right.

For once I left my mind out of it and it felt good. I felt like I was home... I kept my cards to myself initially, I couldn't possibly make another mistake. It wasn't long before I finally felt I'd turned a corner, I'd found the feelings that I was looking for, which I believe can only be based on a precedent set by Charlie himself all that time ago, that simply no one else had managed to meet. It was tough to know what to do!

"I think we should go on holiday."

"What!"

"We need to see if this is real, Natalie. We need to know!"

He had the same thinking as me. I knew it was a good idea but it all seemed a bit soon. We discussed it and I decided I really had to put myself first and not worry about what anyone else thought for a change. I agreed and we started looking at options. Charlie's were way more luxurious than mine and I told him I couldn't afford them. He said he was paying and so we booked to go to the Maldives. The hotel was beautiful, the setting idyllic. Nothing could be faulted. We were escorted to our beautiful beach villa, with outside bathroom, lounge area and just a couple of steps to a stretch of immaculate white sand and a little further the clear as tap water sea. I'd been worried about how we were going to deal with the reality of being somewhere that was so obviously romantic for several days but we'd vowed to remain friends regardless and when things are meant to be, they just happen. And so they did. We chatted, ate, swam, sunbathed and messed around. Breakfast under the sun, lunch by the pool, cocktails at sunset and dinners on the beach. And just as we thought things couldn't get any better, they did. An incident occurred just outside our room, that although unwanted, brought us a bonus. An intruder jumped the wall to our bathroom in an attempt to get to our room, which led to them giving a complimentary upgrade to the honeymoon suite. If this wasn't a sign — what was? An incredible luxury sea villa, on stilts at the end of a long pier, with a glass floor, infinity pool, deck and private staircase to the sea. I actually did pinch myself several times and yes it was really happening. What was even more important though was that

Charlie and I just seemed to get along. I didn't have to try to be. I was just being without having to think about it. God, it felt good. Each day was convincing me more that after all these years of not realising it, perhaps we really were meant to be. It was becoming clearer and clearer. How could I have not seen it before? The time just clearly couldn't have been right.

One evening, we took a walk along the beach to the bar for a last couple of amaretto sours before settling back in our villa for the night. We stopped for a moment to watch the stars.

"Let's sit here." Charlie gently tugged at my hand, guiding me down to the sand. "See if we see a shooting star."

We sat close on the soft sand, huddled together, the warm evening breeze caressing our bronzed skin as we gazed admiringly into the beautiful stillness of night sky. I'd never physically seen a shooting star before so wasn't exactly sure what I was looking for. Suddenly, I froze, a shudder of excitement rushing through me. There it was right before us: a glistening star falling between our gaze. As it disappeared into the glimmering folds of the ocean, spellbound, we turned to each other and I heard my grandmother's voice whisper in my ear... 'il destino'.

A Falling Star
There are those who do not believe
That a single soul, born in heaven
Can split into twin spirits
And shoot like falling stars to earth,
Where over oceans and continents,
Their magnetic forces,
Will finally unite them into one.
(Lord Byron)

Home at last

Holidays are one thing but what happens when you return from an exotic place and get back to the daily grind? I remember sitting in Charlie's house watching TV with him not long after returning and thinking, "I could do this forever." Restless, party girl Natalie was not squirming to get away or thinking of tomorrow or the next thing. I was surprised at how content I was. I'd never given Charlie a chance at school; I'd thought he was 'too nice' a bit boring even but actually if I had, I would have found out there was excitement, spontaneity and fun but the important thing was it felt like I'd come home. And I had. I'd pushed him away often but here he was and we were meant to be.

And that is how it works. If someone is really meant for you, they will be.

I am still very close to almost all the people related to in this book. I very much value their friendships, love and respect them with their strengths and weaknesses. I only hope that the inclusion of their experiences may be of benefit to others going through similar situations.

CPSIA information can be obtained at www.ICGtesting.com
Printed in the USA
BVOW05s1046010216

435000BV00023B/202/P